Maybe I Should . . .

Maybe I Should . . .

Case Studies on Ethics for Student Affairs Professionals

Second Edition

Edited by
Mimi Benjamin and Jody Jessup-Anger

LEXINGTON BOOKS
Lanham • Boulder • New York • London

Published by Lexington Books
Copublished with American College Personnel Association
An imprint of The Rowman & Littlefield Publishing Group, Inc.
4501 Forbes Boulevard, Suite 200, Lanham, Maryland 20706
www.rowman.com

6 Tinworth Street, London SE11 5AL, United Kingdom

British Library Cataloguing in Publication Information Available

Library of Congress Cataloging-in-Publication Data

Library of Congress Control Number: 2019952415
ISBN 978-1-4985-7900-1 (cloth)
ISBN 978-1-4985-7902-5 (pbk.)
ISBN 978-1-4985-7901-8 (Electronic)

To Mike Howland (Mimi) and
to Olivia, Sydney, and Eric Jessup-Anger (Jody)

Contents

Preface

It seems trite to say this, but ethical issues abound in our world. They are also evident in the work of student affairs professionals, whether graduate assistants or senior student affairs officers. While some of these dilemmas end up in the news, most of the "everyday ethics" that professionals encounter may seem only mildly concerning at first glance. And therein lies the potential problem, because a deeper look at the issue may surface very troubling circumstances that require careful efforts to address. Professionals must use their own ethical compasses as well as the guidance of professional standards and trusted colleagues to come to appropriate conclusions about ethical challenges.

The intent of the second edition of *Maybe I Should . . . : Case Studies on Ethics for Student Affairs Professionals* is the same as the first. Our goal is to provide primarily new professionals with situations to ponder and opportunities to work through the kinds of challenges that they may encounter in their student affairs roles. The first edition of this book offered readers a brief overview of ethics and ethical decision making, strategies for analyzing ethical situations including a framework for considering ethical dilemmas and a sample case analysis using the framework, and opportunities to consider an array of ethical dilemmas written largely by newer professionals. Additionally, we included resources and suggestions for facilitators and instructors for incorporating ethical decision-making activities into their professional development or classroom instruction. The second edition offers readers the same, with all new cases, some of which reflect current situations on our campuses while others illuminate challenges that seem enduring.

The first edition of this book grew out of a course assignment more than ten years ago. Second-year master's students were asked to write short ethical situations that were relevant to graduate students and new professionals.

They shared these cases with their classmates and then facilitated discussion to sort through the issue(s) and identify appropriate strategies for addressing the situation. This assignment was effective for several reasons. First, these students had the opportunity to identify an ethical dilemma about which to write, and many of those cases were based on their real experiences of challenge as young professionals. Second, they had the chance to puzzle through the situation with others, which is a helpful way to work through ethical dilemmas. Finally, although they may not have had a team in place to consider the situation when and as it really happened, as a group they came to conclusions about ways to tackle these challenges by consulting each other. Foregrounding ethical elements of student affairs work served as a reminder to students that their work will likely require their consideration of professional ethics, and it was important for them to be aware of and review the profession's ethical standards as well as hear thoughts and ideas for resolving these situations from their colleagues.

The cases in the second edition highlight ethical dilemmas that primarily graduate students and new professionals may encounter in their work in such functional areas as admissions and orientation, advocacy and inclusion, career and academic support services, residence life and housing, and student involvement and student conduct. Although professionals at any level may find these cases valuable, a newer professional serves as the lead character in each case, the one who has a challenge to identify and address. In contrast to the high-profile, public situations that often are used to frame case studies, most of the conundrums professionals will address will be less sensational, manifesting more in the daily variety of dilemmas that make professionals take pause. We believe that graduate students and new professionals are those most likely to encounter surprising situations, although professionals at any level can undoubtedly tell stories that start with, "You won't believe what happened today!" Time and intentional training about ethical situations are presumably offered to those newer to the profession, who might find themselves in situations they had never considered. Circumstances in these cases affect a range of roles, from student organization advisor to supervisor, colleague to classmate.

In spring 2018, a call for cases was sent out to a variety of listservs and colleagues. We particularly encouraged graduate students and new professionals to consider submitting cases, and many did. As well, a number of cases are coauthored with these students and newer professionals by graduate faculty or professional mentors and some are solely written by these faculty and administrators as well. A special thanks goes to those faculty and administrators who took the time to work with these individuals, for many of whom this is their first professional publication. As editors, we attempted to honor elements of the cases that clearly were deliberate on the part of the authors.

As such, in some cases authors specify character pronouns; in others, they have intentionally chosen to use the plural "they" to refer to characters.

There are numerous people who contributed to the publishing of this book, and we are so grateful. The assistance provided by our current and former graduate assistants, Noreen Siddiqui from Marquette University and Kaitlyn Martin, formerly of Indiana University of Pennsylvania and currently with the Sigma Chi Fraternity International Headquarters, provided support for this project on a level that is difficult to describe. We are so thankful to these two women for their attention to the administrative tasks associated with an edited book that included more than 120 submitted cases. We also are grateful to our colleagues who allowed us to tap into their knowledge and expertise and served as case reviewers: Courtney Baum, Ben Chamberlain, Jenny Ciesiulka, Hannah Clayborne, Coreen Newman Coronado, Kipp Cox, Laura Davis, Jamie Elftman, Monica Fochtman, Juan Guardia, Suzanne Harle, Lisa Ingarfield, John Janulis, Gabe Javier, Kim Jeffrey-Peirce, Susan Lammers, Jenna Lassila, Kirsten Leih-DiMartino, Kyle Oldham, Kacie Otto, Heather Phillips, Nicci Port, Terri Potter, Valyncia Raphael, Sara Smith, D. Tobiassen-Baitinger, Brian Troyer, Lance Wright, and Graice van Spankeren. Additionally, we want to express our thanks to Florence A. Hamrick, who conceptualized and coedited the first edition of the book and trusted us to carry it through in its second edition. Finally, we both wish to thank our families, in particular our spouses Mike Howland and Eric Jessup-Anger. Your support for us as we engaged in this project was instrumental.

Mimi Benjamin, Indiana, Pennsylvania
Jody E. Jessup-Anger, Milwaukee, Wisconsin

Chapter One

Overview

In this chapter we introduce ethics and the need for addressing ethics in higher education, exploring the various ways in which attention to ethics in student affairs professional preparation and throughout one's career may ameliorate or mitigate some of the vexing ethical dilemmas faced by student affairs professionals. We then turn to defining ethics and discussing the philosophical underpinnings. After clarifying the definition of ethics, we examine the role of ethics in professional identity, and then explore avenues for ethical decision-making. Finally, we discuss the need for guidance in ethics and ethical decision-making—especially for new professionals in student affairs. Although it is beyond the scope of this book to provide comprehensive coverage of the development of ethics and ethical decision-making, we hope by introducing readers to the concepts broadly, providing a framework for ethical decision-making, and ethical dilemmas to consider in their professional lives, they will become attentive to the tacit values that guide their decision-making.

THE NEED TO ATTEND TO ETHICS

A quick scan of higher education news sources like *The Chronicle of Higher Education* and *Inside Higher Ed* reveals a complex ethical landscape within postsecondary institutions. Certainly, high-profile ethical transgressions like admissions scandals where unqualified students were granted admission in exchange for money, sexual violence committed by trusted university personnel, and financial improprieties within financial aid disbursements come to mind readily when one considers the ethical impropriety and lapses in higher education. Although all these scenarios have heightened the public's awareness and scrutiny of postsecondary institutions and are important to

1

address, they do not paint an accurate portrait of the everyday ethical dilemmas faced by administrators and faculty.

Student affairs professionals, who are tasked with promoting the welfare and success of students in postsecondary contexts, are often at the forefront of ethical dilemmas in postsecondary education. Eberhardt and Valente (2007) surveyed student affairs professionals through professional association listservs and found that half of those who responded indicated they faced ethical dilemmas routinely in their work. The professionals worked in every facet of student affairs and held new, mid-level, and senior-level positions. Overwhelmingly, respondents to Eberhardt and Valente's study cited conflicts between supporting students and attending to the needs and policies of the institution as a central theme of reported ethical conundrums. Examples of such dilemmas included justifying the variation in enforcement of alcohol policies throughout the academic year, with strict enforcement as the norm on campus but then lax enforcement occurring when alumni were on campus or during home football games (Eberhardt and Valente 2007). Another example from the study related to confidentiality of student records, and specifically when federal policy prohibited the sharing of student information across offices, but student well-being necessitated it.

In the first edition of this book, Hamrick and Benjamin (2009) encouraged readers to consider that not all ethical dilemmas are easily identifiable, and, furthermore, not all choices include a dilemma or ethical dilemma. They posited that ethical dilemmas are vexing because there are "multiple, plausible, 'right' answers, and making choices, setting policies, and reaching decisions can certainly present or raise ethical dilemmas" (Hamrick and Benjamin 2009, 2). A fictitious account of such an example might be: Suppose after a high-profile and dangerous stunt was performed by a student organization with no advisor, Felicia, a student organization coordinator, recommended that all student organizations must have advisors in order to be recognized and have access to university funds. However, after a two-year phase in of the requirement, student organization data revealed that the policy disproportionately disadvantaged identity-based student organizations, as two-thirds of these organizations ceased to be recognized because of the advisor mandate. Upon realizing the unintended consequences of the policy shift, Felicia faced an ethical dilemma. Although she believed that advisor oversight made the student organizations safer, the policy also inadvertently harmed other groups who may not have needed such oversight in the first place, many of which were already marginalized on campus. After realizing the unintended harm, Felicia may have wondered how to hold her value for fairness with her value for equity. This example illustrates that, although it is clearly important for professionals to attend to ethical dilemmas by reflecting on their personal values, often these values are insufficient for addressing ethical conundrums, thus, it is also critical that they understand ethics from a broader perspective.

DEFINING PROFESSIONAL ETHICS

Underpinning professional ethics are theoretical models of moral development that are widely used in the student affairs field. Liddell and Cooper (2012, 14) explained that, although moral and ethical development are often used interchangeably, moral development is rooted in cognitive development, whereas ethics are "a set of moral principles used by an individual or group that provides a framework for behavior." Because of the connection between moral development and ethics, we provide a synopsis of moral development here and then further define ethics.

Models of moral development commonly taught in graduate preparation programs help to make the case for the importance of focusing on ethical development of student affairs professionals. For example, Kohlberg's (1976) model of moral development, with its emphasis on an orientation toward justice, and Gilligan's (1982) model of moral development, with its focus on an orientation toward care for self and others, illustrate how moral reasoning develops from simple to more complex over time. This temporal development happens as a result of both exposure to higher levels of moral reasoning and added complexity in situations containing a moral dimension. Thus, to encourage moral development, individuals should be exposed to others' meaning making about moral decision-making as well as increasingly complex problems that have a moral dimension to them.

Both Rest and Mathieson expanded on Kohlberg's foundational work to consider new dimensions of moral development in addition to the constructs of reasoning and judgment. Rest's (1979) model is more comprehensive than Kohlberg's, and includes moral sensitivity (how one situates circumstances related to the well-being of others from a moral perspective and works to find alternatives); moral motivation (one's decision to follow a moral path); and moral action (the implementation of a moral plan). Mathieson (2003) introduced the concept of moral maturity and identified seven factors related to its development, including: (1) Moral agency and sense of one's self as a moral being; (2) Ability to utilize cognition in decision-making; (3) Ability to apply emotional reserves and sensitivity toward others; (4) Capability to employ social skill to convince others; (5) Capacity for identifying and utilizing higher-order principles to guide decision-making; (6) Respect for others; and (7) Development of one's life purpose. These neo-Kohlbergian models are more contextual, situating the self as a moral being with the capacity to weigh the circumstances of others, the agency to act in ways aligned with one's moral beliefs, and skills to engage with others. This complexity helps to position moral development as a foundation that informs frameworks of ethical decision-making and behavior.

In their study of ethical decision-making of administrative staff in post-secondary education, Reybold, Halx, and Jimenez (2008) made connections between morality and ethics, explaining that morality includes judgments of right and acceptable behavior that are situated in broader cultural contexts and religious standards, and that ethics were the principles or standards drawn from moral perspectives. Reybold, Halx, and Jimenez (2008) explored thirteen student affairs administrators' perceptions of ethics in student affairs, specifically exploring how they defined ethics and their experiences with professional integrity in their specific institutional context. They found that the administrators drew upon myriad sources to define ethics, including perceived standards of professionalism based on the contexts of their institution and of the student affairs profession as well as personal morality guided by their religious beliefs. Further, the researchers found that most administrators described considering a combination of personal values and professional socialization on their workplace ethical reasoning and conduct. They noted that on the job training, professional development, trial and error, supervisors, and experience all helped to refine their ethical decision-making.

Reybold, Halx, and Jimenez (2008) articulated three dimensions of ethics the administrators drew upon in combination to describe their decision-making and behaviors, namely (1) regulatory ethics—specific codes and workplace regulations that are externally set, (2) situated ethics—situated in the institutional culture and mission, and (3) collective ethics—based on collective critique from sources like professional codes, principles, and shared values. Based on their findings, the researchers argued that additional support is needed to help student affairs professionals to become more conscious about professional ethics. Although several of the participants in their study knew about professional standards abstractly, many did not describe using these standards to guide their professional decision making, instead relying on personal values. Reybold, Halx, and Jimenez contended that by providing student affairs professionals with opportunities to consider ethics and discuss them publicly with colleagues, these professionals will be more inclined to utilize a more complex and nuanced approach to ethical decision making, rising above the divisive rhetoric that often accompanies ethical dilemmas.

ADVANCING PROFESSIONAL ETHICS

Given the religious, cultural, and moral plurality of student affairs professionals, the ways in which they approach ethical dilemmas would likely vary widely if they were to solely use their personal moral foundations to guide decision-making. Thus, professional ethics become necessary to promote consistency across the field and a base from which to consider ethical dilemmas. Student affairs professionals have several different avenues to pursue for grounding in professional ethics. Perhaps the broadest is advanced by the Council for the Advancement of Standards in Higher Education (CAS). CAS includes membership of forty-one active professional associations related to postsecondary education. Many of these associations have their own codes and standards of ethical conduct, therefore CAS developed a statement of shared ethical principles that focuses on the overarching themes of the CAS member association codes, including: autonomy, non-malfeasance, beneficence, justice, fidelity, veracity, and affiliation (see appendix B). The first five principles are drawn from Kitchener's (1986) work, who derived her principles from biomedical ethicists Beauchamp and Childress (1979). Kitchener describes autonomy as having the right to act (as long as that choice does not infringe upon others) and the freedom to act. Kitchener (1985) connects the principle of autonomy to right of self-determination, privacy, and informed consent.

Non-malfeasance, or what Kitchener (1985) refers to as "do no harm," means that one does not engage in activities that run the risk of harming others, either physically or psychologically. Kitchener highlights the potential for "subtle psychological harm" (1985, 22), which she indicates can come from the negative consequences of university policies that impinge upon academic advancement.

Beneficence, or what Kitchener (1985) calls "benefitting others," is connected to advancing student development by enhancing the well-being of others. Kitchener cautions student affairs administrators that often beneficence can conflict with institutional priorities, and suggests a balance between various groups' priorities, with the outcome highlighting a benefit for individual, group, and university.

Justice is often equated with fairness, but also connotes that the rights of the individual are balanced with the rights of the group, thus equity must also be considered. Kitchener encourages ethical decision makers to recognize that "guaranteeing equal treatment, equal access to facilities, or due process for all does not always guarantee an equal outcome for everyone, nor does it ensure an outcome that seems intuitively to be fair" (1985, 25). She encourages weighing fairness with acknowledgment of difference.

Fidelity, or "being faithful," as determined by Kitchener, involves "issues of loyalty, truthfulness, promise keeping, and respect" (1985, 25). Kitchener argues that student affairs professionals, as part of a helping profession, are bound by fidelity because of their role. She encourages readers to imagine the role of a helper as an informal contract with those whom they work "not to exploit, lie to, or otherwise deceive those in their professional care (Kitchener 1985, 25–26).

Kitchener's influence on the foundation of ethics in student affairs is unparalleled. In addition to her work supporting the CAS statement of shared ethical principles, it also informs, or has historically informed, the work of student affairs professional associations. ACPA—College Student Educators International and NASPA—Student Affairs Administrators in Higher Education, are two umbrella professional organizations that support student affairs professional development.

ACPA's *Ethical Principles and Standards* are intended to "assist student affairs professionals . . . in regulating their own behavior by sensitizing them to potential ethical problems and by providing standards useful in daily practice" (n.d., 1). The statement (see appendix C for full statement) encourages ACPA members to model ethical behavior in their work using the four standards for guidance. These standards of ethical practice include: "1) Professional responsibility and competence; 2) Student learning and development; 3) Responsibility to the institution; and 4) responsibility to society" (ACPA 2006, 1).

As illustrated in appendix C, the first standard, *professional responsibility and competence,* addresses the tenets of professional conduct and includes such areas as professional service, development, and effectiveness, adherence to legal and policy mandates related to the student affairs profession, and providing accurate and timely information related to one's own and others' professional advancement. The second standard, *student learning and development,* concerns the capacity for student affairs professionals to attend to the needs of students in well-informed ways. The tenets of the second standard include developing the capacity to address the needs of all students, maintaining clear boundaries in relationships in order to best serve students, and attending to the need for referral to others and the limits of confidentiality in working with students. The third standard, *responsibility to the institution,* situates student affairs practice into the context of the institution and promotes the notion that student affairs work is conducted in accordance with the institution's mission, goals, policies, and procedures. The standard outlines the potential conflicts that may occur between colleagues and encourages student affairs professionals to weigh competing demands when development of students and support for the institution's policies and interests come into conflict with one another. The fourth standard, *responsibility to society,* addresses the need for student affairs professionals to act with integrity in their personal and professional lives, working to improve their communities as advocates of social justice.

NASPA voted in 2006 to adopt the *CAS Statement of Ethical Principles,* detailed above and featured in appendix B, to guide professional ethical practice. In 2012, a task force on ethics reviewed the statement, along with other documents, and created an ethical framework for the association (Saunders and Wilson 2017). The task force shied away from universal principles, instead opting to focus on the content and process of ethical decision-making, with an emphasis on recognizing plurality, potential conflicts in global context and one's own ethical behavior, and the need for accepting ambiguity. Three reflection questions advanced by the task force were: "1) What would the greater good, benevolence, or compassion look like in this situation? 2) What thoughts, ideas, behaviors, and relationships will be expanded from what is created by my decision? What will be reduced? And, 3) Does the decision respect my individual values and the integrity of all people being affected by it?" (Saunders and Wilson 2017, 97–98).

In 2009, ACPA and NASPA utilized their collective expertise to develop professional competencies to guide the development of student affairs professionals. Personal and Ethical Foundations is one of ACPA/NASPA's ten professional competencies (see appendix A for the full text of the competency). Originally, the competency was separated into Ethical Professional Practice and Personal Foundations, but because of their interrelatedness, a decision was made in the 2015 edition of the competencies to combine them. ACPA/NASPA explain that the Personal and Ethical Foundations competency

> involves the knowledge, skills, and dispositions to develop and maintain integrity in one's life and work; this includes thoughtful development, critique, and adherence to a holistic and comprehensive standard of ethics and commitment to one's own wellness and growth. Personal and ethical foundations are aligned because integrity has an internal locus informed by a combination of external ethical guidelines, an internal voice of care, and our own lived experiences. Our personal and ethical foundations grow through a process of curiosity, reflection, and self-authorship. (2015, 12)

As with the other professional competencies, ACPA/NASPA outlined foundational, intermediate, and advanced outcomes that student affairs professionals should demonstrate as they achieve proficiency (see appendix A for the Personal and Ethical Foundations competency in its entirety). Whereas the foundational outcomes emphasize "awareness and understanding of one's values and beliefs, especially as related to professional codes of ethics and principles for personal wellness," the advanced outcomes are more complex, demanding the capacity for critique and self-awareness, and modeling and mentoring with others (ACPA/NASPA 2015, 12). The trajectory of proficiency from awareness to articulation and critique illustrates the need for new professionals to practice ethics and ethical decision-making from the start of their careers. Our hope is that this book will serve as a resource for graduate students and new professionals to practice their ethical decision-making by providing contexts for and details of ethical dilemmas for them to consider, and in doing so identify their own beliefs and commitments related to ethical dilemmas, how these beliefs align with or diverge from professional standards, and how they can manage areas of incongruence between personal, institutional, and professional standards.

REFINING AND REMOVING BARRIERS TO ETHICAL DECISION-MAKING

As discussed earlier in this chapter, Reybold, Halx, and Jimenez (2008) posited that more should be done to support student affairs professionals gaining awareness and practicing ethical decision-making. Without this awareness and practice, student affairs professionals in their study reverted to reliance on personal values, which may have not been congruent with university or professional ethics. By providing opportunities to consider, discuss, and practice ethical decision-making, Reybold, Halx, and Jimenez contend that student affairs professionals will advance a more complex approach—one that balances the regulatory, situated, and collective ethics, which were described earlier in the chapter.

New student affairs professionals, defined as "first time, full-time staff with 5 or fewer years of experience" (Renn and Jessup-Anger 2008, 319), are in a complicated situation as it pertains to ethics and ethical decision-making. Many are still in a process of identity formation (Chickering and Reisser 1993) and early self-authorship (Baxter Magolda 2001), yet they are also in positions where they often serve as advisers and supervisors to undergraduate students who are only a few years younger than they are. Thus, they both *are* mentors and *need* mentors for ethical decision-making. Liddell, Cooper, Healy, and Stewart (2010) frame the possibility of situating *ethical elders* on campus, or those who can serve as mentors who help provide guidance for moral and ethical decision-making. Liddell and colleagues borrow from Sharon Daloz Parks's work to define a mentor as someone who (1) sees a learner as capable but perhaps not yet refined in cognitive authority, (2) provides support for growth while challenging to provide momentum toward a learner's potential, (3) encourages the learner to meet high expectations, and (4) is authentic and caring while the learner works through challenges. In sum, a mentor holds space and provides support for a learner to step into deeper cognitive complexity and ethical clarity.

Ethical elders may address two needs new professionals have related to ethical decision-making. First, an ethical elder can provide that space and support for new professionals to grow in their cognitive complexity and ethical decision-making. In this role, the ethical elder serves as a mentor, helping new professionals work through the day-to-day ethical dilemmas they face by encouraging them to draw from different ethical foundations and weigh competing demands. Second, an ethical elder can serve as a role model to help new professionals understand how they (the new professional) might serve in that same capacity for the students with whom they are in contact. By providing new professionals with mentorship as well as an example of mentorship, these ethical elders serve to promote both cognitive and professional development of new professionals, while also helping new professionals attend to potential barriers to ethical development.

Among these barriers to ethical development identified by Liddell and colleagues (2010) are personal dimensions, including such issues as conformity and a lack of ethical awareness. Conformity—the pressure to fit in—can result from a fear of being perceived as an outsider to an organization. Lack of ethical awareness arises from a lack of practice using ethical principles to guide decision-making, either because of a lack of certainty about the ethical course of action or because of inconsistent application of ethical principles. Both barriers might be mitigated by using case study analysis to practice ethical decision-making (see appendix D for an example of a professional ethics continuum exercise for ethical decision-making). As we will discuss in the next chapter, case study analysis helps to create space for alternative pathways and realities in a situation. It may also promote awareness of the different dimensions of ethics, be they regulatory, situated, or collective (Reybold, Halx, and Jimenez 2008). The following chapter provides a systematic approach to case study analysis and reflection, which may be used to promote awareness of one's ethical principles and potential courses of action. The approach may also be used to reflect on actual situations.

Chapter Two

Analyzing Case Studies

Student affairs practitioners encounter many challenging situations, but not all dilemmas are ethical ones. Deciding, for example, whether or not to abide by the speed limit is not necessarily an ethical conundrum, although it may be legally problematic. We agree with Nash and Jang (2016, 49) who assert, "Most of your genuine ethical conflicts will produce considerable 'emotional disturbance,' so be prepared for the hard cases, while hoping always for the easy ones." The cases in this book, many of which are likely based on real but deidentified experiences, may produce this kind of disturbance for readers. Some cases may seem, at initial glance, to be "the easy ones," but we anticipate that they will be more challenging than what may appear in an initial reading of the situation. Although the cases themselves are relatively short, the ethical dilemmas within each case have complexities that likely require multiple readings to fully consider and address the concern, as these situations typically impact individuals beyond the person/character immediately dealing with the conundrum. Some of these complexities are highlighted by Pope, Reynolds, and Mueller (2019, 269), who asserted, "Understanding concepts like power, organizational culture, social identities, social influence, systemic biases, and organizational change adds to an in-depth analysis of any cases or problems involving dynamic and sometimes complicated human interaction and organizational structures." The framework provided offers questions to guide the reader beyond what might appear on the surface, such as the characters or the institutional setting, to the deeper considerations noted above, including the short- and long-term implications of each potential decision for all involved as well as for the department and institution.

The ACPA/NASPA Professional Competency Areas for Student Affairs Educators (2015) identify foundational outcomes in the area of Personal and

Ethical Foundations (appendix A), noting that professionals must be able to identify ethical issues in their work and use appropriate resources for solving ethical dilemmas. Case studies are useful mechanisms for helping student affairs professionals understand how they might go about making important decisions and practicing that decision-making in low- to no-stakes circumstances. Vaccaro, McCoy, Champagne, and Siegle (2013) suggest that while some professionals rely on instinct to make decisions, others rely on a process that they have perfected over their career. Often, though, it takes considerable experience to incorporate such a process into one's work, and while ideally professionals will not encounter numerous ethical dilemmas, realistically we know that readers will be faced with some ethical challenges in their student affairs work (Eberhardt and Valente 2007). Practicing decision-making by working through case studies results in a greater level of experience than not testing our knowledge, skills, and instincts through such activities. Being able to practice decision-making, in a situation that is not an emergency or critical, will allow for a better understanding of the decision-making process and the opportunity to maybe not perfect an approach but to gain skills in thinking through actions readers might employ in similar real-life situations. Imagine encountering a significant dilemma for the first time as a professional without having given thought to the various elements one must consider when faced with this type of situation. The cases in this book allow graduate students and newer student affairs professionals to encounter such dilemmas, providing valuable time for consideration of the situation that often is not afforded to practitioners when addressing similar circumstances in their professional work. In reviewing the cases, readers will be asked to consider their morals and ethics and create a decision process they can internalize and draw on for future ethical dilemmas, a process that is informed by relevant professional standards and competencies.

FRAMEWORK FOR CASE ANALYSIS

The purpose of this chapter is to assist emerging and current student affairs professionals in identifying important considerations when analyzing a case study. Using the framework noted below, we offer readers a method for case analysis, recognizing that this framework is just one approach to considering the situations presented. Others (Jacob, Centola, and Werkmeister 2018, Nash and Jang 2016, Stage and Hubbard 2012, Vaccaro, McCoy, Champagne, and Siegel 2013) also provide helpful guides for considering professional dilemmas and case studies, and we recommend that readers consult those valuable resources.

In the previous edition of this book, the coeditors provided this framework for case analysis that we again recommend in this edition. Readers are encouraged to give thought to the situational characteristics presented in the case in order to unpack what seems evident and discover issues that might be less apparent, and then move to analyzing the issue itself. During this analysis, readers will want to consult ethical statements, principles, and competencies such as those provided by ACPA, NASPA, and the Council for the Advancement of Standards (CAS) (appendix B). As readers make decisions about a course of action, they should consider recommendations for case characters that will limit the likelihood of future similar occurrences since we always hope to learn from experience. These recommendations may be helpful to newer professionals as they encounter similar situations in their professional work.

Case studies are often used for courses or training, and thus analysis of a case study is usually a team or group task. As such, we suggest that individual members of the team address the questions of the framework for case analysis independently, keeping notes about their rationales for decisions and approaches, before discussing the case with the larger group. This approach provides the team with multiple views and perspectives on the case, which may result in identification of nuances that could be missed without that individual review. Referencing individuals' notes about rationales, opinions, and interpretations that are important to the group's consideration of the situation will result in a rich discussion of options.

The framework for case analysis (Hamrick and Benjamin 2009) is provided below:

Identify Relevant Situational Characteristics

- Who are the main characters in the situation?
- Who are the supporting or peripheral characters?
- What are the reporting, advising, or other work relationships relevant to the situation?
- What kind of institution, program area(s), and work settings are specified, and in what ways are these relevant to the situation?
- What are the temporal characteristics involved (e.g., time of semester, relative experience level(s), requests for meetings, or other contact), and in what ways are these relevant to the situation?

Analyze the Situation

- What is troubling, disturbing, or of concern to you in the case? Identify and describe the problematic aspect(s) as you see it (or them).
- What makes certain aspects of this situation troubling or a concern for you? Consult your own background beliefs and core values.

- Are there aspects in this situation that, while perhaps not troubling to you, might be troubling to others involved in this situation or impacted by it?
- Who is engaged in and/or affected by the situation?

Consult Ethical Principles

- Act to benefit others: In what ways are people benefited, disadvantaged, or disserved?
- Promote justice: In what ways is the cause of justice advanced, promoted, stymied, or threatened?
- Respect autonomy: In what ways is autonomy protected, advanced, violated, or curtailed?
- Be faithful: In what ways is faith or trustworthiness present, absent, or compromised?
- Do no harm: In what ways are individuals' well-being, worth, or dignity advanced, threatened, or ignored? (Kitchener 1985; see also appendix B and appendix C)

Identify and Consult Relevant Ethical Standards

- Which of the specific ethical standards or provisions from the ACPA or CAS statements provide guidance for understanding and addressing this situation? Do ethical standards or provisions from other groups such as specialty associations apply, and if so, which groups and which standards?
- In what ways do the relevant standards or principles reinforce each other as applied to this situation? In what ways are the relevant standards or principles inconsistent, and how do you reconcile any conflicts among them?

Identify the Decision Makers

- Who, if anyone, should make decision(s) and/or take action(s) in the short term? In the long term?
- Who should be consulted about this situation and potential short-term decisions or actions? Long-term decisions or actions?
- Who, if anyone, should also be called upon to make decision(s) and/or take action(s) about contextual situations or concerns (e.g., policy considerations, contributing or aggravating factors)?

Recommended Actions and Strategies

- What actions should be taken?
- What are your rationales for recommending that these actions be taken?

- What actions, while perhaps tempting, should not be taken?
- What is your rationale for cautioning against taking those actions?

Appraise the Decision

- Revisit the five ethical principles above to evaluate your recommended decisions and actions. In what ways do your decisions and actions serve to benefit others, promote justice, respect autonomy, demonstrate faithfulness, and do no harm?
- What, if any, changes would you suggest for the characters or case settings that could minimize the likelihood of a future, similar occurrence?

Contextual Factors

- Suggest hypothetical changes to the events, circumstances, or characters, and brainstorm how these alterations may impact your analyses and ethical decision making. Such challenges can amplify certain aspects or raise additional issues in the cases, ultimately reinforcing the contextual sensitivities of perceptions and judgments.

CASE STUDY AND ANALYSIS

Using the case study below (Dougharty 2009), we put the framework for case analysis to use in an example application, which can serve as a resource for considering the cases in the book. From the analysis, we offer explanations of our decision-making and recommendations for action, using the framework as our guide. As a practice opportunity, we suggest that readers review the case completely and carefully while taking notes regarding important information and readers' personal responses to and interpretations of the situation presented.

Who Is Living Here? By W. Houston Dougharty

Balancing the demands of life as a first-year, full-time graduate student and resident coordinator in family housing at the Principal State University's campus at San Tomas (a regional Hispanic-serving university enrolling seventeen thousand students in the western United States) is no easy task, but Adrian thoroughly enjoys her position. Having a partner who works full-time at a local bank and a very active two-year-old toddler also makes her life very full.

One of the things Adrian likes best about her job is the wide variety of residents with whom she works—PSU students, mostly graduate students, and their families from several countries. The four apartment buildings that Adrian oversees house people of a variety of ages and life experiences who speak many different languages and study a variety of academic disciplines. She has gotten to know many of her residents well, and she regards many of them as friends and close neighbors.

PSU's family housing apartments are in high demand, and the university maintains clear eligibility requirements for residents. At least one resident must be a full-time PSU student, and they may reside with legally recognized partners or spouses and/or up to four children for whom the PSU student is legal guardian. Furthermore, the policy specifies that residents who violate this policy are subject to eviction. So far, only minor issues have arisen with family housing residents, and Adrian has realized that most of the problems have resulted from misunderstandings or misinterpretation of PSU policies.

Bernardo Gabaldon is a chemistry graduate student from Central America. He shares his apartment with his spouse, Margarita, and their two elementary school-aged children, Inez and Luis. Both Bernardo and Margarita are very active in the apartment complex and the university community. They have volunteered for many committees, participated in social events, and offered to watch other residents' children on occasion. Recently, they coordinated a program where they spoke about the current political and economic strife in their home country, and the difficulties faced by citizens there—including many of their own family members and friends back home. Bernardo added that he was an active member of the political opposition as a college student before coming to PSU for graduate work. He said, "Sometimes we fear for the safety of our relatives. I don't think we should return until the current ruling party is out of power."

Adrian's next-door neighbor's seven-year-old son, Drew, often played with the Gabaldon children and spent a great deal of time at their apartment. One evening, Adrian and her partner invited Drew and his mom Kimberly over for a barbecue. In the middle of dinner, as they were talking about the larger than usual numbers of people in some of the apartment buildings this year, Drew added to his mom, "Yeah, and there are new people at Inez and Luis's house to play with now, too."

Adrian smiled and thought nothing of it, assuming he was referring to other children living in the complex. However, after dinner, Drew and Adrian's partner and their two year old went into the living room to watch a video. Once they had left the kitchen, Kimberly told Adrian quietly, "There are rumors in the complex that there are non-students living at the Gabaldons' apartment, Adrian—people who only leave the apartment after dark." Kimberly added that neighbors think they are relatives who are in the country illegally. Kimberly begged Adrian not to tell anyone because "everyone loves Bernardo and Margarita, and we don't want to see anything happen to them."

Adrian ran into Bernardo around midnight in the community laundry room, where Bernardo was carrying two large stacks of folded clothes and also holding Luis's hand. Luis yawned deeply and rubbed his eyes. When Adrian commented on his heavy load, Bernardo replied, "Yes, our kids go through a lot of clothes." He hesitated and then added, "And we have company. Margarita and I have a couple of relatives staying with us temporarily. But it won't be long. Their documents should come through any day now, and they can move on." Bernardo hurried out the door, telling Luis that he will go to bed soon.

The next morning Adrian attended the monthly Graduate Student Services meeting which included representatives from Residence Life, the International Students Office, Enrollment Services, and the Student Health Center. On a monthly basis, this group gathered to discuss student services issues related to the international student population at PSU. Before the meeting started, Ted, an International Students Office staff member, took a seat beside Adrian. After saying hello, Ted said to Adrian, "I've been notified that there may be a problem with Bernardo Gabaldon's visa status, I need for you to send me verification of his residence at the student apartment complex—just an e-mail will be fine for now. And could you let him know that he should contact me ASAP? He hasn't responded to my phone messages or e-mails from yesterday. Have you seen him lately?"

What should Adrian do and why?

Identify Relevant Situational Characteristics

Adrian and Bernardo Gabaldon are main characters in this case, and supporting characters include Margarita Gabaldon, the Gabaldon children (Inez and Luis), Kimberly, the Gabaldon's visiting relatives, and Ted. As the resident coordinator in family housing, Adrian oversees the area where Bernardo and his family live, and as such she has responsibility for, among other things, providing support to residents as well as enforcing housing and university policy. Adrian's personal relationship with Kimberly, another resident of the housing area, results in her hearing the rumor about the visiting Gabaldon family members, although Bernardo himself makes a comment to Adrian about having temporary family visitors. Other important relationships to consider include Bernardo and Margarita's familial relationships and concern for their well-being as well as the working relationship of Adrian and Ted. Additionally, Adrian's relationship with other residents of the housing area must be considered, as her actions in this case may be relayed to other community members, affecting their assumptions about support, their decisions about policies, and their perception of consequences for policy violations.

Principle State University at San Tomas, a Hispanic-serving institution, is located in the western United States and, with seventeen thousand students, could be considered medium to large in size. Identifying an institution as a Hispanic-serving institution (HSI) provides information about the students served by the university, meaning that a significant number of Latino/a students are enrolled; Bernardo is part of that population. Hirt (2006) emphasized that professionals at HSIs work with both students and their families, which she noted as uniquely different than other institutions at which professionals often engage with students and their parents (as opposed to larger family units). As noted, Bernardo and his family are primary characters in this case. The case is situated in residential life and housing, specifically in a family housing unit, which is relevant because of the eligibility requirements residents on campus must meet for living there. As noted, each resident must be a full-time student or be the legal partner or child of a full-time student; Bernardo and his immediate family meet this requirement as he is the full-time student, and his wife Margarita and his children Inez and Luis are his legal partner and children. However, visiting family members are not permitted to reside in the housing area. What is not noted in the case is any type of visitation policy; for example, are there limits on the number of nights visitors can stay/visit in an apartment? Fire safety standards may also be at play as, depending on the number of visitors, fire safety codes may be violated. Finally, there is a current issue regarding Bernardo's visa status, although we do not know if this is in any way connected to his visiting family members. Ted's asking for confirmation of Bernardo's residence may be benign, but what may feel more concerning for Adrian (and ultimately for Bernardo) is the request for Bernardo to contact Ted.

Analyze the Situation

There are a number of potentially troubling elements to this situation. First and foremost, an issue has arisen with Bernardo's visa status. Although Ted does not communicate this as an emergency, he says there "may" be an issue and asks Adrian to have Bernardo contact him. In her role as the resident coordinator for family housing, it would be common for Adrian to be asked to convey information to her residents. For Bernardo's benefit, it is important that Adrian convey this message quickly to him.

Secondly, Adrian must consider her responsibilities, if any, regarding the visiting Gabaldon family. Adrian is initially informed of the rumor about Bernardo's visitors, and then the rumor is confirmed by Bernardo himself, although he assures her that these individuals are visiting temporarily. In her role as the resident coordinator for family housing, Adrian could be concerned that the Gabaldon family may be violating residence life policies regarding who can live in the housing area. Additionally, she does not know how many people are visiting. As a result, in the event of an emergency like a fire, for example, she would be unaware of how many individuals to be concerned about. Given that Kimberly, another resident, was the first to inform Adrian about the visitors, Adrian is aware that others within the living community are aware of the situation. Not addressing the situation may reflect on her professionalism and send messages to community members that Adrian will allow behaviors that may violate policies to go unaddressed, compromising her role. Finally, Adrian recognizes the contributions of the Gabaldon family to the family housing community and may worry that they will be sanctioned in some way, potentially through removal from the community. As a parent herself, Adrian could be troubled by the resulting upheaval, especially for Inez and Luis, if the family is removed from the housing area. Student affairs professionals who are parents and partners may have beliefs and core values affected by those roles that influence their opinions.

Political beliefs may impact the way a student affairs professional views this situation, particularly specific views one may hold about immigration as immigration questions are potential elements of this case; the case study itself was written more than ten years ago, and the current focus on immigration has made these issues even more thorny today. Beyond the possibility that the Gabaldons may be allowing family to live with them and thus violating the housing policy, Bernardo has noted that the family members are waiting for their documentation, which they anticipate receiving in a few days. What Adrian does not know is what that documentation is. Although their lack of documentation may lead Adrian to assume that they are undocumented aliens, that may not be the case; "documentation" could be anything from new visas to permission to work documents. Adrian's knowledge of these visitors staying in the family housing area may be troubling her, but the fact that she is employed by a Hispanic-serving institution might suggest to her a duty to aid the family. Ultimately, she must decide if she is going to delve into the situation and perhaps surface a policy violation or something even more concerning.

Others who may be affected by this situation include residents in the family housing community. First, an increase in people using the resources and services in the community (for example, laundry facilities) can create tensions. As well, additional residents can result in an increase in noise and a decrease in available community space, although Kimberly noted that the visitors stay inside during the day, suggesting that they are trying not to be seen. While it may seem extreme to think that a few visitors could cause much upheaval, if other residents invite or allow their family members to similarly visit, the overall effect on the community could be considerable.

Ted's inability to reach Bernardo, and the fact that Bernardo has not responded to Ted's outreach, adds to the problem. Ted indicates that there is a concern about Bernardo's visa status, although he does not indicate what the problem actually is. Adrian may fear that any attention to Bernardo at this time could raise subsequent questions and issues associated with his family members' visit. However, what Ted has requested—confirmation of Bernardo's student residence—is a reasonable request that is intended to aid the student. Additionally, regarding his visa status, Bernardo should be able to approach a staff member who he trusts to talk about changes in his visa or his status. His lack of response to Ted may suggest that a trusting relationship does not exist, or that no relationship exists at all. Given the size of the institution, it is plausible that Bernardo does not know Ted or others in the Office of International Students very well, particularly if he has not had questions or issues for which he needed their assistance.

The potential stress of the situation also may be affecting Bernardo and his immediate family. The reader does not know, and Bernardo may not either, what consequences are possible if he and his family are in violation of an institutional policy or law. As a graduate student, Bernardo likely has academic obligations that may go unmet because he is caring for visiting family members. It also appears that the situation may be affecting his children, as Adrian sees a very tired young Luis with Bernardo in the laundry room at midnight. As a graduate student herself, Adrian may experience concern for Bernardo and his ability to be successful as a student because of the additional pressures he may be experiencing.

Consult Ethical Principles

Professionals will naturally consider their own personal theories as they think about this case, but as Ignelzi and Rychener (2018, 6) noted, "the personal theories of individuals are primary and valuable, but are insufficient when not informed by the more formal theories, research, and standards of a profession." As such, formal professional principles and standards, such as those provided by the Council for the Advancement of Standards (CAS), ACPA, and other professional associations, must be considered.

The CAS Statement of Shared Ethical Principles (appendix B) notes three principles that are primary considerations in this case. Two principles, non-malfeasance and beneficence, can be jointly considered. The principle of non-malfeasance requires us to do no harm, and beneficence requires that we seek beneficial outcomes and be thoughtful in our consideration of others. Not conveying the potential visa concern information to Bernardo could result in harm to him and his family. As well, Adrian has to consider how reporting a visitation policy violation, if one exists, may result in harm to Bernardo and his family. Seeking positive outcomes for everyone is critical and collaborating with her supervisor and other university personnel is imperative in this situation. Sharing the information she currently has with her supervisor, who likely has greater knowledge of the resources available to assist Bernardo and his family, is a good starting point assuming that the Gabaldons need that assistance. At a minimum, if they are visiting for an extended period of time and that is not permitted in the family housing community, aiding them in finding other appropriate accommodations can help. As well, Ted and his colleagues in the Office of International Students may be able to assist. If there is an immigration issue with either Bernardo or his extended family, it is likely that this is not the first time the institution has had undocumented family members within the community, and they may already have a process in place for helping these individuals. Adrian also must be thoughtful about the impact of visitors on other students living in the community.

The principle of justice is a critical consideration in this case, as well. Preserving the dignity of the Gabaldon family must occur and treating them respectfully and fairly is of the utmost importance. At the same time, the principle notes that professionals must abide by laws and policies. We do not know if Adrian is informed about immigration law, but as a staff member she would be aware of institutional policies and must perform her policy enforcement role if a policy is being violated. Again, given that Principle State University at San Tomas is a Hispanic-serving institution, it is possible that professionals at the university have tackled similar situations in the past, and thus working with her supervisor and others will likely benefit both Adrian and the Gabaldon family.

Identify and Consult Relevant Ethical Standards

Ethical standards provided by professional organizations help guide decisions in this case and often mirror the principles highlighted above. Adrian has a responsibility to the institution to upholding the policies of Principle State University (e.g., ACPA 3.1) and to alerting appropriate staff members about situations that may be disruptive or affect her ability to be effective in her role (e.g., ACPA 3.5; ACPA 3.6). She also has an obligation as a steward of university resources, and as such must ensure that university facilities are used for the benefit of the students (e.g., ACPA 3.18). Adrian also may have strong views about immigration and must ensure that her actions do not suggest a conflict of interest (e.g., ACPA 3.19) by either causing harm to the Gabaldon family if she holds negative views about immigration or acting in unlawful ways if she holds positive views. Social responsibility is noted by professional organizations as well, and ACPA notes the benefits of diversity within our communities. ACPA (n.d., 5) also indicates that professionals must "demonstrate concern for the welfare of all students and work for constructive change on behalf of students," while also highlighting the expectation that professionals must recognize the effect of violations of legal standards on both the professional and the institution. In this case, concern for Bernardo and his family, as well as her legal obligations, may weigh on Adrian.

The Association of College and University Housing Officers-International (ACUHO-I) offers ethical principles that are specific to the functional area of the case. According to ACUHO-I (2015, 8), "Staff members are knowledgeable about and remain current with respect to the obligations and limitations placed upon the institution by constitutional, statutory, and civil law, and by external governmental agencies and institutional policies. This includes 'duty to accommodate' legislation," and legal advice should be available to staff members. As well, the organization indicates that clear written contract terms as well as procedures for contract cancellation must be conveyed to residents. If a visitation policy exists and if Bernardo is violating that policy, he should have been made aware of both the policy and consequences for violating that policy when he entered into his housing contract.

Although the immediate issue in the case is regarding the housing situation, Ted also may have an ethical dilemma when he ultimately is able to reach Bernardo. As a staff member in the Office of International Students, Ted may be aware of and expected to use as a guide the ethical principles provided by NAFSA: Association of International Educators. These principles include a commitment to educational success, integrity, respect, and creating inclusive environments as well as legal compliance (NAFSA 2019).

Identify the Decision Makers

A number of different decisions must be made in this case, with various decision makers involved. Ultimately, Adrian is a decision maker as she must decide whether or not to discuss her potential concerns about Bernardo's visiting family members with him or with her supervisor. She also must determine if she will share what she knows about the Gabaldon family with other university personnel, which may include Ted or other members of the Office of International Students, her direct supervisor, or the university's legal counsel. Adrian's decisions may jeopardize her own position as both a graduate student and a residence life staff member, which may lead her to consider consulting with her academic advisor as well.

Bernardo also is a decision maker in this case, although he may feel that he has limited choices. He may choose to continue keeping his family visitors out of sight as much as possible in the hopes that a policy violation, if one exists, is not noted and the documentation he mentioned does arrive. As an alternative, he might consider seeking assistance and guidance from campus officials, perhaps in the Office of International Students, or even someone within the community who may be a supporter of immigration.

Another decision maker in this case is the director of housing, who may conclude that Bernardo and his family are violating institutional policy and thus may choose to sanction Bernardo in some way, including canceling Bernardo's housing contract. As well, if the visiting family members are violating immigration laws, the director may choose to report them to the police. Conversely, the director may make the decision not to sanction Bernardo if a policy is being violated. With either decision, the director may opt to help Bernardo seek assistance for his family. Ted also may be a decision maker once he is able to make contact with Bernardo. Like others, he may be able to assist Bernardo and his family or report them if he believes a policy or law has been violated.

Recommended Actions and Strategies

Adrian's first action must be to contact Bernardo and ensure that he is aware of the potential visa status issue. While it is possible that this information will cause additional stress for Bernardo, it is imperative that any immigration issue be resolved so that he can maintain his student status and complete his degree if that is his desire. If Bernardo seems hesitant to contact Ted, Adrian might offer to assist him by inviting Ted to her office for a meeting with Bernardo or accompanying Bernardo when he goes to meet with Ted in the Office of International Students.

Next, Adrian should consult relevant policies as well as her supervisor to identify potential housing policies at issue. As Adrian is a graduate assistant, it is likely that her supervisor is not the director of housing, and thus that individual also may need to be brought into the situation if there is more than a housing policy to be addressed or considered. If the visitors' immigration status is a concern, Adrian's supervisor or the director of housing may need to contact legal counsel and also should make contact with any community agencies that provide assistance to immigrants so that the Gabaldon family has support. Clearly, the family's attempts to remain unseen within the community suggest a desire for secrecy, which may be connected to Bernardo wishing to help his family but not alert others of a policy violation, or it could suggest fear related to immigration issues. As previously noted, these family members may be legal immigrants awaiting needed documentation, but they may be concerned that even their legal immigration status will not protect them from discrimination if they are seen. Decisions must be made about how quickly or if the non-students will be asked to leave and if Bernardo and his family will have their housing contract canceled or if any other consequences will result if an institutional policy is being violated. If there is a legal issue at hand, Adrian and her professional colleagues may find that this situation creates a need to revisit policies and procedures to ensure that staff are prepared should similar situations occur in the future. In this current situation, readers may assume that this preparation has not happened, but we are not privy to information about Adrian's training.

When considering recommended actions, readers must also consider actions that should not be taken. Ignoring the situation is not an option. Adrian might want to convince herself that she need not act because what she heard from Kimberly was a rumor, but when Bernardo himself told her that his family members were staying with him, Adrian became obligated to address the situation. If Adrian jumps to the conclusion that Bernardo's family members are illegal immigrants, an action Adrian could take is to simply call the police without consulting a supervisor if she assumes that the documentation issue presents a violation of the law. This step is discouraged; Adrian (nor the reader) does not have sufficient evidence to assume that the awaited documentation confirms that the Gabaldon family has violated immigration laws.

Appraise the Decision

By prioritizing Bernardo's well-being and identifying conveying the information about his visa concern as primary, Adrian addresses the ethical principles of non-malfeasance and beneficence. Not providing the information to Bernardo or not encouraging him to meet with Ted could certainly result in harm to Bernardo; not resolving the visa issue could prevent him from achieving his educational goals and potentially result in termination of his visa and removal from the country. Adrian's concern for Bernardo's overall well-being should be preeminent. By consulting her supervisor for next steps, Adrian also is abiding by the principles of non-malfeasance, beneficence, and justice as she is seeking to aid and support Bernardo and his family in an informed way. Her intent with this action is to assist the Gabaldon family in their desire to remain in the country, as their pending documentation suggests this as a goal. As well, aiding her resident and his family acts to promote their dignity and preserve their welfare. Eliminating barriers to student learning also is an element of the justice principle, and one barrier to learning that Bernardo may be experiencing is his concern for and need to aid his family. Helping him address the situation, whether it is simply one of too many people in one household or something more difficult, will contribute to the elimination of such barriers to his success.

Contextual Factors

Factors not noted in the case may be important considerations. Would the decision change if the university was not Hispanic serving? Would it be less likely that a professional would encounter extended family members living with students or visiting for a lengthy timeframe? As noted, HSI professionals tend to interact with family members beyond students and parents. Professionals at HSIs might be accustomed to this, but at a different institutional type, this could be a novel issue. What if San Tomas was a sanctuary city?

Chapter Three

Admissions and Orientation Cases

CAN SHE POST THAT ON FACEBOOK?
CLIFF HAYNES

Rena has served as a coordinator for international admissions at the University of the River for four years in the Department of Enrollment Services, which includes admissions, financial aid, and the registrar. She was excited to be promoted last year as the assistant director for international admissions. The University of the River (UR) is a public regional comprehensive university and classified as a research university with higher research activity by the Carnegie Foundation for the Advancement of Teaching and an emerging research university within the state. Its 35,000 students choose from 90 bachelor's degrees, 80 master's degrees, and 10 doctoral degree programs. It is located in a growing community of 60,000 people in the suburbs of a major city. The campus is unique in the state as a river runs through campus and the town, providing recreational activities for students throughout the year. Its access to a large metropolitan city also provides access for commuter students and a growing international student population.

In her new role, Rena supervises four full-time coordinators and a program assistant. Additionally, the office employs several work-study student employees. Rena hired all of the coordinators after beginning her new position, except for her program assistant, Cathy Schwimmer. Cathy has been at UR for close to twenty years and is quite competent at her job. She provides the "historical knowledge" for the unit and is generally well liked among the rest of the department. Rena relied heavily on Cathy's knowledge of the unit to help her transition into her new role as assistant director.

Cathy is well liked among the other veteran front-line staff within the Department of Enrollment Services. This group of veteran staff affectionately call her "Chatty Cathy" when they eat lunch in the break room. However, new hires often comment about her being "stuck in her ways" and not very welcoming to changes. Other unit directors have commented that their new secretaries purposefully plan their lunch so as not to be in the breakroom with "Cathy's clique." Rena recalls from her experience as a new staff member in the unit that Cathy always seemed "untouchable," even if she did not follow the new protocol or was less than welcoming of new staff.

Three months into the semester and Rena's new position, a local newspaper publishes an article about a drug bust in which twenty people were arrested, including some UR students. The story has been the talk of the town and around campus. Many students, faculty, community members, and administrators have made their opinions known over social media. A few days after the newspaper article goes viral, Rena arrives to find a printout of a Facebook post in her mailbox. It is a thread of the comments to a post from the local newspaper, which includes the following exchange:

Ima Local: Wow, I can't believe this is happening.
Cathy Schwimmer: Me neither! 2 of them are international students that are here on legal visas and I can confirm that. I work at UR.
John Q Public: Cathy, lol. International students who are confirmed drug traffickers. Guess UR's admissions standards aren't what they used to be.

Cathy's comment is circled in red with a note "Is she allowed to discuss students like this?" The printout is anonymous, and Rena has no idea who would have put it in her mailbox.

Rena notes that Cathy's comment is time stamped as posted at 6:43 pm, and Cathy gets off work at 5:00 pm. This is one of Rena's first major challenges in her new supervisory role, so she wants to respond correctly. She recalls from her legal issues class that state employees have the right to freedom of speech after hours, but this post troubles her in regard to institutional policy and FERPA. Additionally, Rena knows that the university has a social media policy that allows a supervisor to discuss any social media use outside of official work hours to address employees' activities that are illegal, against university policy, or against professional standards.

What should Rena do?

UNDOCUMENTED AND UNWORTHY?
NICOLE MARTINEZ

Central State University is a mid-sized public institution located in the mid-western United States. Though the state in which CSU is situated is politically conservative, the town where the school is located tends to be more progressive. CSU has an active Office of Diversity and Inclusion, headed by Wayne, who has worked diligently to increase the number of minority students on campus and ensure support services for non-English-speaking students. Under Wayne's leadership, the university even received a federal grant to recruit and mentor migrant students from local communities around the CSU campus. The program, called CASE (Central Aid for Student Excellence), works in high schools to help students prepare and apply to CSU their senior year. Once on campus, CASE students meet one-on-one with program staff for their freshman year to ensure a smooth and successful transition to college life. To incentivize enrollment Wayne even secured funds to award scholarships to first-year CASE students.

Juan is a sophomore at CSU and participated in the CASE program. He is the first in his family to attend college. His mother and father work seasonally as agricultural workers in a town about an hour away for eight months out of the year. In the winter his parents relocate their three children to Florida, so they can find work. Juan has lived in the United States for the majority of his life but is not a U.S. citizen. When he was sixteen years old, he and his younger siblings were able to gain temporary legal status through the Deferred Action for Childhood Arrivals (DACA) program. Juan has a work permit and a part-time, off-campus job, in addition to attending college as a full-time student. Even with the support of the CASE program, Juan had difficulties in his first year of college, earning a 2.5 GPA for the year. The scholarship he received in his first year from CASE enabled him to attend the university and continue to contribute financially to his family, but with his grades during his freshman year he has not been able to secure any additional funding for the upcoming year.

The CASE program referred Juan to the CSU financial aid office to explore his financial options. Juan met with a financial aid counselor and was told that his options are few. Per federal law, students with DACA status, like Juan, cannot receive federal financial aid. Other students might consider private lender loans through a bank or credit union but that would likely require the applicant to have citizen status and an established credit history, which neither Juan nor his parents have. While some colleges offer scholarship opportunities for students with DACA status, CSU offers no such program. In fact, most CSU institutional scholarships stipulate that recipients must be in-state students or U.S. citizens to receive the award.

After his meeting with financial aid, Juan contacts Wayne to inform him that he will likely need to leave CSU due to finances. Juan is not the only student in this situation and Wayne decides it is time to seek out a solution that could help many former CASE students. Wayne contacts Laura, a senior officer in the Development and Giving Office, who helped Wayne secure funding for his first-year CASE scholarship from a member of the community a few years ago.

Although she thinks the idea of a DACA scholarship may be a hard sell, Laura sympathizes with Juan's situation and would love to help. She agrees to write a proposal to raise funds to support a scholarship for financially needy students who have an undocumented citizenship status, to encourage diversity and financially support under-served populations. When she takes the idea to her supervisor, the director of Development and Giving, he says a similar idea was actively pursued about ten years ago and created an uproar. After hearing of fundraising to financially support "illegals," several high-profile donors issued vague threats of pulling funding from the university and the project was ended.

After hearing of Juan's plight, the director of Development and Giving suggested scholarship funds be found for Juan and awarded on the basis of his first-generation status. It is the director's preference to try and help students with undocumented status individually, if possible, to avoid any appearance of impropriety. At this news Wayne is very upset and calls for a meeting of campus leaders to draft a plan of action to better support DACA students. He asks Laura to explore what peer institutions do to help students with undocumented status and prepare a fundraising plan to solicit donations, when approval is given. He requests that the CASE program be placed on the university president's calendar in the upcoming months and intends to bring CASE students, including Juan, to the proposed meeting. Laura is torn. She recognizes the need to fundraise for students who have DACA status and is personally drawn to the project, but she believes that following Wayne's directive might be seen as insubordination by her supervisor.

What should Laura do?

NOT SO HONORABLE HONORS COLLEGE
JEFFREY KYLE GRIM AND DANIEL HARTLEP

Melissa entered her office hurriedly to prepare for her first admissions meeting. She is excited to be behind the scenes to see how students are selected. As she catches a glimpse of her name plate, "Melissa Jones—Northwind University," she feels great pride. As a first-generation student of color growing up just thirty minutes away, Northwind always seemed out of reach until she secured her first job there. Melissa recently graduated from her two-time alma mater Eastern Market University (EMU) with a MA in student affairs administration. She was starting to feel comfortable in her role as program manager for the Honors College at Northwind University (NU), and now Melissa is unsure if she misjudged whether this role fits with her values of social justice and equity. NU is the flagship university in a midwestern state and has a renewed focus on recruiting high academically achieving students, while also ensuring racial and socioeconomic diversity of the undergraduate student population. The Honors College is an academic unit that reports directly to the associate provost and dean of undergraduate studies and was designed to attract and retain high-achieving students to NU from some of the local private school competitors. The Honors College makes up about 6 percent of the undergraduate student population at NU but does not have the same demographic profile. Melissa was particularly excited to grow the racial and socioeconomic diversity amongst the high-achieving Honors College student population that is not as diverse as the institution itself.

Every year during the final week of the fall semester, the Honors College Admissions Committee convenes to admit a small and competitive pool of applicants. This admissions cycle is for first-year students currently on campus as well as future NU transfer students. The Admissions Committee is composed of the director of student services for the Honors College and three faculty members that represent the college's interdisciplinary nature. Melissa's role was solely to provide administrative support and quick access to applications and supplemental materials for the committee members to judge.

As all members of the committee convened in the cramped conference room, Melissa could feel anxiety in the air as everyone was exhausted from the end of the semester and eager to begin their summer break. There were only twenty-three spots for second-year students in the Honors College, and there were 144 first-year and transfer applicants. Each student application was independently reviewed by two members of the Admissions Committee. Professor Contreras, a professor of biology who has been working at NU for twenty-five years (with the Honors College for fifteen years) and chair of the Admissions Committee started the conversation. He began describing a Latina student as "resilient" and a "future scholar." Professor Contreras identifies as Chicano and works closely with college access programs for underrepresented students interested in STEM fields and is known to be an advocate for students of color in the Honors College. Melissa was glad Professor Contreras was advocating for students of color until she noticed another pattern. When a young Nigerian American woman was discussed, Professor Contreras described her as "not articulate" and mentioned her "wild hair and appearance."

Melissa could feel her neck and back tense. She looked over to see her own large braids reflected in the glass door. She sighed and was about to challenge what "wild hair" meant, but Dr. Boseman, Melissa's supervisor and director of student services for the Honors College, interjected to let the committee know that the Nigerian American student also had two noise violations from her residence hall, even though conduct files were not supposed to be part of the Honors College admissions process. Previously, Dr. Boseman was the assistant director of the Office of Student Conduct and had access to student records that are normally not considered in the Honors College admissions process. After Dr. Boseman interjected, the student was quickly denied admission into the program.

Next, Professor Covaci, an associate professor of psychology whose research centers on identity development and social media usage in millennials, noted that he had found evidence of underage alcohol use in six of the applicants' Facebook pictures; additionally, three other female applicants wore "short" dresses that were not "dignified" of honors students. Melissa was confused because she did not think the committee agreed to look at applicants' Facebook profiles, but she also knew that Professor Covaci was new to the Honors College Admissions Committee, although he had been at NU for nine years. Unfortunately, no one challenged him, and the committee agreed that those nine students could be eliminated from the admissions process.

As the admissions conversation progressed, there were two students in particular who did not take challenging classes in their first semester, nor submit strong personal statements, but were involved in the Sailing Club. Professor McNulty, professor of ceramic arts and faculty advisor to the Sailing Club, shared that she knew the students had exemplary leadership skills and she asked the committee to admit them based on their "intangible" skills and her informal recommendation. She also said the two women would "fit in" well with the Honors College. Since Professor McNulty had worked with the Honors College for six of her seven years at NU, she "knew who a good fit would be," and it seemed the committee agreed with her by admitting the two students.

A few more students were discussed, and then they got to Harrison, a White student with whom Melissa had interacted before. Melissa shared with the group that Harrison contacted her to see what types of activities he should engage in during his first semester in order to increase his chances of being admitted to the Honors College for his sophomore year. Melissa shared with the committee that she gave advice to Harrison and it seemed like he enacted it. With minimal conversation, Harrison was admitted because of the advice Melissa gave and a comment Professor McNulty made about his influential parents. Melissa's stomach dropped. The conversation about this student was much shorter and less critical than that of the previous Nigerian American student who had not been admitted. It did not seem that anyone in the room was noticing the inequity inherent in the committee's decision-making. With thoughts from the entire meeting running through her head, Melissa had an emotional reflex. Before she could even think about what exactly she wanted to say, she cleared her throat and said, "Excuse me." The committee stopped to look at her.

What should Melissa do?

NEW SPACE FOR NEW STUDENT
CHELSEA JORDAN AND MICHELLE J. BOETTCHER

David is in his first year as a coordinator in the Office of New Student Events (NSE) at Faith College, a small private Christian institution in the Southwest. His primary responsibility is to coordinate logistics during campus visits, which includes assigning housing for students and their families at orientation. Although David's undergraduate and master's programs were at public institutions, he is enjoying working at and learning about a new institutional setting via the religiously affiliated environment at Faith.

David is in his second of three orientation weeks when he gets a call from the front desk of the hall where students are checking in for their visits. Tabitha, a second-year orientation NSE team member and a junior at Faith, says, "We have an issue with a student's room. I need your help." David is surprised since Tabitha has been a strong leader all summer and, in fact, has helped him learn a lot about processes and policies at this institution.

When David gets to the desk he sees Tabitha talking with a student in a lounge near the desk. Nathan, another student worker, pulls David to the side and explains, "Tabitha is with Payton who told us that they are a gender non-conforming student. They were assigned to room with another new student, Elizabeth, because their registration paperwork says 'female,' but Payton says they would prefer to room with a male. They are being really cool about it, and they said that this happens all the time. But neither Tabitha nor I knew what to do, so we called you."

Nathan goes on to tell David that he heard some orientation students and their parents making comments about Payton. The parents mentioned they do not feel comfortable with Payton staying with their children, and the student staff members are unsure of how to address the parents who are upset. Nathan shares that Elizabeth's parents went up to get settled, but that they are coming back down and want to make sure that Payton does not room with their daughter, despite Elizabeth assuring them that she is fine with Payton.

Payton doesn't seem to mind the response, saying, "I'm used to these kinds of reactions. Especially from parents. It's not a big deal." However, the student staff member is concerned about Elizabeth's parents' reactions as well as what could happen if Payton were to be moved. Though Payton may be comfortable handling this difficult situation, David worries that Payton's parents will hear about it and have some concern about Payton feeling comfortable on campus.

David checks the roster for the building and finds that there are empty spaces in rooms with men in the building, empty spaces with women in the building, one empty single room on the women's floor, and no empty single rooms on the men's floor. David calls his supervisor, Susie, and explains the situation. Susie says, "Just put that person in the single on the women's floor.

It's all we can do since Payton is identified as female on the documents we have. In situations like these, we go with what the paperwork says and that's what we will do here."

What should David do?

WHEN "KEEPIN' IT REAL" GOES WRONG: #PCPOLICE
KELLY ALVARADO-YOUNG AND LOUISE MICHELLE VITAL

Maria is the first director and only professional staff member of the newly formed Office of Student Leadership at Assumption Central College (ACC), which is a big undertaking for a student affairs practitioner. New Student Orientation is one of the programs run out of the Office of Student Leadership and the office relies heavily on volunteer student leaders to manage the program. Prior to Maria's arrival two years ago, New Student Orientation was completely student run with only advisement from the dean of students, John, who directly supervises the Office of Student Leadership. Maria chose to work at ACC because it was a mid-sized, private, religiously affiliated institution on the West Coast with a student population of approximately 4,500 undergraduate students, which reminded her of her own undergraduate institution.

ACC is a selective, primarily residential campus with a two-year residence requirement for all students. Students move into their residence halls on the first day of New Student Orientation. New Student Orientation is a four-day, weekend-style orientation program and runs from Friday through Monday. Approximately 1,500 new students participate in the program. Supporting 1,500 students' transition to ACC in a short period of time is a major undertaking. Because of this, New Student Orientation requires several levels of student leader volunteers to ensure a smooth process and an impactful experience for the new students. The program is planned with a five-student Core Team. Matt, a senior, serves as liaison between the Core Team and his supervisor Maria. The Core Team trains over 250 student leaders. Leaders in these positions include fifteen major leaders who report to the Core Team and arrive a few days early for more intensive training. The major leaders are each responsible for training and supporting a group of fifteen orientation leaders, who will lead reflections, run team-building sessions, respond to questions, and manage the orientation leaders during New Student Orientation. These 200 orientation leaders work in pairs to manage a small group of 15 to 18 new students. In addition, there are 35 logistics leaders who act as ushers at major events, set up events, and answer questions across campus. All the student leaders return to campus for training a few days before the new students arrive. The major leaders receive a total of four days of training that includes two days of major training and the two days of general leader training. The orientation leaders and logistics leaders only receive two days of general training immediately before the arrival of new students. A majority of the student leaders are first-semester sophomores who have not previously held a student leadership position at ACC.

During the last day of orientation leader training, with all 250 students present, there was a Diversity and Equity session just before lunch. ACC is a predominately White institution (PWI) but is experiencing rapid demographic shifts. The incoming class boasts 30 percent students of color, 7 percent international students, and 20 percent first-generation students. These numbers have doubled within the last five years. Information shared during the session included statistics on the demographics of the incoming class, ways to use inclusive language in small group sessions with new students during orientation, and how the university mission embraces the dignity of all people. The Diversity and Equity training also addressed the focus of the university's mission "to create a more just and equitable world through recognizing the infinite worth of every person we interact with, especially the marginalized." As such, students were asked to consider difference through a lens of power and privilege.

For many of the first-time student leaders, the Diversity and Equity training was their first exposure to identity development and privilege. Each student was asked to fill out an identity wheel and discuss their most and least salient identities. The training lasted a total of seventy-five minutes. There were table discussions and case studies for the students to talk through various situations in which diversity and equity conversations may come up in their small group meetings with the incoming class. John, the dean of students, was attending the training because he was the interim director of the Diversity and Equity Center. John is a White male in his mid-fifties who has worked at ACC for more than fifteen years in various roles. This was the first time he was directly supervising the Diversity and Equity Center.

Toward the last fifteen minutes of the student leader training, Matt approaches Maria with a look of worry. Matt asks Maria to step out to the hallway for a minute. Maria is concerned because Matt walked all the way up to the front of the room to pull Maria out of the session. When they were in the hallway, Matt shows Maria a series of tweets from @ACC_ToughLove that were live tweeted throughout the Diversity and Equity training session. The profile for @ACC_ToughLove reads, "Fighting the PCness and keepin it real at @ACC!" Everything the Diversity and Equity trainer had shared during the training had been counter argued by @ACC_ToughLove and all of the tweets had included the orientation hashtag, #ACCOrientation. The final tweet argued that the increase in students of color was unfair because "those charity cases were taking the spot of smarter, better White kids that should have gotten into @ACC." The post had been on Twitter for twenty-two minutes and had already received 541 impressions, 22 likes, and 4 retweets. Matt looks at Maria and asks, "What do we do?" Although there are only fifteen minutes left in the session before the break for lunch, Maria believes the matter should be addressed immediately. John overhears the conversation and tells Maria that she should ignore the tweets for now "because the students need a break from the mentally stimulating session" and suggests they meet after the training day concludes to discuss next steps.

What should Maria do?

ADMISSION REQUIREMENTS: EXCEPTION TO THE RULE
JAMIE HECK, ANDREA (ANDI) DAVIS, AND ANGIE FISHER

Ann Gibson is a high-level executive at Rowland Medical Center, a prominent healthcare organization in a major city in the Midwest. The organization for which she works is encouraging her to pursue her doctorate of nursing practice, which has a focus on leadership and administration, as part of an overall professional growth and succession plan in which Ann is anticipated to assume the role of CEO. In order to place herself in a position to be a competitive candidate for the CEO position, she must complete a doctoral degree by the time she applies for the CEO position.

Ann called Sarah Johnson, coordinator of graduate programs at Moreland University, College of Nursing, a public research university located in a major city in the Midwest, regarding her interest in applying to their doctoral program. Current enrollment at Moreland University, College of Nursing is approximately three thousand total students. Approximately two thousand students are enrolled in nursing graduate programs. Sarah has been employed at Moreland University for about five years. Although Sarah's educational and professional background is in higher education administration, she has developed a passion for working with graduate students in helping them achieve their academic and professional goals.

Sarah was excited to speak with Ann about her interest in applying to the doctoral program. She had previously communicated with Ann in an effort to foster a relationship with Rowland Medical Center to create clinical opportunities for undergraduate and graduate students enrolled in the college, due to a national shortage of available preceptorships for nursing students. This shortage continues to cause much frustration and anxiety for all involved, including the students, institutions, and healthcare organizations. The preceptorship is a vital experience in the learning process to adequately prepare nursing students for the profession. Ann has been a pivotal stakeholder in the creation of clinical opportunities for Moreland University nursing students.

After pleasantries are exchanged, Ann says, "I feel that the doctorate of nursing practice program would be a perfect fit for me based on the length of the program and the positive feedback that I have received from colleagues who have completed this same program at Moreland University." She acknowledges that completing a doctoral degree within five years would be ambitious, but Ann expresses that her work ethic and perseverance would result in successful completion of this doctoral program within the allotted time frame.

With pride, Sarah discusses the details related to the doctoral program with Ann. As Sarah transitions to the application process and admission requirements, Ann asks about the minimum requirements for GPA and GRE scores. Ann shares that while she was able to complete her bachelor's and master's degrees at other institutions, she had encountered some obstacles in her academic endeavors. Sarah questions, "Can you describe your previous academic journey, specifically providing details related to your undergraduate and graduate GPA as well as the obstacles that you encountered that impacted your academic success?" Ann states, "I earned a 2.6 undergraduate GPA. Like many students, I was becoming acclimated to my newfound freedom during my freshman year and was struggling with time management and balancing my priorities. I also discovered quickly that pursuing an engineering degree like my father was not the appropriate path for me. Unfortunately, I made this decision after multiple semesters of earning dismal grades in courses included within the pre-engineering major." Sarah asks Ann to speak about her experience in her master's program. Ann says, "My graduate GPA was a 2.95. While I was pursuing my master's program, I was involved in major projects at work and raising two small children. I learned a lot about myself during my master's program. In hindsight, I should have established more boundaries at work and at home to be able to focus on my academic endeavors." Ann expresses that she has grown from these prior experiences. Her children are now adults, and she is in a position to dedicate her time and energy to a doctoral program, while remaining in her role as an executive at Rowland Medical Center. In addition, Ann has assumed leadership responsibilities in an effort to continue to grow professionally and place herself in a position to be qualified to serve as CEO of a healthcare organization in the future.

Sarah reviews that the College of Nursing evaluates applications holistically, considering various components, including GRE exam scores, prior undergraduate and graduate grade point averages (GPAs), goal statement, resume, letters of recommendation, leadership roles, and work experiences. The preferred application requirements for entry into the doctorate of nursing practice program is a minimum 3.0 cumulative GPA for both their undergraduate and graduate studies. The doctoral program requires the completion of the GRE exam with a minimum score of 150 on the verbal and quantitative sections and a minimum of a 4.0 on the analytical section. In addition, applicants are required to submit other application materials including resume, goal statement, and letters of recommendation.

There is a long pause after Sarah shares the characteristics of the ideal candidate for the doctorate of nursing practice program and the preferred application requirements. Ann responds, "I don't feel that the GRE provides adequate insight into my ability to successfully complete the doctoral program. Couldn't the GRE exam be waived for me given my professional experience?" Sarah responds, "Ann, I can tell that you are very passionate about continuing your education. I'd like to further review the details of your academic and professional history. I'll call you tomorrow to follow-up on our conversation." Ann concludes their conversation and states, "I'm optimistic that the GRE exam will be waived, taking into consideration my prior academic and professional experiences. I aspire to be a future graduate of this doctoral program, and I look forward to the learning and growth that I will experience as a result of the academic rigor and prestige of this program. In the future, I'm eager to advocate for the nursing profession and to serve as an active alumnae of Moreland University. My hope is that I will be able to address some of the areas warranting improvement locally and nationally. This program will allow me to have a true impact on the nursing profession. I want to provide other students with opportunities. The combination of this doctoral program and my professional aspirations will provide a platform for me to advocate for and to assist students at the College of Nursing to obtain preceptorships more readily. Thank you for your willingness to explore my options and in helping me achieve my future goals to have a direct impact on Moreland students and the local community."

As Sarah hangs up the telephone at the conclusion of their call, she ponders the connection Ann made between completing her doctoral program and the possibility of enhancing preceptorship opportunities availability for Moreland nursing students in the future. Sarah also reflects on the admission requirements for the doctoral program. Although the program conducts a holistic review of application requirements, the applicant pool has been quite competitive in the past for a program that limits the cohort to ten students. In addition, Sarah has never submitted an incomplete application to the admission review committee or advocated to waive the GRE exam previously. Would the integrity and fairness of the admission process be compromised by adhering to Ann's request to waive the GRE?

What should Sarah do?

DO I NOT EXIST? UNDOCU/DACAMENTED LATINX STUDENT EXPERIENCES WITH MICROAGGRESSIONS IN HIGHER EDUCATION
STEPHEN SANTA-RAMIREZ

Brandon, a White man, recently graduated with his master's in student affairs administration and is new in his first professional job as the coordinator of new student programs at Arizona's Northeast State University (NSU). NSU is a predominantly White, research intensive university with an enrollment of approximately 55,000 students. The university is known for having highly ranked undergraduate and graduate academic programs, has strong community relationships with many Fortune 500 companies, and has a university mission that highlights diversity and inclusivity. Brandon's department manages first-year summer orientation sessions as well as ongoing college transition, social, and educational programs throughout the academic year for NSU's first-year students.

Amanda is a rising junior at NSU, identifies as Latinx, and is pursuing a bachelor's degree in ethnic studies with a minor in border studies. Amanda was recently hired as an orientation leader through the Department of New Student Programs. As a former resident assistant managing the social justice living learning community for first-year students, Amanda is excited to begin staff training and embark on this new paraprofessional journey. Amanda arrives at staff training eager to meet and engage with her new colleagues, and after an initial glance of the room, quickly realizes that all of her peers appear to be White. During the commencement of training, Ryan, the associate director of the department who supervises Brandon, welcomes the new team and announces that Brandon will be their direct supervisor. Amanda smiles, still very excited to embrace her new paraprofessional position. Shortly after, during a team-building activity, Amanda overhears Brandon state to one of his department colleagues, "I'm very happy with the recent changes in national immigration laws. I feel like the policies are really working."

Amanda taps Brandon on the shoulder to address the remarks she overheard. Amanda shares her disagreement and states, "I am an undocumented student at NSU under the Deferred Action for Childhood Arrivals (DACA) program, which provides me and many others at NSU with a work permit and temporary reprieve from deportation. Unfortunately, in-state tuition benefits for DACA recipients were recently rescinded, which makes it even harder for us to attend college." Brandon quickly apologizes and states, "I didn't know you are Mexican; you look White. I was unaware that we had undocumented students at this university and on staff." Ryan was close in proximity and overheard the dialogue between Amanda and Brandon. Ryan immediately looked over at Brandon, very surprised by his response to

Amanda. Ryan chose to not intervene since Amanda appeared, at the moment, to be okay. Brandon looked perplexed by the look of disbelief Ryan gave him but chose not to acknowledge it and just move on with the training agenda.

Although very distant and quiet after the encounter with Brandon, Amanda continues to partake in all training activities for the remainder of the day, even though her feelings of excitement and eagerness for her new job have diminished. That evening Amanda e-mailed Brandon and wrote,

> *Dear Brandon, I did not expect to feel this way when I woke up this morning and prepared to travel to campus, but during one of the Orientation Leader training activities today I felt completely marginalized, dehumanized, and culturally invalidated by you. I overheard you state your agreement with the current anti-immigration laws enacted in the recent years, and your assumption of me being White after I shared that I am a DACA recipient. I am shocked that Latinx (or in your words "Mexican") and undocumented students were not even considered to be represented in the space. I wholly disapprove of how I was spoken to and treated by you, therefore, I have decided to resign as an Orientation Leader within the department. Unfortunately, I cannot work for a department and supervisor who does not see me, and others who share similar racial and immigrant backgrounds, as existing or being human.*

What should Brandon do?

Chapter Four

Advocacy and Inclusion Cases

HOW CAN I HELP YOU?
WAYNE GLASS AND MICHELLE J. BOETTCHER

Joy is a cisgender, queer Latinx female, who works as the coordinator of the LGBTQ+ Center at Lake University. LU is a medium-sized public institution of about ten thousand students in the Midwest with a history of progressive work supporting students, staff, and faculty around issues of identity and access. Although LU is a predominantly White institution, it has a variety of centers and offices to serve marginalized students on campus. The campus is generally considered accepting and supportive for students with a variety of backgrounds and identities. However, in the past five years there have been some racist incidents on campus (KKK fliers put on cars on campus, a faculty member who used a racial epithet in a classroom, and a controversial anti-immigration speaker on campus), and some students have talked with Joy about microaggressions they experience from students, faculty, and staff at LU and in the surrounding community.

Joy has been in her position for about a year and has enjoyed the number of students who connect with the Center. She is seen as caring, approachable, and a valuable resource to her students as well as having strong collaborative relationships with other offices and faculty across campus. The lounge space in the Center is often full of students between classes as well as during the ongoing programs and group meetings that provide safe spaces and opportunities for engagement for LGBTQ+ students on campus. Joy reports to the dean of students and after Joy's first few months on the job, she talked with the dean about the fact that the Center was being used nearly exclusively by White students. The dean encouraged Joy to work on this challenge and provided her some additional funding for events and marketing to broaden the appeal of the Center. As a result of outreach and a number of new initiatives, there has been a gradual increase in the number of students of color coming to the Center.

Joy's office is parallel to the lounge area and she always has her door open unless she is meeting with a student who asks to close the door for privacy when discussing difficult issues. One day in the fall term Joy overhears a conversation between students in the lounge about an incident in a class. Tara, a trans woman of color, shares an experience she had in a class earlier that day: "I can't believe what happened in my political science class today. The professor was talking about how history and politics are written by those who are in charge and those who are in charge tend to be the smartest at navigating systems to their own benefit. He said, 'Transvestites are today what Blacks used to be—well, transvestites and Chicanos. They are at the bottom of the totem pole in terms of social hierarchy. They are less than—I mean *seen* as less than because we always have to have someone who is less powerful, less human, and has less autonomy than we do. Now that racism is over, we have to find someone new to look down on, so we choose transvestites and illegal immigrants.'"

The other four students are outraged. "He said *transvestite*?!" one person asks loudly. "So, queers aren't smart?" asks another. "Who is this guy? We need to report him for discriminating against LGBTQ+ students in his class!"

Joy looks out and sees that all of the students, other than Tara, are White. She steps out to see if she can help. All four students besides Tara are on their feet and packing up their book bags. They explain that they want to talk more but have to get to class. Tara stays behind but doesn't respond to Joy's offer to help.

"Tara, do you want to talk more? What do you need and how can I help you? I'm really sorry you had the experience you did." Tara asks to talk with Joy in the office and closes the door behind them once they are inside.

"They don't get it," Tara begins. "They don't even see me."

"What do you mean?" Joy asks. "Who doesn't see you?"

"You heard them, right? They didn't even acknowledge the racist statement that was made. This is not about one piece of who I am. This is about all of who I am. Maybe LU and the Center aren't for me. I feel like I'm always the only person in the Center or at activities or in groups who isn't White. People just don't understand what it's like."

"Have you talked to anyone at the Latinx Center?" Joy asks.

Tara looks at Joy for a long moment and then shakes her head. "You don't get it, either. It's not that I need help with one or the other. I need support for every piece of who I am. I don't know what to do or where to go so that I feel like I belong. I was so excited to come to LU. I received several scholarships and heard about the good work the campus was doing around social justice. Now that I'm here . . . I just feel very alone. Every time I ask for help, I get directed to some other person or department. My resident advisor and I were having a really good conversation, but when I said it was tough being trans even in a housing environment that was supportive, her response was, 'Maybe you should go to the LGBT Center.' When I talked about feeling like an outsider with the Latinx Student Union committee I'm on, two people said I should come over here and talk with you. Now you are sending me to the Latinx Center."

Joy starts to apologize, but Tara interrupts her. "It's okay. I know you're doing the best you can. You don't have a big staff and you just want to help. It's just hard." Tara starts to gather her things and says she has a meeting with her academic advisor. Joy asks if they can talk more after the meeting. Tara says she is busy the rest of day, but that she will come by tomorrow before her class at noon.

As she gets ready to leave, Tara turns and says, "Don't say anything to anyone about what happened in class, okay? I need to stay on that faculty member's good side because I really need an 'A' in the class, and I might have to take courses from him again. Let's just keep all of this between us." In her role, Joy is obligated to report any bias incidents to both the dean and the Office of Equal Opportunity.

What should Joy do?

ACTIVISM OR NOT?
YULISA LIN

Amber was recently hired to serve as the new area coordinator for the Residence Life Office at Osprey University (OU). Having served as an entry-level residence hall director at a small, private college for four years, Amber looked forward to the challenge of mentoring future professionals to the field of student affairs in a different setting. Osprey University is a predominately White, large, public, and urban university located in the southeastern region of the United States, with an undergraduate enrollment of twenty-four thousand. Student activism on campus is at an all-time high, especially given the ongoing contentious national conversation on systemic racial injustice, gun control, and immigration. Political controversy has also emerged at OU, with the most recent activity focused on whether a Confederate monument on campus should be removed. Similar to other universities in this region of the United States, Confederate monuments are commonly located in public spaces, including state university campuses. While the campus climate has remained civil, there is an underlying current of tension on campus due to the increasingly antagonistic rhetoric on multiple sides of the various political issues.

Amber was excited to join the Residence Life team at Osprey University for the opportunity to supervise graduate students pursuing their master's degree in higher education and student affairs. Among her responsibilities as area coordinator, Amber will supervise two graduate hall directors and a full-time administrative coordinator, managing the daily operations of a residential community holding a total of 2,400 beds. Osprey University maintains a first-year living requirement, and 88 percent of residents living in Amber's community are first-year students. Amber's residential community is also the home for two living learning communities, one of which is focused on leadership and civic engagement. Amber identifies as a straight, White woman.

Carter is one of the two graduate hall directors who reports to Amber at Osprey University, returning to the same residential community for his last year in graduate school. As one of the few African American men on staff, he found himself constantly raising tough questions and initiating difficult conversations with his staff, his peers, and his supervisor to consider how their department approaches building an inclusive community. Over the course of his first-year experience on OU's Residence Life team, Carter received positive feedback on how he facilitates difficult conversations with his staff. Several of his resident advisors (RAs) told him that he helped them think more broadly and critically about emerging political issues at the local and national level. At his end-of-year performance review last spring, Carter expressed an interest in helping others find their voices as advocates and allies because he wanted to avoid becoming the "token diversity voice" on staff due to his identity as a person of color. With his departing supervisor's help, they brainstormed several strategies Carter could use to empower his students on finding their own voices and becoming stronger social justice advocates.

The newest member of Amber's team of graduate hall directors is Fran, a biracial Chinese American woman. In light of the strong and increasingly divisive political rhetoric at the national and local levels, Fran and her RAs have focused their programming efforts to help students develop skills necessary to respectfully navigate conversations with people who disagreed with them. So far this year, her staff have strived to hold neutral positions when facilitating community conversations, and they worked hard to create an inclusive environment that respects diverse political thought.

As the fall semester progressed, discourse regarding the Confederate monument on campus became increasingly heated. The student newspaper started to publish a series of letters written by students and alumni expressing their support to either keep, remove, or replace the Confederate monument located in one of the three campus plazas. Even though no cases of vandalism or violence so far have been reported at Osprey University, at least one incident of vandalism had already occurred at a nearby public university in the state. At Osprey, a small group of White and students of color activists submitted a petition to senior university administrators to remove the Confederate monument, however no decisions have been made public. After the state legislature had passed legislation focused on the preservation of public historical monuments two years ago, the process of pursuing the removal of any public monument on state property has become increasingly complex. In the meantime, the administration sent out an electronic memo highly discouraging staff and student workers from participating in any of the upcoming on-campus protests and counter-protests organized by student groups in favor of or against keeping the monument.

In the days following a recent on-campus student demonstration, Fran asked to speak with Amber privately. She shared that in their weekly meeting, her hall council president mentioned appreciating seeing Carter participate in the student demonstration, especially given there had been little to no administration or staff presence at previous events. Fran informed Amber that she had not yet spoken with Carter and felt Amber needed to be aware of what happened. Amber thanked Fran for bringing this to her attention and let Fran know she would look into the situation.

As Fran leaves, Amber recalls the multiple conversations she has had with her graduate hall directors on balancing personal and professional integrity, especially due to their dual roles at the university as students pursuing a degree, and as staff members who lead their residential communities. In light of the administration's directive instructing staff and student workers to avoid participating in the on-campus demonstrations, Amber is concerned about the personal, professional, and departmental consequences of Carter's alleged participation in the protests. While she strongly values an individual's right to civic and political activism, she recognizes that personal values and institutional priorities may not always align. Amber is also concerned about the rising tensions on campus after the memo was released, and she received several community reports that students of color in her area feel marginalized and unsupported by the university.

Personally, Amber feels conflicted about the administration's directive of non-participation, and she knows she is not alone based on her private conversations with her colleagues. While people of color are also underrepresented among the university staff, Amber has observed that neither White staff nor staff of color at Osprey University have spoken out about the memo in a public forum. Concerns about the directive have been raised behind closed doors in senior staff meetings in Residence Life, but the implicit message from her department's leadership is to adhere to the directive. Being a relatively new staff member to the university, Amber is mindful that she is still learning about the institutional culture, and she is trying to be strategic about when and how to challenge established norms. As a White woman aware of her racial privilege and who identifies as a social justice advocate, Amber wants to challenge the status quo, but is uncertain on how to do so.

What should Amber do?

WHEN DOES FAMILIAL SUPPORT BECOME A DISSERVICE?
ADRIENNE KRAVITZ

Angela was a graduate assistant in student affairs completing her master's degree in special education. When Angela graduated, she decided to apply for full-time employment in higher education. Angela became an assistant director in Parent and Family Programs in the Division of Student Affairs at State University. State University is a mid-sized, tuition-driven, private university in New York. The total student enrollment at State is approximately 11,000, about 7,000 of who are undergraduate students. State University highlights "100 percent program accessibility for persons with disabilities" in their campus information. Twelve percent of the undergraduate population is registered with Disability Services. Many students, with their family's support, apply and choose State because of the disability resources available.

State sends paperwork to register with Disability Services to all students in their acceptance packages and many students, or their families, fill out this paperwork upon acceptance. This allows Disability Services to provide accommodations and meet with students on or before the first week of school. This strategy sets students up for success in their first semester. Of course, there is no guarantee of success and many students are surprised to still find themselves burdened by taxing course work. Most families understand that college is difficult and their student with a disability may have additional challenges. Many parents and guardians contact the administrators in the Office of Parent and Family Programs to be the liaisons between the family and the university. The Parent and Family Programs professionals outreach to the Disability Services staff who assist the students. The Parent and Family Programs and Disability Services staff share student information on a need to know basis, while adhering to the Federal Educational Right to Privacy Act (FERPA) and ensuring that written permission is obtained by students before any personal information is shared across offices or with parents. This open communication allows the Parent and Family Program staff to lead the conversations with family members while understanding the whole situation. This system both provides support for the student to take ownership of their journey, while alleviating the workload of the Disability Services staff, who can spend less time troubleshooting with family members. It is important that the students initiate the use of that support. It is also important that family members who have spent almost two decades fighting for their child's needs do not feel alienated by the university.

Angela, in her new position as the assistant director of Parent and Family Programs at State University, with her background in special education, quickly becomes the in-house "expert" in students with disabilities and begins to grow as a new professional and work with many families whose students registered with Disability Services at State. Most of Angela's work with families of students with disabilities is positive and educational. Angela hosts information sessions for new families during orientation, explaining how guardians and family members can best support students by working with the Office of Parent and Family Programs and allowing students to advocate for themselves with the assistance of Disability Services. Angela hands out business cards and continues to connect with many families through the year. Most families build healthy relationships with Angela and the Office of Parent and Family Programs. It is important for family members to feel empowered and welcome to call the Parent and Family Program Office to share any concerns or questions they have about a student's journey at State. However, there are times when some families overstep boundaries by calling multiple offices on a student's behalf before the student has had the chance to develop the ability to self-advocate and ask for support when needed.

Sarah, a prospective student for the upcoming fall term, recently accepted her spot in the new first-year class. Sarah's brother Sam was an engineer, so Sarah would major in engineering. Sarah's family is convinced that State University is the place for her, and that Disability Services would take care of all of Sarah's needs. Immediately after Sarah's family sent in her deposit to State University, Sarah's mom has Sarah fill out the FERPA form, giving permission for the offices to talk and waiving her academic privacy rights to allow the university to release information to both of her parents. Sarah's mom then calls the director of Disability Services to ask to meet as soon as possible. The director congratulates Sarah's mom and remarks that she looks forward to seeing everyone at orientation. Sarah's mom continues to outreach during the summer with many questions about accommodations and supports. Months before Sarah begins her first class, many student affairs offices already knew her name.

The support staff at State decide to host Sarah and her parents for an hour meeting on campus to ensure everyone is on the same page and knowledgeable of Sarah's needs. Administration from four offices attend this meeting to discuss all the ways Sarah will be supported and what Sarah should do to take advantage of these supports. Sarah's mom is informed that she may reach out to Angela in the Parent and Family Programs Office as needed but is gently reminded this will be the time to allow Sarah to begin to self-advocate.

Despite the advice to allow Sarah to lead, throughout Sarah's first year, her mom incessantly contacts Angela, the director of Parent and Family Programs, the director of Disability Services, and numerous other advisors and administrators. Angela learns of new concerns almost daily from Sarah's mom—it is difficult for Sarah to find food she can tolerate, Sarah could not open her mailbox and therefore could not get her medication, Sarah could not stay focused in her afternoon class because she was hungry and tired, Sarah could not focus in her morning class because her roommate goes to bed too late, Sarah could not see her professor in office hours because she had another class at the same time; the list of difficulties grew weekly, and sometimes daily. Almost everyone in student affairs at State knows Sarah's mom—including resident hall staff who received complaints as minor as the blinds not blocking enough sun.

Sarah stops in to see Angela from time to time, rarely mentioning any issues Angela has heard from Sarah's mom. Angela tries to ask about some of these issues, but many do not seem to be of concern to Sarah. Sarah never self-advocates and rarely works to improve her executive functioning skills—as her mom constantly steps in. Angela does her best to support, but many times Angela wonders if Sarah is even bothered or if it is only Sarah's mom who is concerned. Angela works to end every conversation with Sarah's mom by reminding her that Sarah can come see Angela with concerns and it would be okay to allow her to sit with some discomfort and allow her to problem solve.

After midterms, Sarah comes to Angela's office less frequently and only quickly reports she is not doing well in her classes but does not wish to discuss it further. It is clear to Angela that Sarah is not yet fully equipped to handle her academic workload. Angela soon learns that Sarah stopped attending her tutoring sessions and often cancels her appointments with support staff. Sarah will likely fail this semester. Angela thinks it may be time for Sarah to take a leave of absence from the university; perhaps she can try again next term. It will be beneficial to withdraw to avoid beginning her next term with failing marks, which will always lower her cumulative GPA. Additionally, a withdrawal may save her scholarship eligibility instead of the impending academic probation that will result in this failed semester. Angela broaches the idea with Sarah, who seems hesitant to make a decision, indicating she will talk with her mom. A few days go by without any word from Sarah. Angela is torn between her desire to provide room for Sarah to self-advocate, her knowledge that not acting will potentially have lasting implications for Sarah's collegiate career, and her reluctance to reach out to Sarah's parents for fear of further enabling their inclination to overstep.

What should Angela do?

WE MATTER, TOO
ELIZABETH HAMMOND, WEN XI,
AND MICHELLE J. BOETTCHER

Lena is a biracial female advisor in her first year in the Academic Success Center at Midwest University (MU), a large public research institution in a small town in the Midwest. One of the areas of Lena's work involves meeting with prospective students during orientation and campus visits to share information about academic resources, programs, and academic organizations that make MU's campus and student experience unique. In addition, Lena supervises the student academic ambassadors (SAAs) as part of the admissions program on campus. SAAs serve as hosts to students visiting MU and also visit different high schools and communities to talk about their experiences on campus in order to attract students. Lena has developed strong relationships with the SAAs on her team and meets with them biweekly about their own personal development as well as SAA programmatic issues.

Ethan is an SAA who has confided a great deal in Lena. Since they both identify as biracial (Lena's mother is African American and her father is White; Ethan's mother is White and his father is Japanese American), they have talked about how they simultaneously fit and do not fit in on campus. After going over topics related to his SAA work in a regularly scheduled meeting, Ethan shares a struggle, saying, "I feel a little awkward talking to you about this, but I don't know where I see myself represented on this campus." Lena asks him to clarify and he says, "Everything here is either set up for White or Black students. But my mom is White, my dad is Japanese American, and I don't see anything for Japanese American or even Asian American students on our campus." He pauses awkwardly and adds, "I appreciate that you've shared your biracial identity with me and I acknowledge your experiences, too. I just wish there was a place for me."

Lena shares that Asian American History Week is coming up next week, but before she can finish Ethan interrupts her saying, "You mean Asian American History *Day*? There is one Chinese American speaker and one social event on the same day. That's not really a history week. Plus, they lump all of us together. Not all Asians are Chinese or Japanese or Korean. My friend Diana—whose family is from India—and I have talked about how we get frustrated that we are considered part of the same culture on this campus. It's more complex than what this place makes it out to be. We want the university to feel like we matter, too."

Lena has had similar concerns but realizes that this is actually the first year there have been any events around Asian American heritage at MU. She shares that she understands Ethan's concerns. She says that it takes time to build events like this but agrees and shares that she has raised the same concerns with her supervisor, Ken. Lena admits that she is still learning about the campus culture and history and promises to try to learn more and get back to Ethan with information. She acknowledges that she does not have a lot of ability to change the larger campus culture but will share Ethan's thoughts with Ken to identify things they might do.

Ethan says, "I know it isn't your job to fix this or even to have to listen to me. I have had this conversation with other friends who identify as Asian American and Latinx and it seems like every office and space set up for students of color excludes us. I love being an SAA, but sometimes I wonder what I'm actually selling to people and what I'm setting students up for when they look at me and make assumptions about my identities—especially when I might share similar identities with them. Am I lying to them by telling them there is value in coming here?"

Later that day, Ken calls Lena into his office. Ken is an African American man who has been the director of the Academic Success Center for twelve years and is also an alumnus of MU. He says, "Have you seen what Ethan posted?" Lena has not, so Ken reads her Ethan's social media post: "Midwestern University: Celebrating Black and White diversity and Asian-American adversity. #MUAsianAmericanHistoryJoke." Lena notes that Ethan tagged the university president, student government president, and Multicultural Center in the post. Ken shares that he has received calls from about a dozen alumni as well as the President's Office with concerns about the post. He also has been contacted by local media and asked to comment. Ken looks at Lena and says directly, "You need to get Ethan to take the post down and figure out what the appropriate consequence is. I need to get back to others about this by the morning. Let Ethan know that if this behavior continues, he may not be an SAA anymore. We can't have someone like that connecting with prospective students."

What should Lena do?

WELCOMING OR INTOLERANT? BALANCING
FREEDOM OF SPEECH AND DIVERSITY
CLAUDINE MCKINNEY AND DIANE CÁRDENAS ELLIOTT

Northwestern First University (NFU) is a public, state institution situated in a rural community in the Northwest and is home to about nine thousand students. NFU is a predominately White institution, largely composed of first-generation students who are from nearby communities. The university is an hour and a half from a large, urban city from which it recruits students of color, who comprise about 20 percent of the student population. Given its location, approximately half of the student body lives on campus.

Over the past ten years, the university has increased efforts to recruit diverse students, which it conceptualizes broadly to include students of color, religious diversity, and LGBTQ populations. It has striven to be a welcoming environment to diverse students through the provision of a Multicultural Center, LGBTQ Center, Veterans Center, and Women's Center. In addition, in acknowledgment that many freshmen come from very homogeneous home environments and are interacting with diverse students for the first time, three years ago the university restructured core course requirements in an effort to stress appreciation for diversity and teach students about the benefits of engaging with individuals of different mindsets.

In the beginning of the spring semester, "The Way of His Kingdom" appropriately notified campus administrators of their scheduled presence and planned to rally outside of the Campus Common. "The Way of His Kingdom" is an extremist evangelical group that invokes messages of hate toward Muslims, atheists, women, non-Whites, and the LGBTQ community who the group perceives to be sinners. "The Way of His Kingdom" proselytize and propagate their religion through rallying on the campuses of state-affiliated institutions of higher education. The Campus Common is on the academic end of campus, in foot traffic for students shuffling between classes or looking to grab a quick bite to eat. However, after being directed incorrectly, the group found themselves on the opposite end of campus outside East Cafeteria, a highly populated area surrounded by residence halls.

While students ventured in and out of East Cafeteria, the scene around the rally grew larger as the day progressed. There was limited interaction with "The Way of His Kingdom" in the morning hours; however, with an increase in social media postings from passersby, the area became filled in the early afternoon with students engaging with the extremist group. The group bantered with students about issues such as race, roles, and stereotypes of women, sexuality, gender identity, and religion. In one specific instance, the group was overheard to say, "God taught us Adam and Eve, not Adam and Steve," "If you were born a woman, get in the kitchen," and "Transgenderism is a mental disorder!" Some students found the engagement to be comical, while others took offense to the messages. Still other students joined in with members of "The Way of His Kingdom" and defended their religious ideology.

As the event became chaotic, more faces from administration began to appear within the crowd, predominately to disband students and discourage engagement with the group. The rally finally ended approximately ten hours later after having interacted with many students.

Juncture Residence Hall "J-Hall" is located about fifty yards from East Cafeteria. J-Hall is home to nearly three hundred first-year students. In light of the rally, the Office of Housing and Residence Life directed resident directors to engage students in an educational discussion about the ideas presented by "The Way of His Kingdom." Quinn, an openly transgender resident director, discussed in detail the event with students at a residence hall meeting. Quinn explained as a public institution, entities like "The Way of His Kingdom" are allowed to rally as part of their freedom of speech but acknowledged how the hateful words of "The Way of His Kingdom" can make individuals feel. Quinn answered questions posed by the students of J-Hall about hate speech and engaged in a meaningful discussion about his viewpoint, as a transgender male, on gender identity and the importance of being accepting of the LGBTQ population. A few students, including Tabby Sanderson who is evangelical, questioned why they had to be accepting of non-hetero populations given what is stated in the Bible. At this, Quinn bristled, and it was clear from his reaction that he strenuously disagreed with these sentiments. A somewhat heated debate ensued in which Quinn reminded the students of the J-Hall community standard of diversity and inclusion of "ALL" students and how groups like "The Way of His Kingdom" can tarnish the climate of the campus and lead to crisis situations impacting campus safety. By the end of the conversation, Quinn believed students had grown in their understanding and openness to his expression of diverse ideas that negated the messages of "The Way of His Kingdom."

The next day, Quinn received many emails from a group of J-Hall parents expressing frustration that Quinn had a conversation with their children. The Sandersons, parents of J-Hall resident Tabby, are evangelical and have strict ideals. The Sandersons expressed outrage that NFU would propagate ideas counter to their religious beliefs. The Sandersons took to the NFU parent page on social media, which resulted in a few additional emails from other displeased parents of J-Hall students. The parents expressed concern that Quinn attempted to push his personal beliefs on the students and did not acknowledge that some students' views may side with the messages of "The Way of His Kingdom." The Sandersons, among the other parents, threatened to contact the president and pull their children from the university. In addition to the anger of the parents, a group of students living in J-Hall who sided with the beliefs of "The Way of His Kingdom" took to social media and their individual room doors to repost the messages set forth by "The Way of His

Kingdom." These messages greatly offended non-Christian, female, racially/ethnically diverse, and LGBTQ students.

Quinn now has a split body of three hundred first-year students in J-Hall who express strong but opposing viewpoints on this matter. Quinn wants to spread a positive and inclusive message to the J-Hall students but is finding it difficult to respond to the students who are offended while also responding to those who have opposing views. Quinn feels conflicted with how to respond to the students of J-Hall and their parents and is extremely worried that his response may impact his ability to express his identity moving forward as the resident director.

What should Quinn do?

BIAS IN THE GAME ROOM
RICHARD A. STEVENS AND ANN E. WENDLE

Northwest State College (NSC) is a predominately White public institution (PWI) located approximately two hours from Chicago. The college is located in a rural community with limited access to Chicago or other larger cities unless students have personal transportation. NSC is a feeder campus to the state's premiere land grant institution. Although less than 10 percent of the student population self-identifies as students of color, the overall campus climate is generally inclusive of marginalized identities, indicated by institutional data, programming, and climate on campus. Policies and procedures including non-discrimination statements illustrate the university's positions on discrimination against students, faculty, and staff. The president has spoken openly about support for diversity and inclusion and has provided funding for ongoing training for all levels of staff over the past five years. Students of color who attend the institution are predominantly male and predominately recruited for athletic opportunities.

Vanessa Chaaya, who identifies as Lebanese American, works as an assistant director of student activities at NSC. She has close relationships with several students who have worked at or attended programs sponsored by the Office of Students Activities. One of her regular student volunteers, Nancy O'Keefe, stopped in to see Vanessa and say hello. Nancy identifies as White and in addition to her involvement in the Office of Student Activities, she is employed at the Student Union. After talking for a few minutes, Nancy revealed that she wanted to get some advice from Vanessa about a concern. While Vanessa does not directly supervise Nancy, she is readily available to students and often connects them with appropriate resources. Nancy reveals that she is feeling uncomfortable with some African American males who were using a free-standing video game in one of the game room areas in the building and believes that they should be reported to student conduct.

Approximately eight African American male students, who play football together for the college, socialize and play the video game in the Student Union each evening after dinner. Some of the men attended high school together, and all of the students grew up near Chicago.

Nancy says that the African American male students harass other students and make people generally uncomfortable with their behaviors. She provided no specifics regarding the harassing behaviors beyond being louder than other groups who used the area. Additionally, she said she felt too many students were at the video game.

Vanessa has used the game room in the Student Union frequently for programming and has knowledge about the policies concerning use, reservations, and occupancy. She knows that the space where the students were playing the video game is a public space that requires no reservation and that eight students is far below the building capacity signs for the entire floor of the Student Union building. Based on her knowledge of the space, the students have a right to use the space and are not violating any policies. Vanessa is also familiar with the practice for student employees reporting incidents that occur while they are working. They are to contact their supervisor, Student Union director Linda Yancey, to document the incident and work through the student conduct reporting process.

Though Vanessa suspects that Nancy's concern is related to a lack of cultural competency, she refers Nancy to the student union director. Vanessa decides to follow up with Linda about Nancy's concern and check in about how to help Nancy with her cultural competency. Vanessa found that Linda, who identifies as White, also shared the same discomfort as Nancy in reference to the African American students. Through the conversation, Vanessa was able to get at Linda's rationale about the allegedly concerning behaviors at the video game. Linda expressed that there were rumors of loud aggressive behaviors and unwanted sexual innuendos from the men gathering in the public space, though there are no actual reports of this described inappropriate behavior. In that conversation, Linda admitted that she had a low comfort level with African American male students due to limited interaction with African Americans in general. She stated that she was inclined to have Nancy report the behavior to Student Conduct so she would not have to address it directly.

As a part of ongoing, previously scheduled professional development, the next week the dean of students and staff in the Multicultural Student Center facilitated a Student Affairs Division meeting for full-time and graduate student staff members designed to address needs of students of color, concerns on campus, cultural competency, resources, and appropriate referrals. Linda and Vanessa were required to attend the meeting as members of the division.

During the meeting, a staff member from Residence Life shared information about an anonymous concern she received from a parent. She indicated that the parent called with a concern that a male student was making unwanted sexual comments to female students in a residence hall near the Student Union. Before additional details could be attained, Linda stated to the entire division, "It's probably one of the guys at the video game." This anonymous information about the parent call included no mention of race nor any indication that it had taken place in the Student Union. Given these incidents with Linda and Nancy, Vanessa is concerned that student and full-time staff members may be using stereotypes of African American men to hold them accountable for behaviors that have yet to be substantiated. She is concerned about the impact it could have on student success and retention.

What should Vanessa do?

THE ALLOCATION CONUNDRUM
KEVIN SINGER AND ELIJAH JEONG

Samuel was floored when he got the call that he had been selected to be the new associate director of diversity and equity for Lynden University, a large public university in the Northwest. After working as an assistant director for student life at small, predominately White institutions (PWI) for the past four years, Samuel was excited to work at a school that prided itself on its award-winning diversity initiatives. He was also excited to work for an institution that was compositionally diverse; as 60 percent of students identified as students of color. Specifically, Samuel, as a second-generation Korean American, looked forward to experiencing a campus environment that touted a large Asian American population. The Asian American population on campus had a diverse range of cultural representations, including Chinese, Japanese, Vietnamese, Korean, Indian, and Filipino students. He had high hopes to help Asian American students to feel heard and supported on campus.

After a relatively quiet first few weeks, Samuel walks into the Office of Diversity and Equity and sees his immediate supervisor, Karla, extremely anxious and frustrated.

Their weekly in-person meeting was scheduled for just a few minutes later. At the beginning of the meeting, Karla apologizes to Samuel for seeming flustered. She had just come from a meeting with her supervisor, Todd, the vice president of student affairs. The purpose of the meeting was to discuss how to best address the racial tension between White and Asian American students on campus, which had come to a head just before summer break. An altercation had taken place between a cohort of White and Asian American students in one of the most popular cafeterias on campus, which resulted in a plethora of phone calls from concerned parents and university donors. Initially, the altercation involved three White students telling a group of Chinese American students to "speak English, you [racial epithet]. . . . This is America." Reportedly, one Chinese American student, Jason, extremely offended, got up and pushed one of the White students. A scuffle between Chinese American and White students followed, until public safety put a halt to the commotion. Although no student got physically hurt, this negatively impacted the campus climate for all students, especially Asian American students.

Karla happens to be a highly respected voice among minority communities on campus and served as a mentor to Jason, the student who was involved in the altercation. She voiced frustration to Samuel that she and Todd were not seeing eye to eye on how to address the tension. Todd suggested that they first begin by distributing a survey to students about the campus racial climate in the fall and discuss the results and next steps in the spring. Karla, however, feared that putting off an action plan until spring would leave the campus vulnerable to additional flare-ups between White and Asian American students. "White people can delay conversations about race," Karla tells Samuel, implicating Todd. "They can ignore racial issues altogether if they want to. That's the privileged place they are in."

Karla then tells Samuel that his first task as associate director would be to determine how to allocate funds that the Office of Diversity and Equity receives every year to support minority racial and ethnic groups on campus. These funds could be used to reserve spaces on campus, bring in speakers, cover travel expenses for trips, and provide food and entertainment for campus events. Historically, the funds had been equally distributed to support the initiatives of Black, Asian American, Native American, and Latinx students. However, this was an older arrangement that was implemented over a decade ago; Todd and Karla agreed that the allocation of funds could be renegotiated if it was warranted. Karla expected Samuel to have a decision made in two weeks, when he was scheduled to meet with Karla and Todd together.

Just a few hours later, as Samuel was hanging some photographs in his new office, Daniel, a student leader of the Korean community on campus, walked in. "Do you have a minute?" he asked. "Sure!" Samuel happily replied. Samuel was hoping to connect with the Korean student group on campus anyway, so he was overjoyed that Daniel happened to walked in. "How can I help you?" Samuel asked earnestly. "Word has spread that a Korean was hired for this position, and the Korean community on campus is very excited," Daniel remarked. "Oh yeah?" Samuel replied. Shifting to a serious tone, Daniel continued, "We know how pivotal this position is when it comes to how funds are distributed to minority groups, and the Asian American community is very unhappy with how this has been done in the past."

Samuel, wanting to know more about Daniel's complaint, inquired, "Why is the Asian American community unhappy?" "Well," Daniel answered, "We are the largest minority group on campus, but we receive the same amount of funds as other minority groups. . . . It makes no sense." Daniel continued, "We are arguably the most invisible minority group on campus. . . . You know the altercation that happened in the cafeteria? That is the result of both students and administration being ignorant of the diversity within Asian Americans as well as our needs." Samuel, unsure of how to proceed, acknowledges Daniels frustration and simply asks, "How can I help?"

"I understand that there's probably pressure on you to allocate funds equally between all minority student groups," Daniel asserts, "But as a fellow Korean American, I ask you to strongly consider our frustrations when making your decision." Daniel proceeds to directly ask Samuel to change the current funding structure that is allocated for minority student support. In fact, Daniel asks Samuel not to distribute the funds equally between the various racial groups on campus, but to give Asian Americans a bigger share of the funding due to the recent events and, since they are, objectively, the largest minority group on campus.

What should Samuel do?

THE DATA DOESN'T LIE
KRISTA BAILEY AND DARBY ROBERTS

Southern Research University (SRU) is a research institution in the South with a campus population of twenty thousand. The community surrounding SRU is very conservative, and SRU has active alumni. SRU provides a solid education for students both in and out of the classroom. About two-thirds of the student body are involved in student organizations. At the same time, university administrators realize that they need to be more proactive about diversity and inclusion efforts. In terms of demographics, only about 20 percent of the undergraduate population is students of color. About 40 percent of the students are first generation. Most of the students come from within two hundred miles of campus, and men make up about 50 percent of the population. While the university does not have exact numbers for their LGBTQ+ population, there has been an increase in the membership in the LGBTQ+ student organization in the past five years. There are also several ethnic identity–based organizations.

LaDonna, the coordinator for student organizations, works in the Department of Student Involvement overseeing student organization recognition. LaDonna identifies as an African American woman and has been working at SRU for a year. This is her first position post-master's degree. She has struggled with her transition to SRU and has worked hard to establish a positive relationship with her supervisor, Victor, the director of the Department of Student Involvement. In addition to overseeing student organization recognition, LaDonna advises two student organizations, one of which focuses on LGBTQ student needs. Based on her informal conversations with students, LaDonna decides to disaggregate the data from a recent campus climate survey. As an active member of the division's assessment committee with an interest in statistics, LaDonna is able to access the raw data. The survey not only addresses LGBTQ issues and experiences, but also addresses race, gender, disability, and religion.

Victor, who identifies as White and male, is out of the office when LaDonna analyzes the data. Having worked at SRU for ten years, Victor has been in and out of the office during the last year dealing with a health issue. He has tried to provide support to LaDonna, but due to his medical issues he has been unable to provide much mentoring and feedback. Dr. Karen Smith, as the assistant vice chancellor and Victor's supervisor, has been providing supervision to the Department of Student Involvement during Victor's absences. She identifies as a White woman, has been working at SRU for twenty years, and is an alumnae of the institution. Dr. Smith is aware of LaDonna's interest in learning more about the campus climate and tells LaDonna to keep things moving forward while Victor is out of the office.

When LaDonna analyzes the results, she sees several concerning issues in addition to some positive points. Overall, most students feel welcome at the institution and think they are treated fairly by faculty, staff, and other students. In addition, most students would recommend SRU to their friends and would be proud to graduate from the institution. On the other hand, students of color feel more isolated than White students and more frequently hear stereotypical remarks about their identity. In addition, LGBTQ+ students specifically report hearing and experiencing threats based on their identity. Students of color, non-Christian students, and students with disabilities report feeling excluded or unwelcome when trying to join student organizations. These results are disappointing because of the recent statements by the university president about how inclusive, diverse, and positive the campus climate is. The president has made these claims to the Board of Regents, the faculty, community leaders, and students. Although not surprised, LaDonna is disheartened to see the significant discrepancy in the findings when they are disaggregated by underrepresented students. Having talked to LGBTQ+ students directly, LaDonna knows some of the students are struggling to find their sense of belonging at SRU and are considering transferring to another institution.

LaDonna shares the results with Victor, who does not support sharing the information more broadly. Victor reminds her that the Department of Student Involvement is already under scrutiny about budgets, assessment, and student learning documentation, and he thinks they would get even more scrutiny and potentially bad press by being in conflict with the president's recent remarks. Victor also mentions to LaDonna that he does not think he has the physical or emotional strength to address the potential controversy releasing the results will cause, given his medical condition. He acknowledges the need for change on campus but tells LaDonna now is not the time to release information that contradicts the president's message. He says, "I'm disappointed that you didn't talk to me before you started this project. I would have stopped you before you wasted your time. I expect you to hold onto this and not share this beyond our conversation today."

The students she works with are asking her about the results and want to know what action the university is going to take to improve the campus climate. Not only do they want a mandatory diversity class as part of the curriculum, they want the student organization recognition process revamped, which would require mandatory student leader training on diversity, equity, and inclusion topics. They also want to pressure the university to revamp the university rules regarding speech in order to prevent students and others from having a forum to express hateful ideas that make some students feel unsafe. LaDonna thinks Dr. Smith will be expecting her to share the results of the disaggregated data at the next assessment committee meeting, but Victor specifically tells her not to share the results with anyone, including Dr. Smith.

What should LaDonna do?

AN INTERNATIONAL INCIDENT
ELIZABETH HAMMOND, WEN XI,
AND MICHELLE J. BOETTCHER

Bill is a White, cisgender, male staff member currently serving as the assistant director in the Office of International Student Support Services (OISSS) housed in the Division of Student Affairs at a mid-sized public institution in the Midwest. He is in his second year in the assistant director role after working previously for two years at a small, private institution doing academic advising for international students and scholars. This is his first position in the field of student affairs.

Bill was particularly excited for this position as it focuses on the experiences of international students on campus. He coordinates educational and social programming, advises international student organizations, and brings groups together to engage in dialogue around issues related to campus, community, national, and global issues affecting international students. The other assistant director in the office is responsible for paperwork, TOEFL, and other academic, government, and administrative support of students. They each supervise one graduate student and the director of OISSS also oversees study abroad experiences.

One of the major events on campus that is coordinated by Bill's office is the International Festival. This is the tenth annual festival which has historically had tremendous attendance from campus and community members. Several faculty who have been consistently involved in the planning and execution of the festival have shared with Bill how excited they are for the event.

Chris, a graduate assistant in the student affairs graduate program whom Bill supervises, shared with Bill a current event that was discussed in class. A recent protest on a campus in Massachusetts has sparked debate around international student festivals where the students feel further marginalized by being positioned as providing food and service to a predominantly White campus and community populations. During the class, a cohort member asks Chris if conversations have taken place in her office about implications of their campus festival. Chris admits that other than logistical planning for the event they have not talked about it, but now she feels compelled to bring this up.

Chris shares with Bill that at the Massachusetts school, protesters held signs saying, "Who's Serving Who?," "Pay to be Entertained," and "Culture Is More than Snacks." In addition to student protests, faculty there have started a petition which has put even more of a spotlight on the event. Chris provides the following timeline to Bill about the events at the other institution.

January—planning committee for annual event identified; planning begins

February 10—one committee member and two international student organization leaders send a letter to the campus paper saying the festival has problematic implications related to privilege on campus

February 12—the rest of the planning committee members submit response to letter to the editor focused on the positive history and institutional pride in the International Festival

February 17—campus dialogues are hosted about the event

February 19—committee member who raised concerns in the original letter to the editor withdraws from the International Festival committee

March 21—International Festival takes place. Twenty-five students and three faculty protest the event

Chris shares with Bill that she had not considered this before and wonders if they need to make changes for their upcoming event. Bill says he had not heard about the protest and will let Chris know after he has talked to others in the office about this. Bill meets with his supervisor, Lynn, the next day during their one-on-one, and presents Chris's concerns. Lynn says the Massachusetts institution is a small private school whose policies and history are different. In addition, key faculty and administrators on campus support and are invested in this event, and OISSS does not want to alienate them and potentially lose financial support for the event.

What should Bill do?

INTERSECTING IDENTITIES AND SEXUAL ASSAULT
KATHRYN S. JAEKEL AND MOLLY B. HOLMES

Located in the rural Midwest, Linden University is a mid-sized regional institution, enrolling about twenty thousand students, located fifty miles outside of a large metropolitan city. Forty percent of the students identify as first generation and more than 60 percent identify as White. Recently, Linden has attempted to diversify its student population and has engaged in marketing campaigns to attract students of color from neighboring states.

While Linden has historically been thought of as a politically conservative institution, there has been a growing group of students interested in issues of equity, access, and social justice, particularly after the recent presidential election. In particular, the queer and trans students on campus have started to raise visibility about the lack of gender-inclusive housing, accessible restrooms, and inclusive name policies. These students staged marches in the college free speech zone and organized walkouts from their classes. In response to the students' outcry, university administration has convened a gender equity committee, made up of faculty, student affairs professionals, and students to come together to make recommendations on how to better support queer and trans students on campus.

During one of the task force meetings, Betty (she, her, hers), who identifies as a White, cisgender lesbian, and who is the new assistant director of Linden University's LGBTQ Center, listens to Todd (he, him, his), an undergraduate student in women's and gender studies, talk passionately about the importance of queer people of color's visibility on campus. While Betty is a new student affairs professional and has only been in her current role for three months, she has worked closely with Todd and knows how much he has done to transform the campus for queer and trans students. Todd, who identifies as a Black transman, has been a leader on Linden's campus ever since he was a first-year student, three years ago. In a short amount of time, Todd founded Spectrum, a LGBTQ student organization, and has been an outspoken advocate for queer and trans students' rights.

As Todd continues, Betty notices that another undergraduate student, Kai (they, them, their), who also serves on the taskforce, is more reserved than they have been in previous encounters. Betty, who is also the advisor of Spectrum, has had multiple encounters with Kai at Spectrum meetings and events. Kai, who identifies as a White, pansexual, genderqueer student, is a first-generation college student majoring in political science, and is typically engaged in meetings; however, recently they seem withdrawn. Betty also remembered Kai had not been at the past two weeks' Spectrum events. During the meeting, when Betty asks Kai what they thought about the committee's questions around what queer students need more of on campus, Kai simply shrugs their shoulders and stays silent.

After the meeting, Betty asks to talk with Kai alone. Betty shares that she has noticed a shift in Kai's demeanor and in their levels of engagement both in the task force meeting and in the Spectrum events. At first, Kai shares they are just stressed and that they have several class projects that are due. As Betty continues to talk with Kai, suddenly Kai starts to cry. They share with Betty that a month ago, Todd had sexually assaulted them at an off-campus party. Betty immediately asks Kai if they had reported the incident to the police or contacted the sexual advocate on campus. Kai says, "Well, no. Not exactly." Betty discusses the value in getting connected to resources, and provides a number of reporting options to Kai and places to seek assistance. Betty also tells Kai that she is a mandatory reporter.

Kai shares that they told their academic advisor, and the advisor, who also knows Todd well, told Kai, "Be careful. That student is famous on campus for his activism. You don't want to ruin his reputation." Kai goes on to tell Betty that they understood what the advisor was saying and that "Todd is such an important campus figure, and he stands up for such important issues, if I report it, so many students won't have a voice on this campus. I mean, Todd is a women's studies major. No one would think he would ever do that. He's the last one anyone would suspect to hurt anyone. I'm afraid I will be accused of being racist and transphobic because I am not attracted to him like that. No. I'm not reporting this, and I would appreciate you holding it in confidence. Todd does too much for this campus." As a mandated reporter, Betty knows she can't hold onto the information Kai shared. That said, since Kai told their academic advisor, Betty wonders if that negates her responsibility to report the information to Title IX, since technically the academic advisor should have. Betty wants to preserve her relationship with Kai, and fears that reporting it to Title IX will put it in jeopardy, further isolating Kai.

What should Betty do?

Chapter Five

Career and Academic Support Services

THIS LAND WAS MADE FOR YOU AND ME
GRAICE VAN SPANKEREN

Having almost wrapped up her first semester as an instructor of a career development class for first-year and sophomore students, Fiona, a career advisor at Lewison University, is relieved to have the experience under her belt. With only fifteen students in the class, and a very malleable syllabus, Fiona has persevered through a semester filled with students whose engagement seems to vacillate as wildly as springtime temperatures in her midwestern, mid-sized, college-town city. She never knows which days she'll walk into a room full of spirited, engaged young people, excited to discover more about themselves and the world of work, or which days she'll be met with blank stares, one-word discussion responses, or students nodding off in class.

Fiona chose to pursue career advising after finding a great sense of meaning in the process of learning about students in all domains of their lives. She appreciates the variety in her job: some appointments are straightforward resume critiques, and others have students digging deep to exhume closely held beliefs, values, and self-concepts that alternately aid or hinder their progress. Fiona sees her work as helping students discover their purpose in the world and partnering with them as they make career and academic choices that will allow them to craft a meaningful life. This framework is largely informed by her religious beliefs, as Fiona is a practicing Christian with a deep commitment to improving the human condition through her services to students. The way she sees it, if students leave Lewison University as more thoughtful, compassionate, and principled young adults, they will use their professional skills in ways that enrich and improve the lives of others, working toward the common good for all.

Although Fiona sees her work as satisfying a personal spiritual dimension, she knows to tread carefully when discussing such matters with her colleagues and students. Religious and spiritual identity can be fraught topics for a variety of reasons—especially at a university without an official religious identity. Although Lewison formerly maintained a Methodist affiliation, it ended fifteen years before Fiona set foot on campus.

The Center for Professional Development staff comprises a director (Mary, in the role for three years), an assistant director (Demetrius, a longtime Lewison employee and Fiona's supervisor), and six career advisors, all of whom are senior to Fiona. As a graduate student, Fiona completed a practicum placement in the Center for Professional Development. While she is only in her second year as a full-time career advisor, she has known her colleagues and supervisor for two years before being hired onto the permanent staff.

Demetrius has always been a transparent and encouraging supervisor, something Fiona greatly appreciates. When thinking of ways to personalize her section of the career development class, Demetrius was the first to support Fiona's idea of introducing approaches to decision-making pulling from a variety of spiritual and religious traditions. Though none of her fellow career counselors had broached this topic in their courses, Demetrius saw Fiona's passion and worked with her to develop learning outcomes and a lesson plan that would help students engage as personally or with as much distance as desired. Fiona was nervous and excited to conduct the class session, but she couldn't get a read on what the students thought of it, as only a few of them really engaged in the discussion and activities.

Although Fiona has sometimes been frustrated by her students' behavior in class, and disappointed at how difficult it has been to earn their trust and respect, there are a handful who make her hours preparing for class feel worthwhile. One of those students is Ricardo, a young man the same age as Fiona's younger brother. Ricardo has turned in every assignment on time (unusual compared to the rest of the class), writes with great candor and self-awareness in the variety of autobiographical journal assignments, and always participates during discussions—even when his classmates stay silent in their seats. In short, Ricardo is the type of student that makes Fiona feel like she is doing her job well, a welcome respite from the challenges of being a new professional barely two years out of graduate school.

One day, Fiona sees Ricardo's name on her appointment calendar. He arrives at her office, right on time, and Fiona begins the appointment as she always does by asking, "What would you like to talk about today?"

Ricardo pauses for a moment, takes a deep breath, and says that he really needs to speak to someone about his interest in joining the military after he finishes his degree at Lewison. He indicates that he feels like he can trust Fiona because she has done so much to help him clarify who he is and what he can contribute to the world. He describes how he grew up seeing pictures of his grandfathers in their uniforms, displayed in ornate frames on his living room wall at home, and how proudly Ricardo's father spoke of their family's contributions and sacrifices during multiple global conflicts spanning decades. While neither of Ricardo's parents served, Ricardo grew up admiring the various branches of the military, playing with soldier toys, and reading history books about famous battles from World War II. Now, seeing the ROTC programs on campus representing the Army and Navy branches of the United States Military, Ricardo states he is interested in getting involved either on the campus level or by enlisting straightaway following graduation. Ricardo credits Fiona's class with helping him find his passion. He explains that the session that incorporated spirituality helped him to see a way forward in his life, one where he could envision doing good for others while also exploring the world.

Upon hearing this, Fiona's stomach drops. Part of Fiona's religious beliefs include an ethos of nonviolence, around which she organizes a lot of her life. She has been a vegetarian since age fourteen, only shops secondhand, and is an activist in pacifist movements. Hearing Ricardo speak about his plans prompts a swell of sadness and fear for this student with whom she feels especially close. While Ricardo spoke, she saw pieces of her younger brother reflected in his excited hand gestures and big grin. How could she let Ricardo, a young person so full of life and potential, enter into a career where he might be harmed or killed, or harm or kill other people? Fiona wants to respect Ricardo's desires and plans for his life, but also wants to act with integrity according to her own beliefs.

With Ricardo having spoken at great length, the appointment concludes before Fiona can respond to Ricardo's ideas. They schedule a follow-up meeting for a week later, and Fiona is grateful for the time so she can process how to respond.

What should Fiona do?

NOT QUITE A SUNSHINE STATE OF MIND
KATARINA ZAMBANINI, KATHERINE DOWNING, AND DIANE CÁRDENAS ELLIOTT

Sunshine Community College (SCC) is located in a rural area in the Southeast and serves approximately 1,200 students. The predominant employer in the area is a fish cannery, and although the cannery provides a steady source of income for many employees such as parents of SCC students, wages are generally low. Like many community colleges, SCC attracts many first-generation college students whose families struggle to provide guidance to students as they navigate college. In addition, due to the relatively low socio-economic status of the student body, financial aid is awarded to nearly 90 percent of students. Nonetheless, many students work in excess of twenty hours per week to help their families make ends meet. Annually, about 85 percent of freshman students are deemed underprepared for college and placed in developmental education coursework. Thus, many of SCC's students possess multiple risk factors. In spite of the many challenges students face, student satisfaction is very high at SCC largely due to the small, tight-knit college community and the sense of support students feel from faculty and staff.

To address the needs of the student population, the college offers students free tutoring services. Due to the scarcity of upperclass students, the college struggles to find qualified tutors, so they are often forced to hire outside tutors who have sufficient knowledge in that subject. These tutors are well utilized and often become mentors to students, providing guidance on studying and life management skills. As a means for sustaining additional support for their students, five years ago SCC received a large grant to enhance academic support services for its students. With the funding, SCC created an academic coaching center (ACC), which serves as an intermediary between tutoring and advising services. The ACC provides supplemental personal and academic services that fall outside the purview of the advising and tutoring offices. The ACC's five professional coaches offer academic counseling services and run workshops that help students develop academic and psychosocial skills (e.g., time management, study skills) to be successful. The coaches also meet with students individually to help them manage the stress of being first-generation college students.

Lily is a first-generation freshman nursing student. Her mother does not work or collect disability and her father, with whom she has little contact, provides at best irregular financial support. As a result, she is forced to work to help cover household bills. Fortunately, her grandfather owns a restaurant, which provides her with a steady stream of work. However, she is expected to frequently work long shifts as well as cover shifts when other servers are not available, regardless of if she has class or needs to focus on upcoming tests and assignments. Lily is a conscientious and academically successful student. Based on her high school grades, she earned an academic scholarship to SCC that covers her entire tuition. Continued funding of the scholarship is contingent upon maintaining a 3.0 overall GPA. Last year, Lily earned a 3.4 GPA, meeting the required 3.0 necessary to ensure continued funding of her studies, but this year she has struggled in her foundational science courses. Of all her courses, biology has given her the most trouble. As a result, Lily consistently makes time in her very busy schedule to attend tutoring.

Early Monday morning, Lily arrives at the academic coaching center and meets with Rachel, her science tutor, to prepare for her upcoming biology test. Rachel is a part-time tutor who was hired by SCC after graduating from the institution and has been tutoring science courses for the past two semesters. By all measures, Rachel is a successful tutor and receives glowing feedback from those she tutors.

Rachel has tutored Lily throughout the semester and perceives her as a hard-working and capable student. She is also aware of Lily's hectic schedule. Throughout the semester they've grown close, so when Lily seems preoccupied, Rachel asks Lily what is bothering her. Lily explains that her schedule has been busier than normal due to her mother's failing health and she is worried about her grades.

Concerned, Rachel suggests that Lily schedule an appointment to meet with Adam, an academic coach, to discuss time management and studying techniques. Rachel and Adam converse frequently, given that their positions are housed in the same office. Adam is in his first year as an academic coach at SCC—a job he accepted even though the grant supporting the ACC was in its final year. His supervisor has suggested a permanent position for him may be available after the grant lapses, contingent upon satisfactory performance in the role. His personal experience as a first-generation college student struggling to navigate the world of higher education has helped him empathize with students experiencing similar struggles.

Adam is familiar with Lily due to his involvement as a committee member who evaluates the academic scholarship program which Lily receives. He remembers Lily's application because she was the most qualified scholarship candidate by far. During her session with Adam, Lily discloses information about her personal life. She tells Adam she is a first-generation college student and that there is a lack of understanding and support from her family. Adam empathizes with Lily. Further exacerbating her concerns, Lily indicates that if she receives below a B+ in any of her nursing courses, she will have to retake them before she can move forward in the curriculum. Lily frequently finds herself overwhelmed and questioning how she will complete her courses while maintaining the required GPA.

While conversing with Adam, Lily pulls out her planner to show how she is keeping herself organized. At that moment, a packet slides out and falls to the floor. Adam glances at the packet on the floor and, although it is hard to see, he believes it reads, "Biology Chapter 3 Test—Professor Smith." Lily notices his observation, nervously laughs, and says, "Oh, one of my tutors gave me this to help with studying for an upcoming test" while quickly snatching up the packet.

As a relatively new employee, Adam feels very conflicted. He knows the faculty sometimes give the tutoring center old exams so the tutors can help students prepare, but he also knows the tutoring center's policies strictly prohibit release of these tests directly to students. In an effort to understand the situation better, Adam asks Lily for more information. Lily explains that during her tutoring session Rachel showed her the test to study during their session. Near the end of their session, Rachel got a call that her sister, who lived locally, had gotten into a minor car accident and needed a ride home. Rachel quickly began packing up her things and upon seeing this, Lily began packing up too. Claiming she did not understand how the process worked, Lily packed up the test because she thought the sample was hers to use as a study tool until her next tutoring appointment.

After a moment, Lily takes a deep breath and explains that while she was packing up her things, she considered whether or not it was okay for her to take the exam along. However, because Rachel hadn't collected the exam when packing up her things and had been the one to show it to her in the first place, she thought it would be acceptable for her to take the exam.

Adam understands that Lily's action not only violates the college's academic integrity policy, but also jeopardizes the terms of Lily's academic scholarship. At the same time, he understands how difficult maneuvering college can be for first-generation students who don't understand how policies and procedures work. He does not want to appear insensitive to Lily's circumstances that are working against her. He is equally concerned about the possibility of securing a future position at SCC. On the one hand if he does not report possible cases of academic integrity violations, he may be deemed unsuitable for a future position at the college. But, given how well regarded Rachel is as a tutor and Lily as a student, he is concerned about the potential future impact associated with charging such serious allegations against them, especially if it really was just a mistake.

What should Adam do?

WELDING ISN'T FOR SISSIES
MOLLY C. WARD AND DAVID J. NGUYEN

Metro Technical and Community College (MTCC) is a community college located in a large metropolitan area that serves approximately ten thousand students. MTCC has a mission to prepare students to directly enter the workforce, but also has developed additional degree programs to support students who wish to pursue bachelor's degrees. MTCC offers more than sixty degree programs and twenty-five certificates which include programs such as HVAC, welding, automotive engineering technology, nursing, and hospitality management. Metro Technical and Community College has made a commitment to helping to fill the current and growing skills gap connected to the skilled trades. Therefore, the institution has made a commitment to enhanced recruitment into programs such as welding. Gloria (she/her/hers) is a student who was recruited last year to participate in the welding program and attended an orientation event where she met Sam (she/her/hers).

Gloria is in her second year of the welding associate's degree program. She is situated in a male-dominated field. Currently, she is participating in a degree-required work-based learning program at a local manufacturing company and plans to work at a manufacturing company at the completion of her associate's degree.

Sam is the assistant director of admissions and student services and reports to the director of admissions and student services under the leadership of the vice president of enrollment management (who both identify as male). Before arriving at MTCC, she worked for two years in career services at a liberal arts college and welcomed a more professionally oriented student affairs role. Though Sam is now working in a mid-level management role, she assists students as they begin their educational experiences at MTCC. Sam met Gloria during Gloria's orientation and encouraged her to realize her dream of being a welder. Gloria expressed some hesitation about being a female in, as she put it, "a male's world." Taking the conversation deeper, Sam asked Gloria to share her larger academic, career, and financial goals. After this conversation, it was clear to Sam that welding was a good fit for Gloria's future, based on her desire to work with her hands and complete an associate's degree. Providing additional support, Sam told Gloria to pursue her dreams and engage with her faculty as she moved through her educational experience.

One day Sam receives an email from Gloria requesting a meeting "just to chat." When Sam responds, she offers Gloria several time options, and Gloria chooses one for later the same day. When Gloria meets Sam at her office, Sam can tell Gloria is concerned and cautious about what she wants to say and how she is going to convey her thoughts. Finally, Gloria takes a deep breath and quickly reveals, "I just need to tell you something because I don't know what to do and I just can't deal with it anymore."

Based on Gloria's apprehensiveness and Sam's previous interactions with Gloria, Sam shares that she is willing to listen and provide feedback; however, Sam needs to let Gloria know that depending on the information she shares, Sam may need to report it to key individuals. Sam assures Gloria by saying, "If you trusted me to come here today, I hope you will trust me to handle the information you share with me in a sensitive way." After a long pause and another deep breath, Gloria tells Sam her concerns. Sam can see that an immediate weight is lifted off of Gloria's shoulders once she shares her story. Sam knows she needs to tell her supervisor, the director of admissions and student services, what Gloria has shared.

Sam provides the following information to her supervisor regarding Gloria's experience. As a welding student, Gloria knew that she would have to complete an experiential learning component to her degree program. Gloria was placed within the welding unit at a local manufacturing company as part of a required work-based learning experience. As Gloria progressed through her work experience at the placement, she received a chilly response from the all-male staff at the company. Gloria feels like she is not being given the opportunity to complete tasks that she sees her male peers doing. For example, Gloria saw her peers being able to set up and make adjustments to stick and mig welding machines and perform basic spot welds. Gaining experience in these areas is essential for career progression and being a capable welder, and Gloria said she is not getting the opportunity to practice the skills.

When Gloria inquired with her workplace mentor on various occasions about why she was unable to attempt these tasks, he stated that "she just wouldn't be strong enough to do that task; women are too small to be holding the needed tools," and, finally, "he couldn't have her getting hurt because what kind of guy would he be if he let the one girl get injured." Discouraged by these demeaning responses, Gloria decided to talk to the shift supervisor. After explaining her experiences, the shift supervisor said, "Well, welding isn't for sissies. You better figure out how to 'be one of the guys' if you're going to be successful." Sam shares that at this point in the conversation Gloria was almost in tears. However, Gloria continued to share her concerns and stated that she loved welding and can do the work but is not being given the chance.

Additionally, Sam relays that Gloria stated that what is worse is she needs a job when she graduates in a few months and if she doesn't "play their game" she will not receive a favorable reference when seeking full-time employment. Gloria added that she was so encouraged by her faculty. They empowered and taught her about the requisite skills that she needs to be successful. However, now that she has experienced the "real world," the work environment was completely different than she had expected and she felt less prepared to handle her relationship with working professionals.

Additionally, Gloria stated she just did not know where to go because she saw her department coordinator, Dominick, talking and laughing with the shift supervisor last week during his site visit. Dominick is the Work-Based Learning Program coordinator at MTCC. His role supports the academic advising and student support functions within the skilled trades department, which includes students (including Gloria) enrolled in the welding program. Along with feeling demeaned in the workplace, Gloria emailed Dominick two weeks ago saying she had concerns within her placement, but he hasn't responded.

After sharing Gloria's experience with her supervisor, Sam receives a nod in return with a suggestion that she "stay in her lane" and refer the student back to the coordinator despite his failure to acknowledge Gloria's previous message.

What should Sam do?

PHILANTHROPIC ADVISING
KIPP VAN DYKE AND TAYLOR PERKINS

Jordan is in her second year in her role as a multicultural program coordinator (MPC) at Northern University, a mid-sized, public university in the Midwest. There is one MPC in each undergraduate college with the primary role
of recruiting, retaining, and providing academic advising to first-generation
students and students of color. Jordan has done an excellent job in her role by
building relationships with students and is respected for going "above and
beyond" for students.

Avery is a second-year student who Jordan helped recruit to Northern
University and is one of Jordan's advisees. The previous year, Avery reached
out to Jordan as Avery was a member of a student organization which em-
phasizes community service and philanthropy. This organization needed a
new adviser as the previous one had left Northern University and the organization risked losing its status as a student organization if it did not have an
adviser. Jordan agreed to take on this role.

The student organization grew with Jordan's support and was actively
involved on campus and the broader community. As the semester begins, the
students vote to buy jackets with their logo on them to build community as a
team, for recognition when they are promoting their group, and for practical-
ity as many of their events are outside in cool weather. Several students share
with Jordan that the $45 cost is a challenge for them. Jordan emails the whole
organization and asks if anyone saw that cost as a detriment and no one else
responds. Jordan decides to use her personal money to buy the three extra
jackets for these members and says, "Consider this my way of donating to
our group," when the group receives the jackets.

Shortly after midterms for the fall semester, Jordan notices Avery not
fully participating in all the activities of the student organization, particularly
those that have some type of financial obligation. Jordan notices when the
group collects canned food for a food drive, Avery does not bring any donations and is quiet in meetings discussing this activity. Jordan also notices
Avery is absent when the group goes out to eat after regular meetings or after
a volunteer event. When asked if she is going, Avery usually shares she has
homework or other things going on as she politely declines the invite.

Toward the end of the fall semester, Jordan notices Avery has not scheduled her advising appointment to select spring semester courses. Jordan casu-
ally reminds Avery at the next student organization meeting, and Avery says
she will try to get in to see Jordan during the upcoming week. When Avery
does not follow through, Jordan looks at Avery's student record and notices
there is a registration hold placed on her account by the Accounts Receivable
office. Jordan sees Avery later in the day and asks her to stop into the office.
Jordan shares she noticed the hold on the account and reminds Avery she

cannot schedule for spring semester courses until it is resolved. Avery begins to cry and shares she is not sure how she is going to pay off her debt. Jordan asks if Avery has talked with Financial Aid about options. Avery continues to cry and shares she is not eligible for any aid as she is an undocumented student. Jordan asks the amount owed and Avery says, "$395." Avery shares she has talked with her family and no one has any money they can loan to pay off the bill. Avery says she thinks she can have the money by the end of winter break, but that would be too late as she has specific courses she needs to register for that are filling up. Avery then looks at Jordan and says, "Unless you would be willing to loan me that money now? I promise I can pay you back before the spring term. If I must go home, I probably won't be able to come back." As a young professional, Jordan has been wise with her personal spending and saving habits and has the means to donate or loan that amount without any impact to her personal finances.

What should Jordan do?

CANDIDATE CONFUSION
JENNIFER VAN ROY AND ADAM ROSS NELSON

Unlike many of her fellow high school classmates, Alex did not start college the fall after high school graduation. Between high school and college, she traveled abroad to teach English as a foreign language in Budapest, Hungary. After two years of teaching, Alex returned to her home state to attend College University (CU), a flagship, R1, D1 institution located in the Midwest, for a bachelor's degree. Before finishing a degree in international studies with a global health certificate, Alex took a year off to work for a nonprofit as a health educator. Alex's role involved speaking and presenting at high schools about health and safety.

While obtaining her master's degree in student affairs at CU, Alex completed a practicum in the Dean of Students Office and an internship in the Office of Student Conduct. After graduating, Alex was hired into the Office of Student Conduct, where she has been working as a student conduct coordinator for the past eighteen months.

With experience both in and out of higher education, Alex is looking for a new position that will both challenge and keep her motivated; her long-range aspirations are to serve as a director or executive director overseeing student life or student conduct. She believes it is now time to advance her career toward that goal by seeking a position that will be a logical next step on the path to serving as director or executive director. She has been applying and interviewing with colleges and universities nationally for area coordinator and associate director of conduct positions. Alex has a strong affinity for her current institution but is open to moving anywhere in the country if she finds a position that is a good fit.

Recently Alex attended an on-campus interview at Pacific Arts Academy (PAA), a small liberal arts college in the Northwest, for a position as a residence life coordinator. The position would afford Alex greater autonomy but would not provide some of the professional growth opportunities Alex was seeking when launching her job search. Her goal was to obtain a more senior position that includes responsibility for supervision of other full-time staff, oversight of a budget, and responsibility for collaboration with and among multiple functional areas. During the interview at PAA for the residence life coordinator position, Alex felt at ease with the staff and thought the campus could provide a comfortable and supportive environment for her to take on a new role. The hiring committee at PAA explained they were impressed with Alex's credentials.

Alex had also applied for the assistant director of student conduct position at CU. It had been known for almost a full year that the current person in that role was planning to leave for another opportunity. Upon review of the CU position description, Alex noted that it listed as a preference a minimum of three years of full-time professional post-master's experience in a higher education setting; Alex has a year and a half of post-master's experience. However, she hoped that her other full-time experiences teaching English and in health education, and her various internships, would help to make her a competitive candidate.

Alex was selected as a finalist for the CU position and scheduled an on-campus interview shortly after her PAA on-campus interview. Alex knew from conversations around CU's campus that many of the other candidates were highly experienced. Alex focused extra time and energy in preparing for the interviews, knowing that the competition would be tough.

Alex completed her on-campus interview for the position at CU but did not feel confident. She felt that she had fumbled her way through her presentation. She also second guessed herself while answering many of the more challenging interview questions. She self-consciously thought her lack of post-master's experience showed during the interview process. Being her own worst critic, she lacked confidence in the quality of herself as a candidate for the CU position. She chalked it up as a good learning experience and put any hope of getting an offer out of her mind.

Alex was offered the position at PAA and accepted it after successful salary and benefits negotiations where she managed to secure a 10 percent raise above her current CU salary. Alex was also happy for PAA's health insurance and retirement programs that also seemed to exceed the value of those offered by CU. Alex reasoned that even though the position with PAA would not be as much of a career advancement as she had hoped, she knew that the position would expose her to new professional development opportunities and a chance to start fresh in a new part of the country. Alex planned on talking to her director at CU about submitting her resignation by the end of the week.

The day before Alex's meeting with her director, she received a call from the CU hiring committee offering her the assistant director of student conduct position. Having put the prospect of receiving an offer from CU out of her mind, Alex was stunned. In an instant, she pictured herself decorating her new office, imagined fulfilling her new duties, and daydreamed about how she would spend her significantly higher salary. She also had a flash of pride that the search committee had confidence in her. She was so happy that her self-evaluation was apparently overly critical. Also, she was pleased that she could continue at the institution she loved. Alex let out a huge sigh of relief and happiness. Then, she remembered that she had accepted the position with PAA. Her stomach dropped.

What should Alex do?

SURVIVING ON RAMEN
NOREEN SIDDIQUI

Fatima is excited to start her first job out of graduate school as an academic advisor in the College of Business at Bluemound State University (Bluemound), a mid-sized comprehensive university in the Pacific Northwest. The College of Business (CoB) is considered the star of Bluemound's programs with competitive admissions into its majors during sophomore year. The majority of students at Bluemound are in state, but a significant number of students attend the university from its neighboring states, specifically for a business degree. The student population is predominantly middle class, but a growing segment of the student body comes from poor and working-class backgrounds.

During Fatima's training, she learns that one of her duties will be reviewing crisis loan applications within the CoB. Business students are able to apply for an interest-free crisis loan for up to $500 in the event of a personal emergency. Fatima's supervisor, Carla, explains that the purpose of the loan is to help prevent students from stopping out when something unexpected occurs in their lives. Carla lists off examples such as a car breaking down, an unexpected medical expense, or having to fly home for a family funeral. She indicates that the loans are not meant to help students meet basic needs that may be ongoing, but if it seems as though students just need a temporary fix, the loans could be approved.

Carla explains that the money for the loans comes from a large endowment, so there is no concern that they would ever run out of funds for the program. Fatima is impressed that the CoB is able to provide its students with this resource when they encounter an emergency.

After two weeks of training, Carla tells Fatima that she is ready to start meeting with advisees and reviewing crisis loan applications. However, Carla says that because Fatima is new to academic advising and Bluemound, she will review Fatima's meeting notes and application decisions for about a month. After meeting with several students and walking them through the loan process successfully with Carla's approval, Fatima meets with Mauricio, who is a first-generation college student. Looking through his file, Fatima learns that Mauricio easily gained admission to the entrepreneurship major last year with high grades in the prerequisite courses. The last advisor who met with Mauricio also wrote that he works twenty hours a week off campus and has expressed interest in internships.

When Mauricio comes into Fatima's office, he looks exhausted. Mauricio starts out by telling Fatima that he is thinking about dropping a class or two but isn't sure how that will affect his ability to graduate on time. After explaining how the process for dropping would work, Fatima asks him why he wants to drop the classes.

Mauricio responds, "I really want to stay in all my classes, but I need to work more. My mom's hours got cut over the summer, so my parents can't help me with any of my bills. I've been trying to cut back—" Mauricio blinks back tears. "But I can't *not* pay my rent or gas to get to my job. I can't cut back anymore! I've got $10 until my next paycheck and all I've eaten the past two days is ramen. All I can think to do is drop some classes so I have more time to work."

At first, Fatima is unsure of what to say but then remembers the CoB crisis loans. "That sounds like you are dealing with a lot right now," she says. "But the College of Business has something that might help you. We have a crisis loan for students that's up to $500. You'd have a year to pay it back, but there's no interest. Here's the application, and we can fill it out together. I can then review your application today. I'll need my supervisor to look it over, but I meet with her this afternoon."

Mauricio responds that $500 would help him out a lot, and that he definitely wants to apply for the loan. While he fills out the application, Fatima looks up resources online. Surprised that there isn't a food pantry on campus, she prints out a list of local food pantries for Mauricio. They then schedule a follow-up meeting to check in the next week. Mauricio thanks Fatima for her help.

Later that day, Fatima is supposed to meet with Carla for her weekly meeting to review her advising notes. However, Carla has a family emergency that will take her away from the office for the remainder of the day, and likely longer. When Carla calls Fatima to cancel the meeting, Fatima tells Carla that she helped a student fill out a crisis loan application and had planned to share the information and form with Carla. Carla asks if the loan meets the typical criteria for a CoB crisis loan, and if so, to send it through. Carla also indicates that if she needs to see the loan application, she likely won't get to it until next week at the earliest. Fatima pauses. She believes that Mauricio is dealing with a crisis and would greatly benefit from the loan. However, from joking comments Carla has made about "surviving on ramen during college," Fatima senses that Carla might question whether Maurcio's situation meets the loan criteria. Further, Fatima knows that if she rationalizes that Mauricio's crisis is temporary, she can send the loan to the bursar's office without Carla even seeing it.

What should Fatima do?

MISREPORTING FIRST DESTINATION
DATA IN CAREER SERVICES
LINSEY HUGO AND DAVID J. NGUYEN

Each year university administrators anxiously await the release of the latest
national rankings to see where their institution stacks up against the competition. This experience is no different at Sycamore College, a Top-100 research
university with a reputation for strong first destination outcomes for business
major students. Year after year, data illustrated business students find career-
related jobs at higher rates than the rest of the institution. For this reason, the
College of Business is seen as the "crown jewel" of campus resources, including state of the art classrooms, additional tenure-track faculty lines, and
senior administrators' praise.

Camille (she/her/hers), the director of the Business Career Center, sat
down at her desk, opened the latest national rankings issue, and smiled. She
beamed with pride at the steady rise of Sycamore's College of Business from
an institution ranked at 379 five years ago to being ranked 44 in the country.
Camille remembered her interview with the dean of the College of Business
five years ago when she pitched her plan for staffing a business-focused
career center. After she accepted the role as director, rankings became a focal
point as a result of the university's investment in Camille and business-
specific career services.

Recognizing the need to enhance career outcomes, the College of Business at Sycamore invested considerable financial, spatial, and staffing resources in growing the new Business Career Center. In addition to hiring two
career coaches, Camille hired Ernie (he/him/his) as an employer relations
coordinator focused on connecting students and employers through events,
campus recruiting, and on-campus interviews. After supervising Ernie for
two years, Camille recognized his strong analytical abilities and gave Ernie
the additional responsibility of compiling and analyzing data from the first
destination survey, which is distributed to graduating students each year. To
support the first destination collection effort, Ernie hired, trained, and supervised several work-study students to help him contact the six hundred recent
graduates and report first destination information.

When Ernie took on this new responsibility, Camille emphasized the
importance of the first destination data—the first destination survey results
are tied to various national rankings and the rankings influence the financial
resources given to the Business Career Center each year. With Camille's
encouragement, Ernie reviewed the prior year's data in a spreadsheet as part
of his training process. Now, as he has worked with the prior year's data, he
encounters difficulty in replicating the facts and figures reported by the College of Business to the national rankings and other news outlets. Running
analyses with the data, he observes substantial discrepancies between the

reported and actual numbers. After several days of investigation, Ernie identifies that some of the erroneous calculations occurred because someone manipulated the data to be more positive than the reported numbers, for example reporting placement rates that were 10 percent higher than were actually placed. He sends Camille an email outlining some of the discovered discrepancies. She quickly responds, asking him to come to her office right away.

In Camille's office, Ernie shares a long list of questionable data decisions and states that actual outcomes for last year were several percentage points lower or more than reported totals. Camille appears flustered but directs Ernie to ignore the error for now. She also mentions that the problem illustrates how important it will be for Ernie to ensure the correct reporting is done for the upcoming graduating class. Ernie recognizes that the rankings were based on erroneous first destination data, thereby misrepresenting Sycamore's position, but does not want to ruffle feathers or jeopardize the Business Career Center. Ernie cannot believe that the College of Business has been reporting incorrect data.

What should Ernie do?

IMPORTANCE OF STAFF TRAINING
MIRANDA COOK AND JAMES KROTZ

Marley is an academic coach at Mid-Central State University (a large, public research institution of twenty-four thousand students in the Midwest). Marley works at the new Academic Coaching Center (ACC) serving first-year students who are conditional admits to the university. In accordance with state law, baseline admissions criteria are established by the statewide Board of Regents and include ACT or SAT scores, high school GPA, and required proficiency in general education courses. The Board of Regents is a group of people appointed to supervise the public higher education system. Students who do not meet Regents admissions requirements are required to meet with an academic coach biweekly to assist them as they adjust to the academic rigor of Mid-Central's curriculum. Mid-Central is known for its engineering and business programs, which are two of the most challenging academic programs at the institution and require time commitment in and outside of the classroom.

The duties of the academic coaches include checking in with students to assess their academic progress and psychological well-being, connecting them to campus resources, answering questions, and helping students prepare for their college experience. The student requirements for the first semester include signing a learning agreement, enrolling as a full-time student, and enrolling in a first-year seminar. The first-year seminar allows students to build community with peers and create a close connection with their academic coach, who also serves as their instructor for the first-year seminar. The course content of the seminar includes student motivation, study habits, time-management, and other important skills for new students. The program serves approximately six hundred students each semester.

The ACC staff consists of five academic coaches, one graduate assistant, and one practicum student. All of the coaches and graduate students report to Roger, the director of academic coaching. Roger worked as a coach for two years and has been the director for six months. The department was created three years ago and has yet to see increased student retention. Roger has had a difficult time building community and confidence among the newly established team. When he served as a coach, he had success building rapport with his students and developing them into strong students as they advanced. He was selected to serve as the director due to his tenure as a coach and success with students, but he hasn't been as successful in the leadership role due to his team's morale. Because of the lack of morale in the office, Roger tends to be sensitive to staff members overstepping their bounds and making change.

Marley is new to academic coaching, as she is a recent graduate of a master's program in student affairs. Marley's institutional knowledge was strong when she began in her new role because she attended Mid-Central as both an undergraduate and graduate. She knew the job would have many learning curves, but her graduate education prepared her well. Prior to starting in the academic coaching role, Marley served as a graduate assistant in an academic advising office on campus. This is her first year serving as an academic coach at the university and Roger's first hire since starting in the director role. She had a few meetings with Roger prior to starting the role, but her training was sparse. She started to see students after three weeks, and though she feels confident in her conversations with them, she is unsure of the goals she should be setting for student progress. During her training, Marley would meet with Roger in the morning and he would assign her time to review links on websites and spend time at the front desk. Marley's time was full of these activities, but she needed more active learning opportunities to understand her new role. Because of her minimal training, Marley is unsure of what the true goal of coaching is, but she is excited to start in the new role.

Since starting as an academic coach, Marley has noticed challenges facing Cynthia and Jim, the graduate students who work in the ACC. Both are pursuing a master's of science in Mid-Central State's student affairs program. Marley knew them from her master's program but was a year ahead of Jim, a current second-year practicum student who works ten hours a week and has a caseload of twenty-five students, and two years ahead of Cynthia, a first-semester graduate assistant who works twenty hours a week and has a caseload of forty students. Their caseloads consist of students on academic warning (cumulative GPA below 2.0), students in their first semester (first-time, full-time freshmen who did not meet Board of Regents requirements), and students participating in the program voluntarily to gain study skills. The diverse caseload creates a challenge for Cynthia's and Jim's workloads. Marley was concerned both about the caseload diversity and the lack of training the graduate students received before starting to meet with students. Neither Cynthia nor Jim received training on scheduling, communicating with students, or assisting students with time management tools, study skills, and motivational interviewing.

Although Marley earned a coaching certification, she still feels hesitant about her own skills for coaching and thus does not feel qualified to offer the graduate students training or advice. Marley is also concerned because the graduate students are located two floors below the full-time academic coaches in a graduate student suite. She believes the lack of supervision and training, coupled with their inexperience as student affairs professionals, will not improve their skills as academic coaches and be a disservice to their assigned students. She has noticed that Roger is disengaged with the graduate students despite his responsibility to them as the supervisor and director.

Four weeks into the fall semester, Jim comes into Marley's office and asks, "What should I be doing for my practicum?" Jim expresses frustration with his lack of training and discloses that Cynthia feels the same way. After a few questions, it is clear that both of the graduate students are reluctant to approach any of the other coaches, let alone Roger, for fear of creating tension. They sense the tension and lack of community in the office and thus are unsure about who to reach out to. But Jim and Cynthia both believe their lack of training is causing them to be incompetent in their work and that the students who they coach and teach may be struggling academically and psychologically as a result. Both graduate students recently discussed ethical dilemmas in higher education in their classes and were thus motivated to come forward to Marley because of their loose connection from graduate school. Even though Marley is not their supervisor, she hopes to assist them with their training, despite her trepidations and dissatisfaction with her own training.

However, although Marley empathizes with the graduate students and is very willing to help them, she is hesitant to approach Roger. Marley wonders if it is her responsibility to take on the graduate students' training and, as a new hire in the office, she feels inadequate to assist their next steps. She believes intervening would be exceeding her bounds as a new professional, and Roger is notoriously protective of his assigned duties and has been known to swiftly reprimand his subordinates for overstepping or offering unwanted advice. Marley has yet to quarrel with Roger and, despite her strong sense of injustice at the situation, does not want to cause problems in her first semester of work.

Despite Marley's concerns, she reaches out to Roger and sets up a meeting with him to discuss the situation of the graduate assistants further. He politely listens to her concerns and thanks her for bringing the issue to his attention but offers no indication that he intends to fix the issue. Over the next few weeks, Jim and Cynthia continue to coach their students as they have been, and it is clear Roger has not sought to resolve the training issue. Jim and Cynthia continue to muddle through their appointments. A few weeks following Marley and Roger's discussion, Cynthia discloses to Marley that she is actively seeking another assistantship, despite her goal of working as an academic coach after graduation. It appears to Marley that things have not improved for Jim and Cynthia's experience. Additionally, because practicum students aren't guaranteed each semester, the original plan was for Cynthia to assume coaching responsibilities for Jim's twenty-five students after he finishes his practicum and she has had a full semester of experience.

What should Marley do?

OFFICE POLITICS
TAYLOR PERKINS AND KIPP VAN DYKE

Dale works at University West, a small, private institution in the Midwest. He is in his first year as an academic advisor in the College of Liberal Arts and Sciences. Dale and his colleagues, Jasmine and Raymond, hold three of six academic advising positions within the office. They report directly to Taj, director of academic advising for the College of Liberal Arts and Sciences. Though Dale gets along well with everyone, Jasmine is his closest friend in the office.

The assistant director of academic advising position in the office has been vacant for three months and the position was recently posted. Jasmine decides to apply for the position but has a few reservations. Though Jasmine is excited, she is apprehensive knowing that a woman has never held the position of assistant director or director in the office before. Not knowing if her application will be taken seriously, Dale encourages her to be confident in her application. Though Dale is new to the office, he believes strongly that Jasmine, having worked in the office for six years, would be a great fit for the position. He has noticed that Jasmine's evaluations from students always have positive remarks in regard to their advising meetings, she recently designed and implemented a new scheduling system to get more students in during registration, and she consistently responds well to completing tasks collaboratively. Because of these observations, Dale is confident that Jasmine would perform well as the assistant director.

One day in the break room, Dale overhears Raymond speaking with the receptionist, Rob. Raymond has been in his position as an academic advisor for eleven years and is well respected in the office and the institution. Raymond is close family friends with the director, Taj. Their children have attended the same schools since elementary school, so their families have gotten close and frequently spend time together. Because of this close relationship, Raymond benefits from freedom and autonomy in his role, in a capacity that other advisors feel they do not receive from Taj.

In Raymond's conversation with Rob, he expresses his frustration that Jasmine is applying for the assistant director position. Dale overhears Raymond say, "I'm just a little confused as to why Jasmine is applying for the position. We need someone who can be assertive and make big decisions. I think Jasmine is a great academic advisor, but I just don't think she has what it takes to be assistant director." Dale hears this and guesses that Raymond's remarks come from a place of frustration, as Raymond applied for the assistant director position the last time that it was open, about four years ago. The director at the time (as Taj was not yet in his current role) did not award Raymond with the position. Because of the freedom and flexibility that Raymond receives from Taj in his current role, he has decided not to reapply for the position this time around. Making inferences about where Raymond's remarks may be coming from, Dale decides to ignore the comments for now.

In the next all-staff meeting, Taj announces who will be on the search committee for the assistant director position. Dale learns that one of the five members of the search committee will be Raymond. Taj shares that he is looking forward to having Raymond's leadership on the committee, since he is a veteran staff member in their office. Dale knows that Raymond has already made his mind up about Jasmine as a candidate and is uncomfortable with the bias he may bring to the hiring process.

The first search committee meeting will occur in two weeks to start reviewing applications. Dale feels he should say something to the director but fears his concerns will not be taken seriously.

What should Dale do?

WHO WROTE THE PAPER?
AMBER N. RACCHINI

Doug is an academic advisor who is in his first full-time position working at Claysville State University (CSU). CSU is a mid-sized, public institution located in a rural town in the Midwest. Doug's position is in the newly created Academic Support Center (ASC). The ASC serves students who enter CSU with a high school grade point average (GPA) below 3.0 and/or SAT score below 850. These students are part of a first-year experience program where they enroll in a one-credit seminar course and are advised by a staff member within the ASC.

Doug accepted this position because he wanted the opportunity to work with at-risk students and help them successfully transition to their second year. Doug struggled his first year in college, participated in a similar first-year experience program, and attributed his success in part to the mentorship provided by his academic advisor.

As part of his job responsibilities, Doug was assigned a caseload of ten students who finished their fall semester with a cumulative grade point average below a 2.0, and were therefore placed on academic probation. The students assigned to Doug are required to participate in an Academic Recovery Program and enroll in a seminar course focused on learning strategies such as note taking, study skills, and time management.

Joseph is one of Doug's advisees. He is on the football team and needs to finish the semester in good standing to be eligible to play next season. Doug meets with Joseph at the beginning of the semester to discuss why he did so poorly in the fall and strategize on how to improve. Joseph tells Doug that he is only at CSU to play football and he feels a lot of pressure from his coaches because they want him to be a starter next season. Joseph is enrolled in the study skills seminar class that Doug co-teaches. Doug and Joseph plan to meet every week after class to discuss his progress and assignments due the following week.

Throughout the semester, Doug and Joseph develop a strong rapport. Doug is happy to see that Joseph is attending his seminar class, meeting with him regularly, and passing his courses. When midterm grades are posted, Joseph tells Doug that he is passing all of his classes except for ENGL 101: Composition. Doug encourages Joseph to meet with his professor to get feedback about his writing and visit CSU's Writing Center. Joseph seems hesitant to ask for help and says, "I've never been good at writing. There is no way that I can pass this class."

Due to their strong rapport, Doug agrees to review Joseph's next paper and offer feedback before he submits it. Later that evening, Joseph emails Doug the first draft of his paper. Doug reads the paper and makes suggestions throughout, noting that Joseph still has a lot of work to do before it is ready to be submitted. Doug sends the draft back to Joseph and tells him to work on the grammatical issues within the paper, the organization, and to incorporate transitional sentences. Doug asks Joseph to make the revisions and meet with him face-to-face later in the week to discuss his second draft.

Later that week, Doug receives an email from Joseph with the final draft of his paper. In the email, Joseph explains that he does not have time to meet with Doug before the paper is due and the attached paper is the one that he submitted to his English professor to grade. Doug reads through the paper and notices that Joseph has made major revisions and shown drastic improvement in the readability of his paper. Doug also notices that Joseph's writing style has changed significantly, and the paper has taken on a professional tone that was missing in the first draft. Doug is concerned that Joseph did not make these changes on his own and wonders if he should contact the English professor to discuss his suspicions.

What should Doug do?

SUCCESS AT A PRICE
MOLLY C. WARD AND DAVID J. NGUYEN

Green City Community College (GCCC) serves thirty-one thousand students across multiple campuses and educational sites within and around a major metropolitan area. The GCCC administration prides itself on being student centered. Additionally, due to the pressures of a state funding model based on student degree completion and course success rates, rather than solely enrollment, GCCC has increased its commitment to providing proactive student support and has emphasized the institutional goal of increasing enrollment and student success. For example, key departments were established for individuals re-entering academia, including veterans and individuals who are experiencing unemployment. Most recently, GCCC has created a staff position to serve students who are entering the college after being incarcerated, also known as Restored Citizens. This new role is housed within the Student Success and Retention Office under the supervision of Don, the assistant director. Don was excited to have the new Restored Citizens Support Program coordinator, Neil, join the team due to his unique professional experiences.

Within the structure of GCCC, Neil officially reports to Student Success and Retention, however, he also has a dotted line to the Enrollment Management Office. Neil is responsible for working with students who were formerly incarcerated as they enter into GCCC and progress through their educational journey. Neil has a social work background and many years of experience working in the public sector. He is highly connected with local service agencies and support networks. While this is a new role for Neil, he had been working in Enrollment Management at the college for two years when asked to step into this role due to his extensive social work background.

Neil and Don have weekly one-on-one meetings where Don has often expressed how Neil has been one of his best employees due to how quickly Neil has gotten the Restored Citizen Support Program off the ground. This is no small compliment as Don is in his fifth year as assistant director of student success and retention and has spent the entirety of his student affairs career at GCCC.

One practice that impressed Don was Neil's development of a caseload management system. Through the system Neil is able to support a variety of students, including Shannon, who was recently released from prison and is attempting to start her experience at GCCC. Shannon is currently living in a halfway house and doing her best to simply survive each day.

On Monday morning, Don arrives at the Student Success and Retention Center. He sits down at his desk with his cup of coffee and begins checking his email from the weekend. As he scrolls through emails, he sees one from Shannon, who wanted to contact Neil's supervisor to provide positive feedback about Neil's support and guidance as she started her academic experiences at GCCC.

In the email, Shannon explains how Neil has gone above and beyond what she thought was possible for a recent parolee. The email details examples of Neil providing resources for food assistance programs and writing letters to the people running the halfway house she is currently living in. These letters provide pathways for her to be able to get exemptions to attend business classes at GCCC and meet with the advisors who are helping Shannon find a suitable major that can lead to employment for individuals with criminal records. Finally, Shannon discusses how Neil paid for her college transcript to be sent from an institution she attended prior to being incarcerated. Due to limitations with income and reintegrating into the community, Shannon explains how her transcript being ordered and sent to GCCC removed a significant barrier and that she wouldn't have been able to start school again without Neil's assistance in the process. Shannon closes by again sharing her gratitude and stating that Neil is a true example of how staff should support students.

Don knows there are no college funds allocated for Neil to pay for transcripts for other Restored Citizen Support Program participants. Don concludes that Neil must have used his own funds to pay for the transcript for Shannon. While there are no college policies about staff providing monetary support to students, Don is concerned with this information and how it may be perceived by students, faculty, and staff. He begins to worry that other program participants will expect the same financial help. Don calls Neil into his office and explains his concerns. Neil begins to worry because, in addition to Shannon, he has paid transcript transfer fees for about ten other students. He also bought books for a few students. He doesn't have kids and has more than enough money to get by, therefore, the fees seem like a small price to pay and he has always considered the amount doled out to students a donation. Neil doesn't believe that Don will find out about the other payments. As Neil ponders what to do next, Don asks Neil to disclose all of the students he provided financial support to and explain his decisions regarding his support of each student.

What should Neil do?

THE GREATER GOOD
CATHERINE DUGAN

Rob worked for four years in the Disability Access Office (DAO) at Normal State University, a mid-sized, mid-Atlantic, Carnegie Doctoral I university. Normal State, serving fourteen thousand undergraduate and graduate students, has a long-term commitment to ensuring disability access which, while not perfect, both provides legally mandated access accommodations as well as holistic advising, advocacy, and other assistance as students learn to navigate higher education. The access services resulted in high student satisfaction, a high rate of first-to-second-year retention, and graduation rates that showed a smaller gap than that of the overall university to national averages. As well as ensuring access, DAO at Normal provides extensive individual support meetings for the eight hundred-plus students they serve.

While at NSU, Rob enjoyed being a part of an experienced staff team that included a long-term director, assistant director, disability access adviser (Rob's role), two graduate assistants, a secretary, and numerous student employees. With shared responsibility for the students whom they served, team meetings often included discussions of issues and support. Differing views were expressed, discussed, and respected. Team members felt comfortable that their leadership had the experience and skills to serve students, advise faculty and the university on accommodations and inclusion, and help their team grow and develop. Both the director and the assistant director enjoyed extensive relationships across campus and a trust with most departments that allowed them to confidentially inquire about unusual and sensitive situations. The vice president for student affairs was committed to ensuring legally mandated access, confidentiality, and support for the department's focus on intrusive/developmental advising services. Normal State's president also openly and publicly advocated for access, while deferring to the professional judgment of the DAO. Faculty from across campus referred students, and other departments understood that the DAO staff needed to provide confidential services such that, to ensure rapport and continued use of services, staff from DAO did not typically refer students judicially for suspected alcohol, drug, or other issues, aside from Title IX or clear Academic Integrity violations. When student offenders were referred, Normal State's conduct policies, while strict, typically allowed for discussion, and focused on alleged offenders' rehabilitation and education, and the "bigger picture."

After four years, Rob felt ready to move on to an assistant director position. He secured a disability services position at Scotland University, a smaller public university of four thousand, also in the mid-Atlantic region. In the assistant director role, he joined the director, who was the only other staff member, in serving a population of about 250 students. Rob didn't like being in a smaller town but did appreciate that the campus was within one and a half hours of several small cities. His plan was to get the additional experience and move on to disability support work on a campus in a larger city such as New York or Boston. His first months in the position have been good, although both the campus and the office director seem more strict about student infractions with regard to alcohol or drugs. As well, questions are not always welcome, particularly if they may indicate a break in "tradition."

Underage drinking and drug use, including cannabis, are illegal in the state in which Normal State and Scotland University reside. Normal State had respected the needs for Disability Access service rapport and didn't require non-observed, secondhand reporting of illegal substances. Scotland University has taken a different approach to conduct, alcohol and drug use, and behavior in general. The administration requires that staff report suspicions of illegal drug or alcohol use, and they advocate for quick and strong adjudication of infractions.

At Scotland, Rob recently began working with a new client, Dan, who came to their first meeting appearing disoriented or "high." Rob knows that Dan is underage, resides in a residence hall, and is an upperclass criminology major, which typically prohibits any prior use of or infractions for illegal substances, as students with infractions were less likely to secure employment in the criminology field. Rob didn't say anything to Dan about his suspicion of Dan's altered state. He reasoned that he wanted to ensure that Dan, who had serious ADHD and academic issues, would return for their next meeting, allowing them to again review accommodation procedures and begin looking at success strategies. Rob also reported nothing because he felt that this could be an isolated incident.

Dan arrives to the next meeting fully alert, but with bad news. He is really upset because he was at a concert off campus but in a university-community jointly managed venue and was arrested with drugs. He was not jailed but will be facing legal and conduct charges. He is both terrified and remorseful about the drug charges. He swore that he rarely used the drugs with which he was found and vowed to no longer use them. Most of their session focused on plans for dealing with the stress of the drug charges while continuing to do school work. Rob began to explore how extensive Dan's drug use was. Dan assured him that his use of ecstasy for the concert was a "one-time" event. With that knowledge, Rob proceeded with their access advising meeting, not mentioning his prior concern about Dan's seemingly having been "high," nor further addressing the drug charge. At the end of their session, Rob did indicate to Dan that he felt that they should meet weekly while Dan worked through these issues and while they focused on improving his academics. Dan agreed.

Dan continued to attend weekly sessions, the focus of which was often his upcoming adjudication for the drug violation at the concert venue, as Dan remained fearful of the results. At each session, after calming Dan down, Rob tried to focus on Dan's use of accommodations for his ADHD, plans for his upcoming assignments, and his future plans. As the semester progressed, Dan calmed down somewhat. He told Rob that he was found in violation of the drug policy but was not expelled from Scotland University nor given jail time. Due to having no prior violations, and his genuine remorse, and his willingness to improve, Dan has been allowed to continue in his major, but was counseled that finding jobs in the field may be challenging. He clearly trusted Rob and began to more willingly track his academic progress. In future meetings, he showed effort in revamping his studies and, albeit slowly, his grades were improving.

Rob had come to care deeply about Dan's progress and was pleased with his small measures of success. Unfortunately, this was disrupted during an early April visit by Dan. During that visit Dan relayed that he had regularly been taking his medication for ADHD. He found it to be fairly effective for increasing his focus, but he still had, he felt, too many intruding thoughts and too much impulsivity. He told Rob that he found smoking weed effective in helping him to decrease those impulses. Rob was taken aback by this information and took a minute to regroup. He indicated to Dan that he was disturbed to learn of this coping strategy, that cannabis was illegal in their state, and that it was unwise and potentially dangerous to take his medicine for ADHD with pot. Further, he indicated that he was supposed to report any illegal drug use. Dan assured Rob that he only smoked "occasionally." Rob told him that he needed to stop his use or Rob would have to report the use. Dan assured him that he would do so.

Despite being very uncomfortable, Rob wanted to be able to keep meeting with Dan and, therefore, said nothing to his supervisor about the conversation, reasoning that Dan would stop using pot. His logic included the fact that, since they had been meeting, Dan's grades had increased from Ds and Fs to Cs. Dan had begun to use accommodative services in a timelier manner and he willingly attended meetings. Nevertheless, being cautious, Rob decided to research Scotland State's judicial policy and to ask his supervisor about their office's interactions with the policy. His supervisor Chuck's response was swift and clear: "I don't care about rapport; we have a zero-tolerance policy. I don't even know why we serve addicts in recovery." Rob's research of the policy revealed that the university did have a "three strikes and you are out" policy, with even "two strikes" ensuring potentially harsh sanctions.

Rob remained tense all week and, upon their next meeting, inquired early on if Dan had implemented their agreement. Dan said, "No, man, I just couldn't, given how useful the pot is. I know that you said that it's not good to mix with my meds, but I am so much calmer when I do both." Rob said nothing more and tried to implement a normal meeting plan.

After the meeting, Rob was even more conflicted. He realized that he had likely violated the university's referral policy, probably would incur his supervisor's wrath, and remained uncomfortable about the fact that Dan's use of pot was potentially harmful with his current ADHD medication. He also realized that Dan had made substantial progress in his grades and overall attitude, appropriate use of services, and that he was contributing to the university by the leadership activities that he began to pursue when Rob recommended him. Dan is close to graduating and would be the first in his family to graduate. He had a potential job lead and graduating and securing a position would help reduce the statistics about undergraduation and under-employment of persons with disabilities. Rob knows that if he reports Dan, Dan will likely stop using services and/or meeting with Rob even if he isn't charged or expelled. He deeply fears that Rob will spiral downward, not continuing his positive progress. He would really like to continue to work with Dan and see him progress during his senior year.

What should Rob do?

THE PROGRAM IS A S.C.A.M.P.
MOLLY JEAN CALLAHAN, JORDAN W. VIARS,
MICHELLE J. BOETTCHER, AND TONY CAWTHON

Robbie works in the Pre-Professional Advising Office at Saddler University (SU), a large, public, predominantly White institution in the Northeast. SU enrolls over twenty-five thousand students. The average SAT score is 1365, 45 percent of the students graduated in the top 10 percent of their high school class, and more than 40 percent receive some type of academic-based scholarship. Additionally, more than 65 percent of the undergraduate students are from in state.

Robbie is the senior pre-medicine advisor in the pre-professional advising office, working primarily with students preparing for medical school. She is one of four professional advisors in the office and reports to the associate provost for undergraduate studies. She has an advising caseload of 242 students. Robbie has been in her position for two years but worked for several years as a registered nurse. She completed her bachelor's degree in nursing at SU and leaned on her mentors to help her transition from nursing to academic advising. Robbie loves serving in a mentoring capacity and strives to support students in innovative ways, including coprogramming with other campus offices to set students up for success.

After spending the morning preparing for a busy week of appointments during registration season, Robbie meets with her first student, Alex, who wants to finalize plans to fulfill the medical school prerequisites and to discuss his upcoming summer.

"Good afternoon, Alex! How's your semester going?" Robbie begins.

"Pretty good so far. I'm feeling comfortable with this round of classes. Midterms went really well." Alex grins. Then pulling out a notebook and finding a page with his registration worksheet, Alex says, "I should be on track to finish up classes for the MCAT by next fall based on our last conversation, so I'd like to take the exam January of junior year. Would that work?"

"That should give you plenty of time," Robbie nods. "Especially if you set up your study plan early enough. What are your plans for the summer?"

"Well, I want to give myself the strongest application possible, but it feels like everyone has different advice. My parents know this doctor from church, Dr. Aston, and she's agreed to let me shadow her this summer," Alex hesitates. "But most of my friends have fancy summer internships and I don't want to fall behind. My advisor, Dr. Burkett, recommended this study abroad program, S.C.A.M.P.—the Saddler Central American Medical Program. He leads it every summer and a bunch of students get the chance to work in a free clinic in Guatemala!"

"Those are two very different summer opportunities open to you. It sounds like you're really excited about S.C.A.M.P. Have you done any further research on the program? Or maybe looked into other study abroad opportunities?" Robbie asks

"I did talk to my cousin and she said her friend went on a S.C.A.M.P. trip a few years ago. He loved it! He got to assist with surgeries and work with a ton of different patients. He's at one of the best programs in the state now. My fraternity brother went too and is pushing for me to go. He said that going on this trip means Dr. Burkett is more likely to write me a letter of recommendation, which would help. I think this would be much better than some shadowing hours. At least this way I can actually work with patients instead of observing all summer."

Robbie has heard of the program before and is unsure of how to advise Alex. She has serious ethical concerns about the program and what it teaches students. The program was created several years ago by Dr. Burkett and has gained significant attention at the university as a great opportunity for students to get hands-on experience. In fact, it was recently selected as a Best Practice in Study Abroad by a nationally recognized international student experience organization.

Robbie's concerns about the program stem from hearing students who have participated mention that there are frequent opportunities for students to assist with surgeries and major medical procedures, order medical supplies, and dispense medications. Students are excited to have this unique, immersive opportunity. She has heard students eagerly share their experiences with peers about participating in medical practices prohibited by U.S. legal and ethical standards. One student came into Robbie's office and proudly proclaimed her intimate involvement in the delivery of an infant during her summer with S.C.A.M.P.

Robbie has previously had conversations with students about how to market their study abroad experience to admissions committees, and she consistently reminds students that one part of the interview is typically an assessment of their ethical decision-making. She challenges her advisees to reflect on how they will respond when presented with an ethical dilemma. Robbie wants to support Alex in whichever opportunity he chooses and feels confident that she will be able to help him market either choice to a medical school admissions board. However, she is worried about future students and the message that the university is sending by promoting this program. Her office is expected to set pre-professional students up for success and better their chances to advance their education.

Robbie raised her concerns last year—her first year on the job—with her direct supervisor, Chris, but was discouraged from taking them further. "You have to understand," Chris began. "This is a really high-profile program for the university and for our department. If you raise concerns, it could close doors for you in the future." While last year she was focused on establishing herself in her new role, this year she feels more compelled than ever to raise concerns about what students are doing during this experience.

By standing idly by, Robbie and the department may be placing their students at a disadvantage as their choice to participate in procedures during this summer program could result in them being denied admission on ethical grounds. Robbie has limited political capital in the university as a young professional, but her network in the department and across campus is strong from her time there as an undergraduate.

What should Robbie do?

A VETERAN AND A SCHOLAR
AMANDA A. TORRENCE

Brooke recently completed her master's degree in higher education at the University of Groveboro, a large flagship institution in the Deep South. Upon graduation, she began a professional position as an academic advisor at South Central University (SCU), also a large flagship institution. During her interview with the Academic Advising Office at SCU, Brooke specifically asked about the supervisors' approach on student advocacy, as that is an important tenet for Brooke's philosophical approach to student advising. She was assured by many people that equitable support of all students was the primary objective in their office. That, coupled with her pre-established familiarity with a large flagship, led to her accept this position.

South Central University, much like Brooke's graduate institution, is a research-heavy and predominately White institution, with a population of around thirty thousand. SCU is also within a two-hour driving radius of several military bases and has seen a recent increase in enrollment of active-duty military and veteran students. These students, along with GI Bill dependents such as the children or spouses of veterans, now make up approximately 18 percent of the undergraduate student population. However, some offices have a reputation for not being military or veteran friendly, and there is no established Veteran Services Office.

As Brooke began to advise incoming students during New Student Orientation throughout the summer months, she noticed the large number of student veterans and active-duty students in her caseload. When she asked to participate in Veterans Advocacy Training, a training to help professionals better understand how to work with military students, her supervisors told her that she wouldn't have any time until after the rush of orientation was over. However, any time Brooke would ask her supervisors a question that related to the direct advisement of her military students, they would respond, "That will be covered in Veterans Advocacy Training."

As summer began to wind down and New Student Orientation came to a close, Brooke started to send emails to all of her students on policies surrounding credit hours, full-time status, and financial aid requirements so her students could meet all the appropriate deadlines before bills for the semester were due to the Bursar's Office. When her students on scholarship emailed her with questions regarding scholarship-specific policies, she referred them to the Office of Financial Aid to best support them, so as to not misinform them.

One morning, Brooke came into work and saw a response to her initial email about payment deadlines from one of her students who was a veteran. The email read:

Hi Brooke,
I am currently trying to get all of my ducks in a row to prepare for the start of the semester. I don't have any questions about my fall semester bill, because I know that my GI Bill will cover it. However, since it has been about six years since I was last in school, I was wondering if you could point me in the right direction to some study resources on campus?
Thanks,
Jackson

Brooke, being new to SCU and unsure about the different university re-sources available to students in this situation, popped into her supervisor Melinda's office to inquire. Melinda oversees the academic advisors in the College of Liberal Arts, for which Brooke is a staff member. When Brooke mentions that Jackson is not worried about the payment, but rather is looking for studying resources, Melinda offhandedly mentions, "Oh, by the way, you will probably start getting a lot of emails from veterans and dependents once the bill deadline passes. The bill for the fall semester is due on the first day of classes, but the United States Department of Veterans Affairs usually doesn't send out checks until at least two weeks after the due date. Those students will have to pay this bill with their own money and then be reimbursed. Otherwise they will be charged a $250 late fee."

"Should I give them a heads up like we do with our students on scholar-ship? Is there someone I can point them to regarding this dilemma?" Brooke asks.

"No," Melinda replies, "that will probably cause more problems and con-fusion. Besides, this is not really our responsibility since we only work with a handful of students within our academic college. This should fall under Fi-nancial Aid's purview, which you will learn in Veterans Advocacy Train-ing."

Brooke feels very uncomfortable with this response. She wants to advo-cate for and support all of her students, especially those students who do not know they will have to pay a $12,000 bill up front with their own money or face a hefty late fee. However, she also does not want to go against a direc-tive from her supervisor and worries about how this would impact her future working relationship with Melinda.

What should Brooke do?

DENTIST DREAMS
ZACHARY UNDERWOOD AND STEPHANIE GANSER

Bradbury University is a mid-sized regional university located in the Southwest with a student population of fifteen thousand undergraduate and graduate students. The institution hosts many undergraduate majors including a
premiere biology department considered to be one of the best in the state.
This particular biology department is considered premiere because of stellar
faculty, undergraduate research opportunities, and a pre-health professions
track. Additionally, the faculty and staff are proud of the high number of
students who are admitted into medical schools after completing their Bradbury University undergraduate degrees. The faculty and staff who work with
the department are committed to maintaining that high standard

Richard, a sophomore at Bradbury University, is majoring in biology.
Richard comes from a family of medical professionals. Growing up, Richard
knew he wanted to join the family tradition of entering the medical field.
Richard's mother is a physician's assistant, and his father is a nurse. His
older brother attends medical school at the flagship university in the state,
earning a full scholarship to attend based on his academic accomplishments
and research experience. Richard has always aspired to be a dentist.

Growing up, Richard would pretend to be a dentist and check everyone's
teeth to make sure they were brushing. He joined the "Future Dentists Club"
in high school and his senior year became the president of the organization.
He wrote about his dental school aspirations in his college application and
was thrilled when he was accepted to Bradbury University, his first-choice
school. Entering college, Richard took introductory-level courses in chemistry and biology. He barely passed with a D in biology and D– in chemistry
and is taking these courses over during sophomore year. He also struggled in
other introductory first-year courses. After his first year, Richard has a cumulative GPA of 2.1.

All students are assigned an academic advisor at Bradbury University, but
students can also have a pre-health advisor to help them specifically with
professional school requirements. Students are encouraged to meet with their
pre-health advisors as soon as their first year so they can begin to plan for
their classes during their time at Bradbury University. These advisors can
also help students with finding internships, shadowing experiences, and programs for students interested in the medical field.

Richard scheduled an introductory meeting with a pre-health advisor at
the beginning of his sophomore year. When meeting with Nancy for the first
time, Richard shared that he was determined to continue on his path for
dental school even though he is repeating introductory science courses. His
major academic advisor suggested he investigate other majors due to his
GPA. Regardless of the major that Richard chooses, Nancy was concerned

that Richard would take math and sciences classes and take the Dental Acceptance Test, only to be turned down due to a poor GPA. A few weeks after the initial meeting, Nancy received messages via the institution's student success management software system indicating Richard does not complete work on time in his science courses and barely attends class.

When they meet for a second time, Nancy brings up the emails and his faculty's concerns. Richard immediately shifts the blame for his poor academic performance away from himself, explaining that the early time of the class, his professor's constant lectures, and the uselessness of introductory courses were reasons for his poor performance. As his advisor, Nancy subtly tries to get Richard to understand that dentists work early in the morning, lectures are commonplace, and introductory courses set a good foundation. Richard insists he will be a fantastic dentist once he gets beyond these introductory courses and he is doing nothing wrong academically.

Nancy is frustrated because of Richard's poor GPA and disappointing performance in introductory science courses. She knows he is not a good candidate for medical school. She perceives he is not addressing his own academic faults by externalizing the situation. He holds onto the idea that getting into dentistry school is an easy process because he has shadowed a dentist in the past. Nancy goes in a different direction and suggests Richard investigate alternative majors or a new parallel academic plan. When Nancy suggests trying other majors, Richard finds her lack support of disheartening and discouraging. Richard wants to continue taking more biology and chemistry courses but avoid professors from his previous courses. He knows his tenacity will pay off and he will be a dentist and enter the medical field, just like everyone else in his family. Richard admits that some of his friends suggested he try other majors as well, but he knows that he will make a great dentist. He wants to follow in his family's footsteps to achieve greatness. As Richard gets up to leave the appointment, Nancy reflects on her feeling that he has not heard her concerns. She is skeptical that Richard will be able to achieve his goals of dental school, but she also acknowledges her role in upholding the positive reputation of Bradbury University's biology programs and their medical school acceptance record.

What should Nancy do?

MORE THAN ACADEMICS
ANTONIQUE FLOOD AND DAVID J. NGUYEN

Remi is a full-time, first-year student affairs graduate student with an academic advising assistantship in the Student Success Center (SSC) at Green University (GU). Nestled in the rolling hills of midwestern Appalachia, GU is a stunning vision of winding footpaths, stately red brick edifices, and picturesque scenery. GU is a predominately White, mid-sized, public institution, serving approximately thirty thousand students. The SSC is situated in the bustling Student Union located in the epicenter of campus. The SSC has a reputation among students, faculty, and staff as being helpful and student-focused, primarily assisting undecided majors and students experiencing academic difficulty. Within the SSC, Remi instructs an undecided first-year seminar, facilitates academic success workshops for students placed on academic probation, and serves as a Student Opportunity for Academic Recovery (SOAR) advisor for recently academically reinstated students. Pairing these responsibilities with a rigorous graduate curriculum makes for a hectic, yet fulfilling, daily schedule.

Serving as a SOAR advisor is a central feature of Remi's assistantship. SOAR is a required intensive academic support program with the expressed purpose of giving academically dismissed undergraduate students an opportunity to complete their degrees. Students are required to participate during the first semester in which they re-enroll and, depending on their academic performance, they are removed from academic probation, continued on academic probation, or academically dismissed. Using an appreciative, strengths-based advising approach, Remi collaborates with students to develop an individualized student success plan. In particular, she teaches SOAR students to develop study skills, self-management strategies, and help-seeking behaviors. As someone who experienced academic difficulty during her undergraduate experience, Remi understands the power of a second chance.

This semester Remi is working with her first SOAR student, Evan. Evan is a junior in the accounting program within GU's College of Business. When the fall semester began, Evan exuded a gregarious personality and discussed a genuine desire to improve his academic performance. Based on his eagerness, Remi felt confident that together they would have a meaningful and successful advisor/advisee partnership. During their first advising meeting, Remi reviewed the program agreement, where she emphasized the required one-hour per week attendance policy. SOAR participants are only permitted one unexcused absence to maintain consistent and intentional interactions between student and advisor. Evan signed the agreement and articulated his commitment to attend every week and engage in required activities. After wrapping up the program's formalities, Remi began a discussion to establish rapport by asking Evan to disclose factors that may have contributed to his academic dismissal. With apparent hesitancy, he revealed that he had recently been diagnosed with clinical depression. Attending GU was his first time away from his family and support networks, and he struggled academically. During his time away from GU, Evan met with a counselor regularly to develop a comprehensive treatment plan involving self-management strategies and medication. He credited counseling as the main contributing factor in his decision to return to school. He assured Remi that he planned to establish a university counseling relationship through Counseling and Psychological Services and to maintain his medication schedule. Remi thanked Evan for sharing and made note of his mental health diagnosis and outlined wellness plan in his SOAR file.

For the first three weeks, Evan attended every meeting on time and demonstrated active participation. Remi felt that they were making progress toward selecting a better major option and expanding Evan's study strategies repertoire. Without advance notice, Evan failed to attend the fourth advising meeting. Concerned, Remi texted him to make sure he was okay. Evan texted her back apologizing and saying he overslept. He promised to be prepared and present next week. As promised, Evan attended the following week, chatty and ready to discuss his courses. Remi checked in about the missed meeting, and he assured her that he was up late studying and really just overslept. She reminded him of the agreed upon attendance policy and encouraged him to notify her in advance if he is unable to attend.

Remi and Evan had a fantastic fifth meeting, which reassured her of his mental and physical well-being and commitment to the SOAR program. Moving into the next week, Remi still felt good from their productive meeting, only to be disappointed when Evan failed to show up again. She texted him but received no response. Later in the day, she followed up via email for program record keeping. Thirty minutes after her email check-in, Remi received a text from Evan saying that he overslept again. He apologized and mentioned that he had not been feeling like himself lately. Remi responded asking if it is possible for them to reschedule for this week rather than waiting until their regularly scheduled appointment the following week. She expressed to Evan that she is concerned about him and his mental health and she would like to make sure he is okay. Evan agreed, and they decided to meet the next day.

To Remi's relief, Evan shows up the next day, but he appears haggard and fatigued. Before she can even begin conversing, Evan apologizes for missing their appointments and acknowledges the academic consequences of his behavior. He explains that he has experienced a loss of appetite and a lack of energy. Remi asks if he had been attending class and Evan replies no; he has not gone to class in two weeks. She then asks if he has been taking his prescribed medication for clinical depression, and he, again, replies no, explaining that he does not like it because it makes him feel weird and not like himself. Remi does not comment, allowing silence to envelop the room. Evan interrupts the silence by saying that he feels lonely, lacks friends in his courses, and sometimes he wishes that he could just disappear. He softly mutters that the world would be a better place without him. Living is exhausting, and he just wants the disappointment to stop.

Remi is unsure whether Evan's admissions are serious enough to complete a Student of Concern report through the Dean of Students Office. Remi perceives Evan's comments to be indicative of harmful thoughts, but there is a chance that her concerns are unfounded. If her intuition is correct, filing a report could connect Evan to the resources he needs, but if her intuition is incorrect, filing a report could alienate him from the SOAR program and destroy the trust in her relationship with Evan.

What should Remi do?

FACULTY RESISTANCE
CHRISTINE PAJEWSKI AND MICHELLE J. BOETTCHER

Chris is an able-bodied, cisgender man. Although Chris does not have learning disabilities himself, he does have experience supporting students with learning disabilities. He recently completed his master's degree in student affairs at Delta University and began a full-time academic advisor position in Public Affairs and Administration at Gamma State University (GSU). GSU is a predominantly White, large, land-grant institution located in the mid-Atlantic. Total enrollment at GSU is about thirty-five thousand students. GSU prides itself on academic success and affordability and has a well-respected Accessibility Center for Students (ACS). Chris, through his primary role as an academic advisor, has developed a highly collaborative relationship with ACS in order to support the students he advises. This open relationship fosters academic success for students needing academic accommodations across campus.

In his first year, Chris thrived in his position. His advising load was one hundred students primarily because the School of Public Affairs and Administration is the smallest school at GSU. As a result, he was able to build strong, trusting relationships with students. These relationships further contributed to Chris's success as a new professional.

One day in the middle of the spring semester, a first-year student named Anna stops by Chris's office hours. Anna frequently emails and visits Chris during office hours, so Chris knows a lot about Anna's academic standing and personal background. For example, based on these conversations, Chris knows that she registered with ACS and has received academic accommodations, including a note taker in each of her classes, extended testing time, and an exemption from spelling errors on graded assignments. Anna is very open about needing accommodations in order to succeed academically, and this helps Chris advise her better because he has a full understanding of her needs.

Anna did very well her first semester. She was worried about succeeding academically, and took full advantage of the resources her professors, Chris, and the ACS provided to her. However, this semester Anna has been struggling with her English professor. The English professor has worked at GSU for more than thirty years and has a reputation for being a very rigid professor. There are no online submissions for assignments in his class and almost everything has to be handwritten.

Chris knew this professor very well. In the previous term Chris had to help facilitate a conversation between this professor and another student with an accommodation. The professor did not want to provide additional time to the student because students had two hours to complete the exam and, the professor added, "It shouldn't take anyone longer than an hour to finish, so I don't need to give this student additional time." Chris hit a dead end; even after meeting one-on-one with the professor to explain the reasoning for accommodations and the origin of the Americans with Disabilities Act, the professor wouldn't budge. Chris decided to involve his supervisor who worked with the ACS and the associate provost to ensure the student received the appropriate accommodation. Chris felt that by involving individuals in more senior positions, the professor would understand the severity of the issue and the requirement for accommodations. However, after the exchange, Chris's supervisor said that he should have been able to handle the situation on his own. She explained, "I shouldn't be dragged into situations like this in the future. We hired you because we thought you had the skills to work with faculty."

Chris has his previous interactions in mind as Anna explains that she received a quiz back, and there were a number of questions marked wrong. Anna was unsure if they were for misspellings or if her answers were simply incorrect. At the end of class, Anna asked the professor, reminding him of her signed accommodations letter that exempts her from grading on spelling. Anna said the professor did not answer her question, and instead threatened to "unsign" her accommodations letter for abusing her privileges. Anna did not know what to say to the professor, so she left class and came straight to Chris's office hours.

Anna shares that she doesn't know what to do next. She wants to be successful and to earn her grades, but now she is doubting herself and whether or not this is a place she can be successful, or if the school is just "too hard." She says, "I knew this might happen because I'm not as smart as most of the other kids—no matter how hard I try." This is not the first time Chris has heard this from a student with accommodations; he's conflicted because he knows that these students have to work much harder to accomplish the same tasks, but at the same time he knows that in order for them to develop autonomy, students need to begin advocating for themselves. Chris wants to go talk to the professor himself; he knows Anna already put in more effort than is typical to receive the accommodations. However, ACS policy also states that any requests must come directly from the student, not a parent, guardian, or university staff member. Chris also knows it is before the drop deadline, and he could advise her to drop the class and take it next semester with a professor who is known to be more accommodating, but he recognizes that the additional course will put more pressure on Anna.

What should Chris do?

MEDDLING WITH HIRING
RENE COUTURE

After completing her master's degree in student affairs, Andrea accepted an academic advising position at River Mountain University, a medium-sized regional, comprehensive public university. Now, after three years as an academic advisor, Andrea has applied to replace the outgoing assistant director of advising. Upon a successful search process, Andrea was named the new assistant director of advising, and part of this role involves hiring and training new advisors. One of Andrea's first tasks is to conduct a search for a new academic advisor to work primarily with undeclared first-year students. Having recently been through the search process herself, Andrea knows she needs to work with human resources to properly launch the search. She forms a search committee made up of four individuals from three offices, which include representatives from academic advising, orientation, and admissions. Next, Andrea calls a meeting with the committee to explain the position's responsibilities and qualifications, as well as to provide the charge. Trusting the search committee to identify highly qualified candidates as finalists, Andrea lets the committee know she will not be involved with the search process until the finalists are identified for on-campus interviews. However, Andrea did not expect that someone else might meddle with this search. This possibility was never discussed in her graduate school training nor any of her professional experiences in higher education.

More than one hundred applicants submitted materials for the advising position by the closing date. Using the same rubric that was used in past academic advising searches, along with the information gained from conversations with Andrea, the committee began narrowing the applicant pool in half by keeping those who met all minimum qualifications. Next, the committee narrowed the pool in half again by retaining those who wrote more persuasive cover letters and had experience working with diverse college student populations, leaving them with their top twenty-five candidates. Finally, to identify ten candidates for phone interviews, the committee selected candidates who possessed the preferred qualifications, which included prior work experience in the functional areas of academic advising, TRIO programs, admissions, orientation, or first-year experience programs. In creating the job announcement, Andrea had identified experiences in these areas as preferred qualifications as they provide important levels of guidance to students.

Andrea reports to Eric, the director of academic advising. Having clear interest in a successful search for the advising office, Eric reaches out to Andrea to ask how the search is progressing. Eric inquires if Sarah, a recent student affairs master's graduate of River Mountain University, will be invited for a campus interview. Sarah has lived her entire life as Eric's neighbor, and Sarah's parents are good friends of Eric's. Sarah's parents are frustrated that it has been nearly a year since Sarah earned her master's degree, but she cannot land a job despite completing several interviews. Eric told Sarah's parents that he would "put in a good word." In turn, Eric politely informs Andrea that he "would *love* to see Sarah land that advising job because she is so perfect for it."

Andrea contacts Stacy, the chair of the search committee, to ask about Sarah's status. Stacy informs Andrea that Sarah will not be invited for a phone interview. Although her materials were satisfactory, the other candidates had more experience relevant to academic advising, wrote more enthusiastic, error-free cover letters, and showed strong commitment to student success. Sarah's cover letter was addressed to the wrong institution, leaving the committee to question her attention to detail. Sarah's resume revealed she left her graduate assistant position in alumni affairs after one year to work two part-time retail positions off campus during her second year. Furthermore, Sarah's materials did not specify direct work experience with first-year students.

Andrea has no prior knowledge of Sarah, but her instincts are telling her that Sarah may not be as perfect as Eric assured. Andrea wants to honor the search committee's work but simultaneously, she feels she must return a favor to her supervisor, who, after all, recently selected Andrea for promotion to assistant director. Although hiring Sarah would show favoritism and bias, going against Eric's wishes would cause friction with him, leaving Andrea uncertain about what could happen to her own career development if she disagrees with him. On the other hand, forcing the committee to invite someone they did not select diminishes credibility, trust, and morale.

What should Andrea do?

TURNING A BLIND EYE TO INTERN ABUSE
BRIAN CAMPBELL

Trixie Wyatt, a new student affairs professional, was hired last year as the internship coordinator for liberal arts and sciences at Hamill University, a liberal arts college in rural Indiana with a population of approximately three thousand undergraduate students. A recent graduate with little previous experience, Trixie is still becoming accustomed to Hamill University's campus culture, politics, and bureaucracy, but has a strong sense of right and wrong and cares deeply about students' well-being. Ten years ago, the university's Political Science Department established a new international relations major that has since become its own department due to high student interest in the program. Students in the international relations program are required to complete an internship through the Diaz Applied Foreign Policy Initiative (DAFPI), which Trixie administers by reviewing applications to the program, helping accepted students compose cover letters and resumes to their preferred internships, and maintaining ongoing communication with participants to track their progress.

Participants in DAFPI spend a semester in Washington, DC, take on a twenty-hour-per-week internship at a government agency or think tank, and attend lectures for class credit. The program was established five years ago with a donation provided to the college by retired State Department Ambassador Benjamin Diaz, a powerful Hamill University alumnus with many connections in Washington, DC. It was Linda Sullivan, director of career services (and Trixie's supervisor), who was instrumental in making DAFPI a reality, thanks to her long-time friendship with Ambassador Diaz. Although the program is required for all international relations majors, students must complete a rigorous application process before participating in the program that includes submitting a personal statement, two letters of recommendation, and completing an interview with a committee of international relations faculty. Students who are not accepted into DAFPI cannot continue in the international relations program. The Career Services Office has its own budget for general programming, but DAFPI is funded entirely separately by Ambassador Diaz's donations. A portion of the DAFPI budget is allocated to the Career Services Office to upkeep the application portal, assign and monitor student internship assignments, and supplement professional development programming for DAFPI participants. Trixie manages this portion of the DAFPI budget.

Halfway through the DAFPI program, Trixie receives mid-semester evaluations from current participants in the program. Five students interning at the Global Development Bank submitted abysmal evaluations of their experience but did not provide any explanation. In addition, Trixie discovers that these same students are struggling with the coursework component and are receiving poor grades. She decides to reach out to one of the students, who, after some hedging, informs Trixie that her supervisor at the Global Development Bank has been emotionally abusive toward the interns. The student describes that she is often yelled at or publicly shamed for simple mistakes. In addition, she is routinely asked to work late on short notice and often ends up staying at the site until well after midnight, which makes it difficult to get up for class the next day. The other four students corroborate the first student's accounts of abuse, but they all say they were too afraid to make an issue of it since the supervisor is a friend of Ambassador Diaz, who used his connections to get the students the prestigious internship. They each also hope to use their supervisor at the Global Development Bank as a reference for their graduate school and job applications and do not want to report the abusive behavior and lose that relationship. All the students believe they can endure the internship until the end of the semester but recommend the site never be used again. Unsure of how to handle the situation, Trixie consults with Linda, the director of career services, during which Trixie proposes that future students not be placed at the site and that DAFPI cut all ties with the Global Development Bank.

However, Linda refuses to believe the students' accounts. She states that the Global Development Bank is too valuable a relationship for DAFPI to sever ties with, and she trusts Ambassador Diaz's judgment in selecting the internship site. She wonders aloud if the students just aren't used to receiving critical feedback and might be resistant to hard work. Because Linda believes her close ties to Ambassador Diaz might be a conflict of interest, she asks Trixie to handle the situation delicately and try to preserve the professional relationship between Hamill University and the Global Development Bank. Trixie believes she is over her head and isn't sure how to get started or who to trust.

What should Trixie do?

LIFE MATTERS IN PROBATIONARY STUDENT ADVISEMENT
HEATHER MALDONADO

Lee, a first-year student adviser, planned to arrive to work early on the first day of the spring semester since the day was bound to be a busy one in the academic advising office. Although it was Lee's second semester as an academic adviser at the college, today was likely going to be full of new professional experiences because it was the day students on academic probation would return to campus needing to adjust schedules and get help with applying for financial aid waivers. Lee remembered the student development theory and the academic advising best practices that had been taught in graduate school in the past two years and was up to the challenge of supporting probationary students in their return to good academic standing.

The institution Lee worked for was a public college that had just recently started offering bachelor's degrees after converting from a two-year community college to a four-year school. Lee knew this added complexity to academic advising because there were different policies in place for students earning associate's degrees and those earning bachelor's degrees, and because the student population still largely reflected the typical demographics of a community college, despite the faculty's and administration's shift in focus to engaging high-achieving upper-division students.

Lee had set aside the morning for drop-in academic advising appointments for students who had urgent matters to discuss before classes got too far underway, and—sure enough—there was an advisee waiting before the office even opened.

"Well, good morning, Mary! Welcome back," Lee said. "You're up early. I take it you need me for something? Let's go into my office and talk."

Mary replied, "Lee, I was stressed out all break because I knew my grades were going to be bad. I'm really worried and confused. I don't know what I should do, but I know I need help because so many things went wrong last semester. I know I can do better if life doesn't get in the way."

Lee said, "Yes, Mary, I have seen your grades and I know you successfully appealed your dismissal—and I'm very glad you're back in school and you've come to see me. There are a few things I need to help you address to make sure you can be as academically successful as possible this semester. We need to talk about your spring schedule, study skill development, financial aid eligibility, and anything else that you think might get in the way of getting back on track academically this semester—but first I'm hoping you can tell me what happened last semester that threw you off course."

As Lee had been speaking, Mary seemed to grow more nervous and once Lee was done talking, Mary asked, "What do you mean financial aid eligibility? I qualified for aid through the FAFSA process last summer, and I get federal and state aid. My bill was paid in full by my aid last semester. I should be fine. I need to know more about that now . . . but I had really wanted to talk to you about what had happened to me last semester."

"Well, you see, Mary, there are actually two parts to a student's financial aid being disbursed," Lee replied. "First, you need to be financially eligible for the aid—that's the annual FAFSA application part—and then you need to be academically eligible for the aid, which means having a certain grade point average and a certain number of passed credits on your academic record at the end of each semester." Lee had been accessing Mary's academic history while answering Mary's question and, after reviewing her record, commented, "Looking at your grades from last semester, I see that you are now academically ineligible for your state aid this semester. Were you aware of that?"

Mary looked at Lee for a moment and then started crying. Lee was not prepared for that reaction and began fumbling around the office for a tissue to offer. "Here, Mary," Lee said, "please take this. Take a minute and then we'll talk through this, okay? Let's figure it out."

After some time, Mary was able to talk with Lee again, and she said, "What you just told me was not good news. Now I'm going to owe the college money. How am I supposed to fix my GPA if I'm worried about this stuff or if I need to work a bunch of hours to make up this money? This bill situation is bad . . . but the reasons my grades from last semester are so bad were worse—and I got through them, so I'll get through this too."

Mary continued, "I'll tell you what happened last semester so you can help me, but I really don't like talking about it. My midterm grades were good, but then I ended up failing all but one of my classes. Well, that happened because up until a week or so before Thanksgiving, things were going really well for me. Then, when I went home for break, someone I knew when I was in high school kept trying to contact me. I ignored them and eventually they stopped, but it brought up really bad memories for me because they had sexually assaulted me when were in high school. I didn't tell anyone when it happened because I was embarrassed, and I thought I could get over it by myself. I realized when they started trying to get in touch with me that I was still really upset by what had happened and I just couldn't keep my mind on my classes when I got back to campus. I just kept feeling worse and worse until I didn't want to leave my room . . . and finals came and went and I failed all of them . . . and I got dismissed . . . but then I appealed and I was allowed to return and I figured I would just come back and do really well and that would fix everything. Now you're telling me I lost my aid, too. It's too much. I can't overcome all of this. I feel a little better having told you all this because now you can tell me what I need to do to fix this mess. You can tell me that, right?"

Lee had been listening intently to Mary as she disclosed all the things that had happened to her at the end of the semester and how she was feeling now.

Lee paused for a moment while thinking about Mary's experience, campus reporting regulations, the documentation required for aid waiver processes, and how to best support Mary now. From Lee's assessment, telling Mary that he had to report what she just told him to Title IX would upset her more, even though he knew it was the policy. But, she didn't seem to be in any danger, and what happened to her was in the past, so he wondered if he could let it slide so that it would not become a bigger deal. Lee then said, "Mary, I'm sorry. That is a lot for you to have had to handle alone, but I'm so glad you told me what's happened. Let's talk about ways to move forward. I want to help."

What should Lee do?

Chapter 5

AN OFFER THAT CAN'T BE REFUSED
KATIE SMITH

Quinten is a career advisor at Towers University, a moderately selective private college in the southeastern United States with an undergraduate student population of approximately six thousand. Towers University prides itself on its relationships with employers and its highly successful campus recruiting program, where external companies and organizations frequently use campus resources to post positions, host information sessions, attend networking events, conduct interviews, and make internship and job offers to students at the institution.

The Towers University Career Center is well utilized by the student body, especially during peak recruiting times in fields such as technology, finance, engineering, and consulting that occur at the beginning of each academic year. The Career Center staff have worked hard to build and maintain relationships with key employers, partnerships that have helped the Career Center build a strong reputation among students and university administration alike.

Among these companies is OPQ Consulting, a global management consulting firm that only recruits from a highly selective group of institutions in the United States. OPQ Consulting began recruiting from Towers University just one year ago, after Career Center staff had been trying to build the partnership for years. In their first year of recruiting at Towers, OPQ hired two students after seeing high turnout for all their campus events and receiving over 300 applications for just two positions. The new partnership caught the attention of the university president, who mentioned it in her commencement speech featuring the accomplishments of Towers graduates.

At the start of the fall semester, Quinten's schedule filled up quickly with appointments from students eager to prepare for and apply to jobs at the highly coveted companies that recruit at the start of the school year. When students mention that they are interested in companies like OPQ Consulting, Quinten reminds students that the process is extremely competitive, with only two open roles for hundreds of applicants. Quinten encourages students to apply to all the positions that match their career and personal goals so as not to limit their opportunities post-graduation.

One of the students that Quinten has worked with for several months is Ashley, a talented senior in biomedical engineering. Ashley is academically successful, involved in undergraduate research, and currently serves as the president for the Towers chapter of the Society of Women Engineers. Over the past summer, Ashley had also completed an engineering internship with a local medical device company, an experience that she talked about often. Quinten knows that Ashley wanted to pursue a career in biomedical engineering since before she even came to Towers University. However, in a recent meeting, Ashley expressed an interest in applying to full-time positions in consulting. When asked what prompted the shift, Ashley told Quinten that she had heard her friends talking about consulting companies that recruit on campus, sparking her curiosity in how she might stack up against her peers for these competitive jobs.

While Quinten didn't want to discourage Ashley from pursuing new career paths, he reminded her that she had originally been interested in biomedical engineering and seemed to really enjoy her engineering coursework and campus involvement, and her recent internship. Ashley assured Quinten that she would be applying for engineering jobs as well and that she was currently working on an application for a competitive position at a biomedical device company called Titan that is close to where she wants to live, that pays well, and that provides great continuing education benefits.

Ashley was a strong candidate for consulting positions, and she was offered an interview invitation with OPQ Consulting. Ashley was thrilled at this news and excitedly reported to Quinten that she was the only one of her friends to receive an invitation to interview. Quinten was proud of Ashley's accomplishment and eagerly helped her prepare for the interview. When Ashley later emailed Quinten to tell him that she made it to the final round, Quinten grew even more excited for her. None of the other students who he worked with had gotten this far in the process with OPQ, and Quinten knew it would reflect well on him to have coached a student through their hiring process.

Two weeks later, Ashley stops by the Career Center to see Quinten, a wide grin on her face. She is visibly excited and quickly shares that she received an offer from OPQ Consulting. Ashley and Quinten high-five and celebrate, Quinten commending her work in navigating the process and Ashley thanking Quinten for his help.

As the excitement winds down, Quinten asks Ashley about how the rest of her job search is going and whether she is going to accept the offer from OPQ. At this point, Ashley mentions that she also just received an invitation for an on-site interview from Titan, but the interview had been scheduled for two weeks away. However, OPQ had only given her one week to make her decision. She shares that she contacted OPQ to ask for more time to make the decision, but they declined her request. Ashley tells Quinten that although she is excited about receiving the offer from OPQ, Titan is still her top choice. Ashley continues, reassuring Quinten that she has talked to her parents about the situation and is going to take their advice. Her parents suggested that Ashley accept the job with OPQ and schedule the interview with Titan. This way, if she gets the job offer with Titan, Ashley can back out of her commitment with OPQ and take Titan's offer instead.

Quinten knows that reneging on a job acceptance is highly unprofessional. In fact, one of the students who he worked with last year had done so, although Quinten hadn't known about it until after the fact. After the student had reneged, the company contacted the Career Center staff, letting them know that this behavior was unethical and that replacing the student at the last minute cost the company significant resources. Although Quinten's supervisor had been understanding of the situation at the time, she had re-minded Quinten that reneging offers was unethical and that one student's actions could affect future opportunities for Towers students. The company had not returned to recruit at Towers again this year.

Quinten knows how hard his colleagues at the Career Center have worked to build a relationship with OPQ and that the partnership is of great interest to the university. He can think of dozens of students who he has met with in recent months who had been hoping to receive interviews and offers from OPQ, none of whom had been successful. If Ashley accepts the job but later backs out, Quinten knows this could strain the relationship between OPQ and Towers University, perhaps ending it entirely. Quinten also knows if Ashley follows through with the plan and ultimately backs out of her acceptance with OPQ, his supervisors will look up her record to see that he had served as his advisor throughout the job search process. Given last year's incident, Quinten knows that Ashley's decision could reflect poorly on him, with potential implications for his job within the Center.

After listening to Ashley's plan, Quinten advises her against taking the job with OPQ and then interviewing with Titan. Quinten tells Ashley that reneging on an offer is considered highly unprofessional and that it would not only reflect poorly on Ashley and her future prospects with the company, but that it could also affect the relationship between Towers University and OPQ, especially since this relationship is new. Although Ashley listens, she seems doubtful and assures Quinten that she knows of others who have reneged acceptances without consequence. Ashley also says she can't pass up the opportunity to work at Titan if she receives the job offer from the company. Ashley leaves Quinten's office saying she'll think about it further.

What should Quinten do?

UNDACAMENTED
ELMER ORELLANA AND MICHELLE J. BOETTCHER

Erik, a Latinx, male-identified, first-generation college graduate recently earned his master's degree in higher education and student affairs from Delta University, an institution in the Northeast. Upon graduation, Erik accepted a full-time position as an academic advisor for the College of Health and Human Services (CHHS) at Phi University, a large rural public research institution in the South. The total student enrollment at Phi University is twenty-six thousand students. The breakdown on campus by race and ethnicity is: White students 77 percent of the student population, Black or African American students 7 percent, international students 6 percent, Hispanic or Latinx students 5 percent, Asian students 3 percent, slightly less than 1 percent Indigenous students (about 1 percent chose not to identify their race). Phi University is a predominantly and historically White institution with a very complex history related to race, power, privilege, and institutional access. Founded by a White philanthropist to provide access to the working-class poor in the state, the institution was initially only open to White students. Additionally, racist and anti-Semitic statements made by the founder in correspondence and speeches during the time the institution was being built and first opened have led to significant discussion on and beyond campus about some of the monuments on campus and the names of several programs at the institution. These historical issues related to power, privilege, and access are a reflection of issues in the region and across the state culturally, politically, and economically.

The university is making efforts to address its complex history of affordable access complicated by racist admissions policies and is trying to recruit more racial and ethnic minoritized faculty and staff. During his on-campus interview, Erik knew that Phi University was the right place for him to be challenged and help him grow to become a better student affairs practitioner. He appreciated the shared structure for advising students in the CHHS. The model involves faculty and professional academic advisors who are paired to advise currently enrolled undergraduate students in CHHS. Students have joint advising meetings with both the faculty and professional academic advisor each term to discuss their progress, their future plans, and any concerns they have. Students are initially assigned an academic advisor but have the option of switching academic advisors after their first year at Phi University.

Erik is one of four professional academic advisors of color in CHHS. He has been at Phi University for two years and has enjoyed the relationships he has developed with his advisees. One advisee Erik has gotten to know well is Joseph. Joseph is a senior health science major with a pre-health concentration. In one of their advising sessions, Joseph disclosed to Erik that he is a Deferred Action for Childhood Arrival student (DACA). Joseph's mother moved to the United States from Korea without getting residency or the documentation required for legal immigration with Joseph, who was an infant at the time. Joseph has applied for and received permission through the DACA process to remain in the United States, and as a result he refers to himself as DACAmented because he has followed the governmental processes and completed all paperwork required. Unbeknownst to Erik, however, is that during Joseph's admission process to Phi University, his college application information was misfiled, and he was admitted and given in-state residency. Phi University does not grant DACA students in-state residency or tuition even if they have lived in state since they were children. Recently some DACA-status students who have enrolled at Phi University have raised concerns about a lack of services for them at Phi University.

DACA was rescinded in the beginning of the fall semester, leaving many DACAmented students with a sense of fear and uncertainty about their lives on campus and beyond. Joseph anxiously enters Erik's office concerned about his future at Phi University. During this meeting, Joseph also discusses the pressure he is feeling about finishing his degree and how his need to finish is intensified by the recent incidents related to DACA students. Joseph shares that he had a conversation with his parents who are pressuring him to continue working toward his physical therapy degree. Becoming a physical therapist would require more education and time—time that Joseph feels like he doesn't have. He is worried about his DACA status impacting potential graduate admissions. In fact, he is struggling with the idea of going to graduate school at all. While Joseph's stepfather is a U.S. citizen, his mother is still in the process of obtaining her own documented status. She sees Joseph's education and medical career as the primary reason they came to the United States. Joseph is worried, overwhelmed, and feels lost.

Joseph has been doing well academically except for his physics class which he has taken twice. As the semester concludes, Joseph found out that based on the final exam, he was two points short of passing. In order to complete the pre-health concentration, students are required to take six science courses and this physics course would be Joseph's sixth. In Joseph's advising sessions he disclosed that he no longer wants to pursue physical therapy but does not want to let his mother down. He is wondering if Erik could talk to the physics faculty member to give him the two additional points so he will have the credits he needs in order for him to graduate. Joseph also asks Erik for guidance on how to talk with his parents.

Erik wants to help Joseph but is not sure how to best advocate for him. Joseph has already talked with the faculty member who has refused to give him the additional points. Erik's supervisor Dian has, on rare occasions, reached out to faculty to advocate for grade changes of graduating seniors who fall short of passing a class, but Dian isn't familiar with Joseph's academic situation, his DACA status, or the concern Joseph has about talking to his family about his future career.

What should Erik do?

QUESTIONABLE PARTNERSHIPS
DEBORAH WORLEY

Founders State University (FSU) is a large public research university located in the Midwest. FSU is a land-grant institution and houses seven academic colleges: Agriculture and Life Sciences, Arts and Letters, Business Administration, Education and Human Sciences, Engineering and Computer Science, Nursing, and Veterinary Medicine. Total enrollment at FSU is 25,150; approximately 5,350 of those enrolled are graduate students.

Encompassed in FSU's mission is a commitment to helping students succeed beyond the college years. To that end, FSU has developed a series of co-curricular experiences to help students develop knowledge, skills, and competencies to increase their post-graduation employment or graduate school prospects. Students can participate in leadership development academies, study abroad, co-ops and internships, service learning programs, and faculty-led research projects, and these programs are a big draw for students to matriculate at the university.

Courtney is an assistant director at the FSU Career Center. She provides career advising and job search guidance to students across academic areas. Courtney has been working in this role for two years after finishing her graduate degree in student affairs. Courtney chose to work at FSU because of the institution's commitment to connecting students to careers throughout their college-going experience. Most recently, the FSU Career Center has partnered with the FSU Alumni Association to develop a networking and mentorship program to connect current students to alumni in their field. Under the direction of the Career Center staff, small groups of three to five students are formed based on their professional interest areas. The small groups are then matched to an alumnus/a who provides career advice and connections to professional networks. The program has been operating for two years and has received glowing recommendations from both alumni and student participants.

Courtney serves as the Career Center's liaison to the Alumni Association and is responsible for matching students to alumni in the network and mentorship program. She works closely with Manny, who is an alumni relations manager with the FSU Alumni Association. Manny was part of the original team that established the network and mentorship program with the Career Center. Courtney and Manny meet to discuss plans for matching students and alumni for the new academic year. Courtney tells Manny that there are more than one hundred students who want to participate in the network and mentorship program this year, an increase of over twenty students from the previous year. She is concerned there are not enough alumni signed up to participate in the program to match with students. Manny tells Courtney about three brothers who are all FSU alumni. They own five successful businesses between the three of them, and they think the network and mentorship program could be helpful in identifying prospective employees, plus they think the program is a great way to give back to FSU.

Courtney is elated to hear this news, and her concern about not having enough alumni partners to meet student demand is alleviated. She returns to her office and starts working on forming student groups who would be a good fit for the three new alumni mentors. She does not know much about the businesses they own so she visits their webpages. Manny was right—the three brothers have been quite successful in developing new technologies for use in the medical field. She can see opportunities to connect students across academic majors with these alumni. Courtney also checks social media to see what news is trending about the three alumni and their businesses. She spends several minutes reading through press releases for new products and watches a video of the brothers breaking ground on a new community health education center that they helped to fund. She sees a link to a blog about rugby that mentions one of the brothers' names. She clicks the link and scrolls through the entries, stopping at a post where he wrote about "male dominance in sports and society." His post was full of disparaging remarks about women, including comments pointing to his position that "a woman's place is in the home." He also claimed that women only talk about sexual assault to get attention, closing with links to a few articles about companies that are reluctant to hire women for fear of being accused of sexual harassment.

Courtney's heart sinks. She calls Manny and tells him what she found. Manny listens then says, "I don't think it's a big deal. He didn't write those things as a representative of his businesses or of his family." Courtney counters, "But we are talking about career mentorship and guidance here. Given what he wrote from his personal standpoint, I don't know that I can trust he would be fair and unbiased in mentoring our students in a professional capacity."

Manny asked if he could have a few minutes to read the blog post. A few minutes later he called Courtney back to continue the conversation. Manny thinks Courtney is overreacting to the blog post, but he understands how the words might be offensive to some people. "I think I have a solution," Manny says. "I know this guy pretty well and he is a good friend to the university. He and his brothers have made several major gifts to FSU that fund scholarships for students. They also support FSU Athletics through donations, plus they are officers of their local alumni athletics booster club. I don't want to discourage him or his brothers from participating in the program nor do I want him to harbor any ill will toward the university. Maybe I can talk to him and ask him to remove the post. If he deletes the post, you would be fine with him participating in the network and mentorship program, right?" Courtney says she will think about it.

Courtney is left wondering if she is overreacting, as Manny says, or if her concern about the blog post is warranted. She is also left wondering if deleting the post alleviates her concerns enough to the point where she feels comfortable pairing students with any of the brothers.

What should Courtney do?

THE RELIGIOUS APPLICANT
CHRISTY MORAN CRAFT

Levi is in his first year as a full-time career specialist at Tallgrass University, a large public research university in the Midwest. About 75 percent of the undergraduate students at Tallgrass identify as Christian—many of who are actively involved in one or more of the evangelical Christian campus ministries. Evangelical Christians believe that Jesus is the only way to God and that people must receive salvation through Jesus in order to be in right-standing with God. They refer to this message of salvation as "the Gospel," and they feel called to share it with those with whom they interact in order to try to persuade them to embrace the message as well. Many evangelical Christians invite others to their religious events (e.g., Bible studies) and other social gatherings in hopes that they will have the opportunity to share the Gospel with them. Given the prevalence of evangelical Christians on campus, many incoming students remark that Tallgrass University feels like a Christian university.

Prior to assuming the full-time career specialist role, Levi worked as a graduate assistant (GA) in the Student Activities Office while finishing his graduate coursework in student affairs administration. In his role as a GA, he was responsible for assisting with the oversight of the student organizations. Last year, Levi became aware of an evangelical Christian group on campus called "Christian Movement" that is affiliated with a larger national religious organization. Through various conversations with the full-time staff in the Student Activities Office while working as a GA, Levi was told that Tall-grass University students, faculty, and staff frequently express concerns to the office about Christian Movement. To be specific, many on campus believe that members of Christian Movement are overly aggressive in the strategies they use to try to encourage students to attend their events. For example, Christian Movement students and staff regularly set up information tables near almost every summer orientation activity. Students and staff of Christian Movement also regularly station themselves near each residence hall during move-in each fall semester, so that they can introduce themselves and ask for contact information (e.g., cell phone number, residence hall room number) from students as they are checking in. Additionally, during the first few weeks of each fall semester, Christian Movement students and staff regularly check in on students who initially expressed interest in the group by calling them and/or visiting students in their residence hall rooms. They particularly "target" those students who initially expressed interest in the group but who have not yet attended a Christian Movement religious meeting or social event.

While Levi was a GA in the Student Activities Office, he was involved in several meetings with the director of student activities wherein some of the student leaders of Christian Movement were questioned about their overly persistent tactics and were reminded of campus policies related to harassment. In those meetings, Luke, the president of Christian Movement, always appeared genuine and respectful of others and stated that he was willing to change some of Christian Movement's recruitment activities. At the same time, he made it clear that his primary purpose for being on campus was "to lead people to Christ." Luke's desire to encourage others to embrace Christianity was not completely surprising to Levi. Levi had, on more than one occasion, spotted Luke at the Student Union, doing what appeared to be a Bible study with other students. Levi had also seen Luke praying with a few students. This never really bothered Levi, though, since such activities did not violate the code of conduct and since he also identified as an evangelical Christian. To the best of Levi's knowledge, during his time as a GA in the Student Activities Office, members of Christian Movement never formally went through a conduct meeting nor were any of them ever formally charged with harassing other students in their efforts to get others involved in their group.

Now, having transitioned to his role as career specialist, Levi is responsible for hiring a group of student workers to work as peer mentors for the Career Center. The peer mentors are typically upper-level students who have strong academic and social skills. They serve as resources for other upper-level students who are preparing to do job searches by reviewing their cover letters and resumes and by providing some basic interviewing advice. Levi supervises two GAs (Kelly and Doug) whose responsibilities include making recommendations to him about who to hire each year as the new group of peer mentors.

One day when Levi returned to the office after having lunch, he overheard Kelly and Doug discussing the peer mentor candidates. They mentioned a candidate named Luke who was "fantastic" in many ways. They talked about his enthusiasm and charisma and about how well he excelled academically. However, they were concerned about hiring him due to his involvement in Christian Movement. In particular, Kelly said, "Those Christian Movement members are focused on only one thing: recruitment. I'm afraid that Luke would use his position as a peer mentor to either try to recruit people to Christian Movement and/or to tell them that they need to become Christians." Doug then replied, "Yeah, I even saw that he had a Bible in the pocket of his backpack when he came to the interview. I really don't think we should hire him. He's too religious."

Levi was torn. On one hand, due to his prior role on campus, he knew that some of Christian Movement's recruitment strategies were troublesome to many on campus. Levi realized that it was entirely possible that Luke could be envisioning the peer mentor role as a way to recruit students to Christian Movement. On the other hand, Levi ultimately agreed with the evangelical ideology of the group, and because of his own religious values and convictions, did not want to prevent the Gospel from being shared. Moreover, Luke was a strong candidate with regard to the required qualifications, and had Levi not worked in the Student Activities Office, he would never have known about the previous concerns about Christian Movement. Levi was facing a hard hiring decision with regard to Luke.

What should Levi do?

Chapter Six

Residence Life and Housing Cases

FOOD AND FRIENDS AND FRICTION
CHELSEA JORDAN AND MICHELLE J. BOETTCHER

Joyce is a third-year hall director at a large, public, land-grant institution on the East Coast. She identifies as cisgender, White, and Christian, and has examined her privilege through her graduate program and now as an emerging professional. During Joyce's graduate program, she did an internship with the Gender and Sexuality Center on her campus and developed a workshop focused on gender and faith, focusing on the role of gender identity across different religions. Joyce was also active in the Students Understanding Beliefs (SUB) group on campus that fostered open dialogue across religious, atheist, and agnostic belief systems. An engaged student activist, Joyce participated in a student-led dialogue group, HERd, which brought women together to discuss the complexities of race and intersectionality.

One of Joyce's collateral assignments in her job this year is coordinating community service opportunities for the Department of Residence Life staff. Both full-time and student staff must participate in three service projects over the course of the academic year, plus a large-scale service activity that takes place each fall during staff training. Joyce has planned an activity each month with different agencies in the county where her institution is located. For the upcoming month, she has partnered with Food and Friends, a local food pantry and dining facility for the homeless.

Although Joyce goes on most of the service trips, she is not able to attend this one, but asks her graduate assistant, Dale, to take the lead the day of the trip, including the staff debrief after the service hours are completed. Dale has co-led some of these trips with Joyce, but is excited to take on this responsibility and apply what he's learned. He also helped identify Food and

Friends as a possible service location because he volunteers there twice a month.

After some logistical planning and going over the learning outcomes of the trip debrief, Joyce asks Dale if there is anything more he needs before the event. Dale assures her he has been taking notes on previous trips and the conversations that have happened and that he is prepared to move into the new role of debrief facilitator. She says to let her know if he thinks of questions or if any other issues come up related to the trip.

Following the event, Joyce gets a text from Dale, who asks if they can meet to talk about the debriefing that happened after the service hours that day. They find a time that works just before staff meeting. Joyce asks Dale if everything is alright and he expresses some frustrations.

"There were some people who were pretty upset after the service we did today," Dale shares. "They didn't feel like Food and Friends was inclusive. I don't know why, but they felt that way. The debrief didn't go very well." Joyce asks for more details and Dale shares that about ten people attended the debrief. Three of them—two students (one student, Joel, is on Joyce and Dale's staff; the other student, Twyla, is a staff member in another residential community on campus) and one area coordinator (Leigh, who is Joyce's supervisor)—said that the prayer led by Food and Friends staff before the lunch they helped serve made them uncomfortable.

Dale said that Joel and Twyla were upset about the prayer and said they felt excluded. Dale told Joyce that he responded saying, "They didn't say that people couldn't eat if they didn't pray. Everyone could attend and have food. They didn't have to leave if they didn't join in the prayer." Dale explained that Joel responded by saying, "I still felt singled out and unwelcome in a space where we were supposed to be working to build community." Dale said that Leigh chimed in, adding, "At the very least, we probably should have been told ahead of time that there would be a prayer."

Joel identifies as agnostic and has encouraged the staff to think inclusively around religious identity several times already as they planned events. Whenever there is a service trip, staff members who attend report out during the next hall staff meeting and Joyce knows Joel is planning to report out on the trip at tonight's meeting. As Joyce is wrapping up her conversation with Dale, she gets a text from Leigh, who says, "I need you to give me a call tonight before your staff meeting."

When Joyce calls Leigh, Leigh starts with, "I am sure Dale told you about today's meeting." Joyce acknowledges that they have talked. "It was clear he was nervous about facilitating the group, but I was really concerned when he told Joel and Twyla that the prayer was 'no big deal' and they could just 'sit there' until it was over." Joyce asks for more specifics, so Leigh shares that Dale said, "We all have to sit through things we don't agree with in this job. That's what it means to be tolerant of diversity." Leigh explains that, from her vantage point, Dale should not be providing thought-leadership on diversity and inclusion efforts, as he clearly doesn't get it. She encourages Joyce to limit Dale's interaction with staff about diversity and inclusion and the service trip until he has a more developed sense of what it really means to be inclusive. Joyce is torn. She sees value in Dale's engagement, especially since he is in a graduate program.

Staff meeting starts in an hour.

What should Joyce do?

WHOSE SIDE ARE YOU ON?
ROGER "MITCH" NASSER JR. AND ERIN P. MANOTT MORRIS

Eduardo has dreamed of being a director of a Residence Life department and has been making intentional professional choices to realize that dream. After two years as a hall director, he received the opportunity to move into an assistant director role last year. He is entering his second year as assistant director at Supply University, a small private university in the Midwest. Supply University has an overall student population of 2,500 (1,700 under-graduates and 800 graduates) with roughly 75 percent of undergraduates living on campus. The institution is well known in the region for a commu-nity atmosphere and strong connections between students and faculty/staff.

Eduardo enjoys many aspects of his job, but two stand out more than the rest. First, he values the professional staff selection process. Although many colleagues question the substantial effort he puts into the recruitment and selection process, Eduardo believes the effort to be worth it. "You are only as good as your people," he would often reply.

Second, Eduardo enjoys training his professional staff. Since he works at a small school, most of his staff are new to student affairs and have many questions for him. He views himself as a mentor and sees these questions as developmental opportunities for his staff members. Eduardo's favorite train-ing topics are social justice and inclusion. He loves to challenge his staff, while supporting their efforts to create a just, inclusive community. He be-lieves self-reflection is essential in understanding situations of bias and ac-tion may take on various forms.

Eduardo currently supervises five professional hall directors. Over the course of the trainings, the hall director staff have shared their identities with the group. Leslie is a first-year hall director from the West Coast who iden-tifies as White, cisgender, and bisexual. Barry is a third-year hall director who identifies as White, male, and gay. Juanita is a second-year hall director who identifies as African American, cisgender, and heterosexual. She is also an alumnus of Supply University and chose to apply for a full-time position after a great experience as a resident assistant. Robert is a first-year hall director from Canada and identifies as male and cisgender. He is the first international full-time staff member in the history of the institution. Tamara is a fourth-year hall director from the Midwest. She identifies as gender fluid or non-binary. She is a strong leader on staff and recently indicated that she will be departing Supply University at the end of the year for a leadership position at another institution.

Early in the fall semester, Supply University received a public safety report regarding a possible hate crime on campus. The incident happened overnight and involved a person or persons defacing the front door of a student's apartment. The graffiti included hateful speech against African

American students and created immediate tension on campus, including students expressing concern over campus safety, the Student Government Association requesting a meeting with the university president, and faculty members communicating anonymously about the incident with local news media. Eduardo's supervisor, Janice, the director of housing and residence life/assistant vice president for student development, notified him immediately of the incident. She also shared the institution's response, which included an emergency cabinet meeting, meeting with the student victims, and investigation by the state police. Eduardo is upset about the incident but is comforted by the institutional response. Janice also shares the perpetrator is unknown at this point, so possibly not a student, and the police investigation will continue. She asks Eduardo to keep his staff updated and leaves him with the following words, "It is important we are all unified in our response to this incident. We do not want to distract from the investigation at this point."

Eduardo returns to his office and prepares to contact his professional staff members for a meeting. Before he can reach out to them, Leslie, Barry, Robert, and Tamara walk through his office door. They remain standing in his office and begin discussing the hate incident and university response. Eduardo senses and connects with their frustration and desire for action. However, soon the conversation turns to perceived inaction on the part of Supply University administration. The staff members believe Supply University administrators should coordinate the investigation rather than the police and/or provide increased transparency to the student body. The staff members become increasingly upset, since Eduardo can only provide limited information about the rationale for the police investigation. "What is the university doing to resolve this incident?" asks a clearly exasperated Leslie. Eduardo explains the response, but the staff do not appear satisfied. Robert exclaims, "This is a sham! Supply administration is trying to sweep this under the rug!" Tamara steps forward and looks directly at Eduardo. "Boss, I have spoken with my colleagues and we are planning a sit in at the dining hall as a response to this incident. You trained us on the importance of action. We wanted to tell you as a heads-up out of respect for you."

What should Eduardo do?

WANT OR NEED A "SUPER SINGLE?"
BETH MCGUIRE-FREDERICKS AND NOVIA RAMSAY

Morgan, a third-year student at Callanra University (a primarily residential private suburban campus), decided to live off campus with three friends for her junior year, so she did not secure on-campus housing during the room selection window of the spring semester. Housing options off campus seemed more appealing to Morgan and her friends, as they would share a spacious four-bedroom apartment, with each room having its own private bathroom, and amenities like a swimming pool and workout room.

Morgan is a psychology major who maintains a 4.0 GPA. For the upcoming fall she intends to carry a full academic load while working part time at a restaurant close to campus to supplement her income. Morgan also has a history of anxiety and is registered with the Office of Student Access Services, as there are times when she has needed accommodations on campus due to a documented disability.

Two weeks before classes began for the fall term, Morgan's friends broke their upcoming lease, opting not to live in the apartment. Scrambling for a new option, Morgan decides to submit a late application for on-campus housing. She specifically requests to be assigned to a "super single," which means she would only have one suitemate, with whom she would share a private bathroom. Morgan was sure to include that this type of room assignment is required because of a documented disability with the Office of Student Access Services (SAS).

Although Callanra has many housing options that students can choose, "super single" suites are the most popular among upperclass students and were all taken during the annual spring housing selection process. Consequently, after reviewing Morgan's accommodation letter from SAS, Chad, an assignments coordinator in the Office of Residence Life, assigned Morgan to a single room as requested, but in a traditional high-rise building where all students on the floor share a common bathroom.

Upon receipt of her housing placement both Morgan and her parents contact the staff in both the Office of Residence Life and SAS, demanding that the assignment be changed to a "super single" immediately or that they should prepare for the President's Office to be contacted because of the lack of accommodation. Staff from both offices explain that no such space is available, and that Morgan's disability accommodation documentation only requires her to be assigned a single and does not specify that it must be a "super single." Both Morgan and the parents demand that another student should be moved to another room to make room for Morgan.

What should Chad do?

ASSIGNMENTS AND ADVOCACY
KENNETH D. GRCICH AND BRITTANY MCDANIEL

David is in his third year as a residential housing manager at Oak University, a highly competitive and diverse private liberal arts university with a residential student population of 1,800. In his role, he conducts the assignment process and manages room changes throughout the academic year. He also serves as an on-call team member and is privy to sensitive and confidential information pertaining to students with concerning behaviors. Like all students, these students are protected by privacy laws such as FERPA, but they are often known to other functional areas (Dean of Students Office, Counseling Center, Public Safety) and may require many resources to function sufficiently, and ideally successfully, at the university.

All members of the on-call team meet weekly to debrief any occurrences requiring staff intervention, review of policies and protocols in responding, and to assess how best to support students with concerning behaviors. David enjoys being on the team and believes the additional insight into students' lives allows him to see his work beyond data in a software program and spreadsheets. He also appreciates and enjoys meeting with students after a crisis to ensure the continuity of care exists.

As a member of the on-call team, David is familiar with Christina, a student on campus who struggles with mental illness. Christina is a first-year student who makes average grades despite a poor attendance record in the classroom. She sees an on-campus counselor every week but still has difficulty managing her depression and suicide ideology. Recently, Christina was hospitalized for a suicide attempt but released to return to campus by the health professionals.

Christina has lived in the same room since she arrived in the fall. Throughout the year, roommates have moved in and requested to move out within weeks. Each student had reasons for why a move was necessary, but only one was forthcoming in sharing with David the heavy burden of living with a suicidal roommate. David suspected Christina was challenging to live with and that she relied greatly on each roommate to support her.

In David's one-on-one with his supervisor, he shares what he knows about Christina and his intuition about why she had several different roommates since the year began. David asks his supervisor if he can place a block on the room to prevent the room from appearing to have a vacancy. He feels guilty for continually assigning the vacancy to other students, when he knows they will likely move out. His supervisor states that nothing can be done since Christina has not violated the student conduct code, nor has she filed for any special housing accommodations. David leaves the meeting feeling frustrated, knowing that if he places someone in that space, it will create a lot of additional work with the same results.

David reflects on his conversation with his supervisor, his knowledge of students with mental health issues, and his ability to prevent this roommate move-in/move-out cycle from happening again. He is well aware of other vacancies in the housing inventory, so it shouldn't be an issue to block one space. David knows that it's better for Christina to have a roommate than to live alone, but is conflicted with the unfairness of placing another student in the room. David believes if he blocks the space, he will prevent the continuous cycle of roommate assignments, and preserve the cherished collegiate and residential experiences for those who may be assigned to share a room with Christina. Additionally, he feels that he will spare Christina the trauma of having another roommate move out after she has started to depend on her for support. He is also sure that his supervisor would not find out about the block.

What should David do?

HEY HEY, HO HO; THIS BUILDING'S NAME HAS GOT TO GO!
ANESHIA JERRALDS AND CHARLIE CLAUSEN

Cameron is starting her second year as a residence coordinator at Rock University, a private institution with approximately twelve thousand students enrolled. Rock University is known for student activism which is one of the reasons Cameron was interested in her position. During her undergraduate and graduate studies, Cameron was a campus activist herself, and she was involved in many protests about issues important to her. It was also important to her that all her protests happen within the scope of her institution's protest policy. Through these experiences, she gained an excitement and love for being on a college campus. Her zeal for student voices to be heard led her to work in student affairs.

In her first year, Cameron struggled to connect with most of the resident assistants (RA) she supervised. The RAs viewed her as an authority figure and an administrator, more than as a mentor. However, one RA, Wei, connected well with Cameron. Wei turned into a top performer toward the end of last year and promised strong potential for being a leader on the team this year.

In an effort to be a more relational supervisor, in her second year Cameron sent requests to add each of her RAs on social media prior to RA training and most RAs accepted her invitation. Cameron believed this action would outwardly display her value of relationships while also breaking down perceived barriers of her role on the team. The department's social media policy had one primary component regarding content, stating that team members "should understand their posted content may be viewed as representing the department or Rock University. As such, team members should refrain from posting any content that could divide or inhibit the development of community."

Last year, peer institutions had protests on their campuses to change the names of buildings whose namesakes' legacies had come into question. Rock University was no different; students identified buildings on campus they wanted to be renamed and formally requested the change to administrators. However, no changes were made, and students perceived the administration ignored their concerns.

In the early morning hours on the first day of class, the students executed a large, peaceful protest on campus. The students involved called for the university to change the name of a long-standing building, Johnson Hall, because they viewed the namesake's words and actions as racially insensitive, contrary to the current climate and aspirations of the institution. Johnson Hall was named after an individual who had contributed money to the institution but also publicly supported slavery. The protest had approximately sixty people in attendance and took place outside the university's administration building. It was unanticipated and came as a surprise to administrators, because it was not pre-registered and occurred on the main quad, which contradicted the university's protest policy.

To maintain safety and gain more understanding regarding the premise of the protest, administrators responded by calling in staff to speak with the protestors. After an hour of discussions between administrators and protesters, the protesters dissipated. Cameron, who was in meetings and unable to respond to the protest, personally agreed with the protestors' request to change the name of the building but kept her views to herself.

In the afternoon, Cameron had her regularly scheduled professional staff meeting, led by her supervisor, Angel. Angel requested and expected any staff member with additional information about the leaders of the protest share it with Angel in a timely manner. If any RAs were involved, Angel expected the residence coordinators to follow up with them to discuss expectations regarding following Rock University's protest policy and guidelines when participating. Cameron again kept her views on the matter to herself as her colleagues were vocally split on what the university should do. A few of the residence coordinators were at the protest as part of the university's response team and they shared the names of the students present that they were able to identify.

Later in the evening, Cameron is at home flipping through social media and sees several posts from Wei supporting the protesters and, upon further profile viewing, finds Wei to be one of the primary organizers. Wei assertively called out the university for contributing to racism and creating an environment at Rock University that is more challenging for students with marginalized identities. Upon further exploration, Cameron sees there will be another protest the following morning, in the same place, and it is unclear if this was pre-registered as required.

What should Cameron do?

MANAGING DUAL RELATIONSHIPS
PATTY WITKOWSKY AND MEGAN BELL

Peak University is a mid-sized, regional state institution with an enrollment of approximately ten thousand undergraduate students. The institution is growing and opportunities for student affairs professionals to engage with students in a variety of settings is present, particularly because of the size of both the faculty and the student affairs staff, whose growth has not kept pace with the institution's enrollment increases. With a focus on student success, the institution requires incoming first-year students to enroll in a first-year seminar class (FYSC) with the goal of providing students with a positive transition to the university through exposure to support resources, discussions about academic and social expectations as members of the campus community, and embedded opportunities to create connections with peers.

As a solution to the limited number of faculty and staff available to teach the growing number of FYSC sections based on enrollment growth at Peak University, a call went out to the campus listserv in search of instructors. Supervisors were encouraged to consider if teaching a FYSC would be an appropriate professional development opportunity for any of their staff members.

Alex completed his master's degree in a student affairs preparation program at a large, research-intensive university and is in the third year of his first professional position in student affairs as a residential life coordinator (RLC) in the Department of Residence Life and Housing (RLH) at Peak University. He has been interested in teaching a FYSC since he started at Peak University, but his supervisor felt he needed to learn his position first and figure out how to manage the intensity and large time commitment required of RLH. This year, however, when the campus-wide call for instructors came out, Alex's supervisor encouraged him to apply. Alex has been teaching the FYSC for six weeks and is pleased with how the classroom community is developing, the relationships he is building with students in a curricular environment, and how he is advancing as an educator in a more formalized role.

Hannah lives in one of the communities Alex oversees on campus, but she is not a student in Alex's course. Since she was an active leader in high school co-curricular activities, she engaged with her hall community early on and joined the Residence Hall Association (RHA) as a floor representative. Hannah moved from across the country to pursue a pre-med degree with the goal of pursuing a career in orthopedic surgery. She met a friend, Jacob, during an orientation event over the summer and the two remained connected over social media until they reconnected in person after arriving at Peak University. Now that they are both living on campus, they have been attending campus programs, eating in the dining hall, and going to the recreation center together. Jacob is a student in Alex's FYSC, but lives in a campus community supervised by another RLC. He moved from a small town about three hours from Peak University, just far enough to get a new start and focus on his education.

Hannah approached Alex one evening after an RHA meeting and asked to meet with him during his office hours the next day. Alex said he had time right then if she wanted to go find a place on campus to talk and Hannah agreed. Hannah started talking about how she is enjoying her involvement in RHA and wondered about future leadership positions for her sophomore year. Alex was unsure where the conversation was leading as it did not seem that Hannah had a specific question or need.

However, once Hannah seemed to feel a bit more comfortable with Alex in this one-on-one setting, she started talking about being concerned about her friend, Jacob. As she described Jacob's background, Alex realized that the student was the same Jacob in his FYSC. As this realization dawned on Alex, Hannah asked him if she could share something confidentially with him about Jacob's home life. Alex said yes but explained the general limitations to confidentiality based on legal requirements.

Hannah shared her concern that Jacob's mom is a drug addict, and once Jacob arrived at Peak University, she relapsed. Hannah explained that Jacob's mom frequently calls him at random hours of the day and night. Because she also had his roommates' contact information, Jacob's mother also recently began contacting them when Jacob would not immediately respond to her calls. Jacob told Hannah that his roommates are frustrated by the contact from his mother and have mentioned wanting him out of the suite.

As an only child, Jacob is feeling responsible for his mother because she is now alone but is limited by his distance from her now that he is at school. In addition to the emotional ties to her, Jacob's mother has also been sharing her financial issues with him and has asked him to send her money every other week when he receives his paycheck from his campus job. Given the various issues that Jacob is dealing with in his home life that are spilling over into his campus experience, Hannah wanted to tell someone about the situation because of her care for Jacob. She trusts Alex from their RHA connection and values his insight as a mentor. Hannah ends the conversation telling Alex that she does not want Jacob to know that she shared his personal life with him because of his private nature, but she wants Alex to know the challenges Jacob is having if there is help he can provide.

Shortly thereafter, Alex notices a change in Jacob's behavior in his FYSC class. Jacob was highly engaged during the first six weeks of class, turned in quality work, and seemed to be connecting well with peers. As the semester has progressed, Jacob's attendance is sporadic and his written reflection papers about his college experience and the course content are weaker in quality than his initial coursework. Jacob seems withdrawn from peers in his course and Alex is concerned about his grade as the semester's end draws closer.

Alex asks to speak with Jacob during his office hours with the initial concern being his declining grade. He can tell Jacob is reluctant about the meeting, but he arrives on time. However, Alex can't break the ice despite attempts to discuss the hobbies Jacob wrote about in one of his reflection papers. Alex moves on to his concerns about Jacob's grade in the course, but Jacob isn't engaging with Alex and only providing one-word responses as Alex seeks to find information to help Jacob succeed academically. Not getting anywhere in his conversation with Jacob, Alex wonders whether to bring up the information about his home life provided by Hannah. On one hand, Alex's instincts lead him to believe that something is really wrong and that Jacob needs assistance. On the other hand, Alex doesn't want to break Hannah's confidence.

What should Alex do?

UNKNOWN STUDENT
REYES J. LUNA AND MICHELLE J. BOETTCHER

Louise is a second-year hall director in a residential apartment community at West Coast University (WCU), a large, minority-serving, public institution on the West Coast. Louise regularly trains her team on a variety of issues and recently conducted a training about suicidal ideation in partnership with the campus counseling staff, which covered campus resources, warning signs, and how to refer residents.

Mary is a first-year RA with lots of friends both within and outside the residential community. During a one-on-one on Monday, October 1, when Louise asked Mary how things were going, Mary initially said fine, but eventually stated that she had something to share. She told Louise that three nights earlier, she had been texting with a friend. During the exchange, the friend shared that he was thinking about hurting himself and had suicidal thoughts since breaking up with his partner over the summer. Mary's friend is a WCU student but not a resident in on-campus housing. Every night, Mary has texted with him, and he continues to make comments about harming himself or just ending things.

Louise talks with Mary about her friend and how Mary might help him. She then asks Mary if she needs any help or support around the issue. Mary says that she has seen counselors before, but she is doing all right for now. She will reach out to counseling services if needed. Louise says she will be checking in with Mary in the next few days to make sure she is doing all right. Mary welcomes the support from Louise and thanks her for listening.

That Thursday (October 4) when Louise fills out her weekly report she includes the exchange with Mary. She focuses on Mary and writes that the RA seems to be doing well and knows what resources are available to her. During Louise's supervision meeting with her area coordinator Joe the next week (Tuesday, October 9), Joe brings up the incident. He says that Louise needs to follow up with Mary and get the name of the student who indicated he might hurt himself. Joe is clearly frustrated that Louise hadn't already done this, but Louise is confused and wonders why Joe didn't call her immediately when she submitted her weekly report if he thought getting the student's name was that urgent.

Wednesday night (October 10), Mary sends Louise an email stating that she is really concerned about her friend and has suggested multiple times that he seek help from the counseling center. However, the friend has declined and stated that he only felt comfortable sharing this with her. Mary has been losing sleep and is worried about him. He will only communicate with her via text.

Louise calls Mary in for a meeting the next morning (Wednesday, October 11). After checking on Mary and how she has been handling this situation, Louise shares that she will need the name of the student who had been texting her about potentially harming himself. Mary becomes visibly upset and says she doesn't want to break his confidence. "He doesn't even live on campus. Why do I have to tell you his name? He'll never trust me again if I share who he is."

What should Louise do?

SOCIAL MEDIA FREEDOM OF SPEECH
KIPP VAN DYKE AND TAYLOR PERKINS

Seth is a first-year hall coordinator in a three-hundred-bed, coed residence hall at Central State University, a mid-sized, public four-year institution in the Midwest. Seth has an undergraduate staff of twelve community assistants and one graduate hall coordinator, Phillip. Phillip served in the position the previous year, as did eight of the community assistants. Seth and Phillip split supervision of the undergraduate staff, and Phillip also coordinates the desk operations of the building. The hall coordinator, graduate hall coordinator, and twelve community assistants make up the "Hall Leadership Team."

During the beginning of the school year, several incidents of vandalism occurred on the weekends within the hall. These included bulletin boards being torn down, signs and flyers having inappropriate sexual drawings added, racial and sexist words/phrases drawn in public spaces, and food being thrown in stairwells. There were some reports from residents of whiteboard vandalism on individual doors, both drawings and racial slurs, but they were always wiped clean before they could be documented by hall staff or the police. The staff discussed these incidents in their leadership team meetings. Both Seth and Phillip stressed having conversations with residents, holding floor meetings, and the importance of documenting hateful speech/language. Phillip sometimes made comments in these meetings insinuating that Seth wasn't doing enough as a leader to create a welcoming culture. Examples included commenting on items that should have been on the agenda about social justice initiatives around campus, making suggestions like Seth could utilize his budget to add cameras to the building, and suggesting more direct communications should be sent to the hall community in response to situations as this would not cost anything, among other comments. Phillip also shared displeasure about the hall climate with his community assistants, other graduate hall coordinators and his classmates. Seth was hesitant to address Phillip from a supervisory standpoint as Seth was a new supervisor and wanted Phillip to feel free to be able to share his thoughts and opinions. Additionally, Seth realized that Phillip, who started graduate school right after graduating with his bachelor's degree, was learning about professional maturity and Seth wanted to provide some gentle guidance in that area. Seth also felt that Phillip's statements, while uncomfortable for Seth at times, were rooted in social change that needed to be addressed and felt he shouldn't suppress those.

Four weeks into the fall semester, three community assistants texted Seth while he was in a meeting, as they were not able to find Phillip in the building. They shared that a student reporter from the campus newspaper contacted the hall desk wanting to talk with Phillip. The community assistants shared that Phillip posted on a personal social media account a photo a resident had posted on their social media account with their whiteboard showing what appeared to be racially derogatory terms written on the board. On the resident's original post showing the photo, Phillip included the comment, "Why did I move to this backwoods school? I'm surrounded by racists!!" Several other graduate hall coordinators shared this post on their social media networks to show support for Phillip, and the community assistants told Seth that "everyone" on campus was talking about the post because the student newspaper had commented on it on the newspaper's official social media account. One resident also commented on the post that was being reshared and identified the name of the resident (Sarah) as the person whose door had the derogatory terms.

Seth stepped out of the meeting and was able to reach Phillip via cell phone. Seth told Phillip it appeared the post on his social media account was set to "public" and not "private" and suggested that Phillip remove the post to mitigate any further issues. Phillip responded that the post was intentionally made public with the hopes it would be shared beyond the hall as he said he was "tired of ignorance and hate not being addressed at this school." Seth also informed Phillip that the desk had been contacted by the student newspaper about the social media post. Phillip told Seth he should not be too concerned, as the posting was to Phillip's personal social media account. Phillip believed these posts were not work related, and he had a right to post them to his personal account. He believed the community assistants could respond to any inquiries by telling those concerned it was made on an individual's personal social media account.

Seth continued checking social media and noticed the post had been shared many times and there was a lot of engagement with the post, both positive and negative. This was happening very quickly and Seth had not been able to consult with his supervisor yet as he felt he should have all the facts and information in order and they had not responded to Seth's initial call to consult. Seth also had several emails coming in, including one from Sarah's parents that went to the entire Hall Leadership Team. In this email, Sarah's parents shared they were coming to pick up Sarah due to Sarah feeling unsafe in the hall given all the attention the viral post was receiving. Her parents said Sarah had received hateful messages and threats on social medial from unknown people calling her a racist for writing those comments on her own whiteboard. They also said Sarah had been gone most of the previous weekend and were 100 percent sure Sarah didn't write that on her door. They also shared their displeasure with a "state employee" creating this unwanted attention toward Sarah through a social media post. They asked if Seth and Phillip could meet them when they arrived to get Sarah to discuss their concerns. Phillip "replied all" to the email and said he was not available that afternoon, adding the post was on a personal social media account so being a "state employee" was not relevant. Phillip also responded in the email that Seth could meet with them to further discuss the situation and to explore options Sarah would have in terms of moving to a different room or out of the hall. Phillip followed that email with a text to Seth and said he felt this would be a good opportunity for the student and their family to experience some of the stressors underrepresented individuals have had to face for many years and hopes his resharing on the post will make the university and surrounding communities open their eyes and address these issues.

What should Seth do?

THE COMPANY YOU KEEP
BRANDIN L. HOWARD

Xavier is currently a second-year hall director at Firesburg Polytechnic University (FTU). Firesburg Polytechnic University (FTU) is an urban, large, land-grant public institution located in the southeastern United States. The residence life department at FTU is one of the largest operations in the region, consisting of an executive director and four associate directors, one of whom is the associate director for residence life. The associate director for residence life, Ava, supervises one senior assistant director for student leadership and conduct as well as four assistant directors (ADs) who each oversee one residential area on campus. At FTU, Xavier is one of the thirty-one hall directors (HD) employed in the department.

During his first year at FTU, Xavier had a difficult time transitioning into his first full-time role as an HD for a variety of reasons. FTU was the first large university Xavier had been at, with over 35,000 students enrolled, 14,500 of which resided on campus. FTU was also the first predominantly White institution Xavier had ever been at, as the institutions he attended previously were Hispanic serving institutions (HSIs). Identifying as a Latinx male, it was important to Xavier to attend an HSI for his undergraduate and graduate careers.

When he arrived to FTU, he was one of four new HDs in the Treeburn Residential Area, and often felt he was the odd one out among the other HDs in his area. Although his AD at the time, Gabby, made every attempt to support him in his role and acclimate him to the department, Xavier still felt like the outcast on his area team due to the challenge of building a connection with the more experienced HDs, who appeared to take little interest in getting to know Xavier. However, over the course of the semester, Xavier became friends with a new HD in the Aquis residential area on campus, Sam. Sam identified as a gender non-conforming, African American staff member and was previously a HD at another institution prior to joining the team at FTU.

As Xavier and Sam's first fall semester progresses, Sam and their AD/ direct supervisor, Faulkner, also begin to socialize outside of work often. Because Sam and Xavier are also friends, it is not uncommon for Xavier to join the other two to hang out. Xavier does not always feel the most comfortable hanging out with Faulkner because of the power dynamics at play. Xavier had been taught in grad school to maintain professional relationships across supervisory lines, but he had never considered hanging out socially with someone above him as often as he did Faulkner. As Xavier starts to get to know Faulkner better, he begins to notice times when Faulkner engages Sam and him in questionable conversations that he feels cross professional boundaries. For example, Faulkner often speaks negatively of other HDs or even other leadership staff in the department. While Xavier does not feel comfortable being a part of these conversations, he also does not want to jeopardize his friendship with Sam, so he keeps quiet during these conversations.

As Xavier enters his second year as a HD at FTU, the department announces a reorganization of the residence life team. The department consolidated two residential areas and one AD will be promoted to the newly created senior assistant director for student leadership and conduct role. Due to seniority and a stellar work history, Gabby is appointed to the senior AD role, and Faulkner becomes the AD for the Treeburn Area. The shuffle of the ADs means that Faulkner becomes Xavier's direct supervisor, which concerns Xavier given their status as "friends." After this shift, Faulkner continues to spend personal time with Sam and Xavier, despite Xavier's increasing discomfort with socializing with his supervisor. As Faulkner's criticism of other staff members in the department and other inappropriate comments continues, Xavier begins to worry the comments are getting out of control and does not feel comfortable challenging his new supervisor.

As the year continues, Ava, the associate director for residence life, begins to hear rumors circulating around the department about Faulkner's engagement with supervisees. She had heard these rumors before and inquired with Faulkner, but the conversation went nowhere. Now, because these rumors mention Sam and Xavier specifically, Ava decides to ask them to meet with her to discuss the rumors. As the meeting with Ava approaches, Xavier is not sure if he should tell her about the conversations with and observations of Faulkner. He is especially concerned because if he confirms the rumors, Faulkner will know it was either him or Sam who told Ava about the conversations.

What should Xavier do?

BEST FRIENDS OR OVERSTEPPING BOUNDARIES
ANGELA M. DELFINE

Mountain Valley College (MVC) is a private, liberal arts institution in the Midwest. MVC hosts 2,500 students, 1,300 of whom live in residence halls on campus. MVC is a predominantly White institution that focuses on core values of community, justice, and sustainability. The college is home to five residence halls, two of which are designated for first-year students. Since the community is small, MVC students, faculty, and staff express that "everyone knows everyone" and frequently talk about how welcoming the community feels. Students often hold doors open for other students, say "hello" to strangers in the hallway, and often express that they feel "at home" within the MVC community.

Marie Williams is a second-year hall director (HD) at MVC who prides herself on engaging with her students and fellow staff members. She has worked to develop positive rapport with many members of the community and is known as being "the friendly and outgoing HD" on campus. Overall, Marie's experience as a HD at MVC has been a positive one, full of personal development and growth. Marie also feels very welcome within the community. She often joins students at on-campus programs and attends professional networking hours with colleagues.

Marie is supervised by Arnold Carter, the director of residence life. Arnold is a very well-known member of the staff community and has worked at the institution for eight years. Arnold served as a HD for four years before moving up to the position of director. Arnold is engaged in the campus community by serving on a few boards, including the Student Retention Committee and the Campus Climate Survey Committee. He also currently serves as the advisor of the on-campus Habitat for Humanity club, which is one of the most popular student organizations at MVC. In addition, the students speak highly of Arnold and how he frequently supports students. Whenever a student needs support in areas such as academics or housing needs, Arnold is always willing to step up and help those students.

One day when she is doing her laundry, Marie is greeted by a student, Louis Jackson, who is upset about his roommate situation. Louis calmly explains that his roommate is disrupting his sleep by playing video games all night and keeps hitting snooze on his phone alarm. Marie tells Louis that she is free to meet about his roommate situation in the morning, since Louis is not immediately threatened or uncomfortable in his room. Louis thanks Marie and says that he will see her in the morning.

Marie meets with Louis the next morning and determines that a roommate mediation would be the best plan of action for the situation. Based on the conversation, Louis explains that he is simply not comfortable in his room at the moment, but that he does not feel threatened by his roommate. Louis mentions that a single room may be better for him, since he is older than his roommate and has taken on additional credits and leadership opportunities this semester. Marie says that she is unable to give Louis a single room, and in fact, the only reason that single rooms are provided is when accompanied by an accommodation letter from the Disability Services Office. After a bit of grumbling and angling to see if Marie will change her mind, Louis seems to come to terms with his reality. He says that he understands Marie's rationale, agrees that a roommate mediation is appropriate, and says that he is free that evening for the meeting. Marie reaches out to Louis's roommate who agrees that there is some tension in the room and that a meeting for later that evening would be ideal. Marie meets with both Louis and his roommate as scheduled later in the evening. After much negotiation, it seems like the students have come to a consensus about the concerns in the room and are willing to meet in the middle.

The next day, Marie arrives in the office and receives an unexpected call from Arnold indicating that he has just spoken with Louis. Marie was aware that Arnold had good rapport with the student, since Arnold serves as the current advisor of Habitat for Humanity and Louis is expected to be the next president of the organization. Arnold says that Louis stated that he was extremely disappointed with how his roommate mediation meeting went the previous evening and had met with Arnold to discuss a private room. Arnold indicated that Louis said he was extremely uncomfortable in the room, despite the agreement, and that this discomfort would affect his academic work. Arnold agrees with Louis, yet assures Marie that he is in no way questioning her decision-making abilities. Arnold expresses that a single would be better for Louis's mental state and that he will need to move over to that space as soon as possible. Marie is confused, since she has not received any indication that Louis is experiencing any mental health concerns, nor has she received an accommodation letter. She is also disappointed that the student felt the need to go above her to the director. She initially questions Arnold about what she perceives as special treatment, but ultimately agrees to complete the switch if it is in Louis's best interests. Arnold thanks Marie for completing the room change.

A few days later, Marie goes over to Arnold's office to ask about another project that she is working on. When Marie arrives, she is immediately greeted by Louis in the office joking around and laughing with Arnold. Both Arnold and Louis seem surprised when Marie walks in, but then greet her. Louis thanks Marie for their initial meeting and raves about how his new single room is already helping with his mental health. Louis also tells her the great news that Arnold has just helped him get a job as a student worker in the main Residence Life Office. Louis says that he is trying to save some additional money for college and that he is more than grateful to take on the job. Marie congratulates Louis on his new job, despite being frustrated that the decision was made without consulting the other staff members in the office, which has been the practice in the past. Marie had been trying to create another work study position in the office for months, since many students had expressed a need for additional income to pay for books and other expenses. Marie is also aware that Louis comes from an upper-middle-class family and may not have needed the position as much as other students. Regardless, Marie trusts Arnold's decision to hire Louis.

Over the next few weeks, Marie notices Louis hanging out more with Arnold. In addition, other staff mention seeing Louis and Arnold out and about together. Even during working office hours, Louis will be in Arnold's office carrying on and laughing about something. At one point, Marie checks with Louis to see how his job is going. Louis answers by saying that it was "amazing, thanks to Arnold" and that "he was basically like the dad that he never had." After hearing this comment, Marie becomes more alarmed about how much time Arnold and Louis are spending together. Marie also notices that Louis is not hanging out with his friends as much in the building and that instead, he is spending more time away from the building.

On a Thursday evening, Marie is walking out of her apartment when she sees Louis entering the residence hall. Marie greets Louis and asks how his evening is going. Louis says that he had a wonderful day and that he just returned from helping Arnold to shop for a new apartment. Louis says that he is doing much better, now that Arnold has taken him under his wing, and that he was looking forward to being able to hang out with Arnold more in his new apartment. At this point, Marie is very concerned that Arnold is over-stepping his boundary as a staff member, especially in his role as the director of residence life.

What should Marie do?

THERE'S A THIN LINE BETWEEN CULTURAL
APPROPRIATION AND APPRECIATION
YOLANDA M. BARNES AND NATHAN VICTORIA

The University of Smithland is a large public institution located in North Texas. Founded in 1932, the University of Smithland is a leading public research university in the vibrant city of Dallas. Each year, the university educates more than forty thousand students in more than three hundred undergraduate and graduate academic programs, on campus and online. Smithland awards more than eight thousand degrees annually and has more than 230,000 alumni.

Every spring, the Division of Student Affairs facilitates a mandatory common leadership training for all student leaders affiliated with a specific department and/or office on campus. Among the students required to attend are sorority and fraternity governing councils, orientation leaders, resident advisors, and campus tour guides. Recently, the division updated the common leadership training curriculum to include intentional conversations around social justice, diversity, and inclusion. These intentional conversations were added after the university suspended all sorority and fraternity activities for six weeks after multiple Greek organizations threw offensively themed parties. One fraternity made national news after throwing a party to commemorate Martin Luther King Jr. Day, replete with racist stereotypes and offensive costumes. The university is working diligently to create a more inclusive campus community by educating its student leaders and staff.

Tori recently completed a graduate degree in student affairs administration and is excited to start work as a residential community director in Student Housing and Residence Life at the University of Smithland. Tori can't wait to implement the many tools and student development theories she learned while in class and as a graduate assistant. The Student Housing and Residence Life department is committed to creating a more socially just living community for all residents. Tori learned about the department's social justice focus when interviewing during her job search and while in training after being hired. Tori's department collaborates often with fraternities and sororities by hosting their group events in spaces operated by Student Housing and Residence Life. It's an intentional partnership cultivated to help provide additional support and a watchful eye to the Greek system, which has experienced campus sanctions and suspensions in the past.

During Tori's weekly meeting with her resident advisor, Sabrina, she learns about an upcoming sorority fundraising event that will be held in the residence hall. Sabrina is a member of this sorority and is the vice president for administration on the College Panhellenic Council. The event is scheduled to take place during the last few weeks of spring classes in the multi-purpose room located in a building Tori supervises. This year's theme is

"Cinco de Mayo." Sabrina lets Tori know that over the weekend, she and other members of the sorority purchased several decorations and costumes— items such as sombreros, ponchos, and maracas. Sabrina is very enthusiastic for the fundraising event, especially because a lot of work has gone into planning it and because they have a university alumna, who is also a member of the sorority, confirmed to speak at the event. This alumna has contributed financially to the university in the past. Tori is aware that University Advancement is in the final stages of confirming a significant donation from this alumna to go toward the creation of a much-needed new residence hall that is scheduled to open in two years.

Tori asks Sabrina to explain the decision-making that went into choosing "Cinco de Mayo" as a theme. Sabrina shares the theme was chosen because the event will take place in May and they want something fun and festive. Tori challenges Sabrina to think back to the intentional conversations facilitated during the common leadership training and the impact of choosing this specific theme. Sabrina says, "As a Latina woman, I do not see anything wrong with the theme. If I'm okay with it, everything should be fine." She confirms their campus faculty advisor will be there to support the event. The event is taking place in three weeks.

In order for the group to have confirmed the reservation, they had to seek approval from the Student Housing and Residence Life Department by providing an outline of their plans for using the space, including theme, and confirmed speakers. Someone in the department has approved the event.

What should Tori do?

WHO GETS TO DRINK AT THE BARS?
BRITTANY MCDANIEL AND KENNETH D. GRCICH

Bailey was starting her second year as a hall director in a first-year residential community at a predominantly White, large, public institution located in a mid-sized Midwest town. Bailey was looking forward to continuing to grow in her position, especially after receiving a very positive performance review at the end of her first year and being told she was already on track for a promotion within the department. Bailey had developed a strong sense of belonging within the department, as well as the division and larger institutional environment. She had formed close friendships with many fellow student affairs professionals at the institution, and residents viewed her as a respected leader within the community. Bailey was thriving in her work within residence life and at the institution.

Bailey knew that university students frequented many bars in town and that several bars were known to serve underage students—including her own residents. Many of Bailey's conduct hearings with residents were in response to alcohol-related violations. Through interactions in the community, and sometimes in conduct meeting conversations, Bailey knew what a typical night out was for her underage residents. Knowing this, Bailey was mindful to not visit bars that her residents frequented.

Bailey soon realized that her colleagues were quite comfortable socializing in nearby establishments, which led her to start accepting invitations at the same places she knew her residents could possibly be drinking, too. During the spring semester, she went only to happy hour to have a few drinks with colleagues. This was a time that she knew her students were least likely to be present. After all, her department did not have a policy stating employees could not drink at bars in town. It was just strongly encouraged by senior leadership that staff be mindful of their behavior when choosing to drink in public. Knowing this information, Bailey felt comfortable in her choice to go to happy hour. Eventually, Bailey started to go out more frequently, meeting friends for happy hour and then staying out at bars until the early hours of the morning. However, she made sure her behavior didn't impact her work performance and was confident that her supervisors weren't aware of her after work activities. Also, Bailey was allowed to legally drink in bars—her twenties were supposed to be a fun time! Bailey found this to be a sound rationale and felt okay with her actions.

A few weeks into the fall semester of her second year, Bailey went out for what had become a typical Friday night with her fellow hall director friends. After grabbing a few drinks during happy hour, she went for a quick dinner and then proceeded to go to one of her favorite bars where she and her friends had become friendly with the bartender, who gave them free drinks. The bar was also a favorite spot of underage students as IDs were not properly checked. Around 11:30 pm Bailey spotted some of her residents, whom she had met at a program the week before and who she knew were under the age of twenty-one. Bailey was having a good time and didn't want to leave—besides she was in the back of the bar so it was unlikely her residents had seen her. Bailey continued drinking, and around 2:00 am decided to call it a night. She remembers stumbling out of the bar a bit but tried her best to keep her composure since she was sure her residents were still at the bar.

When Bailey gets into the office on Monday, she receives a report of an incident where two residents, Alex and Morgan, had been belligerent when returning to the hall early Saturday morning. The incident report notes that the RA could smell alcohol on their breath and the residents' eyes were bloodshot. Bailey schedules a conduct meeting with each resident. During the meeting with Morgan, Bailey begins by sharing the details of the incident report before asking for Morgan's perspective of the incident. At this time, Morgan takes out her phone and proceeds to show pictures of Bailey holding two shots, one in each hand, and a picture of Bailey leaning on two other hall directors for support as they walk out of the bar. The timestamp shows that it had been the night that Bailey saw her residents in the bar. Morgan tells Bailey to drop the conduct case or else she will send the pictures to the director of residence life and dean of students.

What should Bailey do?

WHAT'S THAT SMELL?
STEPHEN WEINMANN

Paul is a twenty-two-year-old White male who recently graduated with his bachelor's degree. He recently started a new position as a residence hall director at a mid-sized, predominantly White, public institution. Most of the residence life staff in Paul's department identify as White and all the public safety officers do as well. There is a small number of students of color on campus.

Paul serves "on call" for the whole campus one night a week, making him the first point of contact for any incident involving students on campus. One evening while on call, Paul receives a report from a residence assistant about an odor of marijuana in a residence hall that he does not typically oversee. Paul arrives and confirms that the odor was indeed marijuana. Paul follows protocol by calling his supervisor to ask for approval to authorize a room search; Paul has carried out this protocol roughly a dozen times before in similar situations regarding odors of marijuana. His supervisor authorizes the room search, which is conducted by two White public safety officers. Per the protocol, Paul and the resident assistants of that floor stand outside the room with the residents, Anthony and Mark. Paul does not know the residents but the resident assistants both know them fairly well. Mark and Anthony identify as Latino. During the search, the residents are overheard by both the resident assistants and Paul saying "fuck all White people" and "they are targeting us." Paul does not want to escalate the situation and decides that neither the resident assistants nor he will address the comments at this point in time. However, he makes sure to document the comments in his report.

The room search results in finding some rolling papers, a small container of marijuana, a lighter, and a bong in a shoebox under Mark's bed. When the public safety officer states that marijuana and drug paraphernalia were found, both residents exclaim that it was not theirs, they had no idea it was there, and suggest that it was planted there. The officers state they were going to confiscate all the contents of the shoe box, and Paul informs the residents that he will be submitting an incident report and that they can expect to hear from his supervisor to set up a conduct meeting. He also explains the conduct process to the students and asks if they have any questions. After submitting documentation about the incident, Paul goes back to his on-campus apartment. The next morning, Paul notices a sign on his door with the word "racist" on it. He removes the sign and brings it down to his supervisor's office, sharing his suspicion that the sign was related to the marijuana incident. Paul's supervisor indicates she will talk to the students.

Later that day Paul goes back to the building where the incident occurred to follow up with the two resident assistants on Anthony and Mark's floor and notices an odor of marijuana coming from their room again.

What should Paul do?

BREAKING THE BINARY
JORDAN W. VIARS, MOLLY JEAN CALLAHAN, MICHELLE J. BOETTCHER, AND TONY CAWTHON

Carson (he/him/his) is a White, cisgender, gay male serving as assistant director of residence life at Lance University (LU), a small, private, faith-affiliated institution in Western Pennsylvania. LU enrolls 1,200 undergraduate students. The student population is primarily female (64 percent), White (94 percent), low-income (88 percent), and first-generation students (72 percent). Students are required to live on campus all four years. LU has made great progress in its efforts to become a more open and inclusive campus community in the past three years. Despite the successes, several senior faculty members have raised concerns that the inclusive excellence initiatives are "getting away from the mission of the institution," referencing the institution's religious affiliation specifically in their concerns.

Carson has worked as a hall director at LU for three years and was promoted three months ago to assistant director. He oversees housing assignments and billing for the Department of Residence Life. Carson received the outstanding employee award two years in a row and believes his reputation has afforded him both political insight and political capital. Carson is an ardent student advocate, centering his advocacy work on social identities and, as an openly gay man, has successfully navigated his identity in the context of the LU culture. With Campus Activities staff and faculty members in the Division of Social Sciences, Carson established a very active student organization—Gender and Sexuality Organization (GSO).

Jesse, a member of the GSO, is a third-year undergraduate who identifies as gender fluid. She uses the pronouns she/her/hers though her university documents identify her as male. This year, Jesse lived in West Hall with her female-identifying best friend, Phoebe (she/her/hers), through a housing request authorized by the former Dean of Students after Jesse made an informal request. Phoebe is transferring to another institution after this year, which prompted Jesse to select Jillian (she/her/hers) as her next roommate. Jesse hopes they can return to West Hall but is unsure how to make a formal request as no formal process is outlined anywhere on the institution's website and the staff she worked with previously are no longer at the university. After talking with friends, Jesse seeks help from Carson, whom she knows through the GSO.

In an email, Jesse informs Carson that she wishes to live in a suite-style assignment with female-identifying roommates, as she does not feel comfortable in the male-only residential spaces where she would be assigned given the documentation on file. Carson reviews the assignment archives and finds no written record of the previous request. Given this lack of documentation,

Carson schedules a meeting with the interim dean of students, Dr. Varnham (he/him/his), to discuss the request.

Dr. Varnham was appointed to the interim dean position three weeks ago, having been a history faculty member at LU for twenty-three years. While he does not have a student affairs background, Dr. Varnham has been a strong student advocate around high-profile campus issues. As interim dean he has been thoughtful, strategic, and politically astute. In the meeting, Carson briefs Dean Varnham on Jesse's situation. Dr. Varnham interrupts Carson and exclaims, "Leviticus 18:22 says it plain as day, 'thou shalt not lie with mankind, as with womankind: it is an abomination.' We make all housing assignments based off the gender listed in the student information system. End of discussion!" Surprised by the response, Carson attempts to redirect the conversation to the institution's value of inclusivity, but the interim dean refuses to listen and instead says, "Carson, while you are well respected on campus, you need to be careful because supporting those people will tarnish your reputation."

Carson staunchly disagrees with this decision and is floored by the interim dean's comments. As a member of the LGBTQ+ Community, Carson is committed to providing gender inclusive spaces so all students feel supported in their identities. After Carson meets with Dr. Varnham for over an hour, the only options afforded to Jesse are to either accept an assignment in the male-only, traditional-style community or reside in a private room in Gunter Hall for an additional $900 single room fee.

Carson returns to his office visibly upset by this decision. The other staff members in the office are worried about Carson as they can tell he is emotionally triggered after his meeting with Dr. Varnham. Carson decides to take the rest of the day away from work. The following day, Carson's feelings and outlook remain the same—tense, emotional, and defeated. Carson feels he has let Jesse down and is not sure how to approach the situation.

With no other options, Carson emails Jesse to meet. Jesse arrives hoping for a positive outcome. With as much professionalism and care possible, Carson informs Jesse the housing request will not be honored. Jesse's face turns red and she begins to cry. In her frustration she exclaims, "Everyone here hates me. They don't understand or help me. Faculty refuse to call me by my name, students look at me strangely, and my parents are threatening to stop helping me financially. I know you've done what you can, but I can't afford a single and I don't want to be alone. I thought this campus was inclusive but obviously only inclusive of some people." Carson sighs, as he knows that Jesse continually struggles to fit at LU. As he reflects on her situation, it occurs to him that no one would know if she paid the $900 single room fee, as the rooms are billed as doubles and the fee is added only when it is solo occupied. He could plausibly put a hold on the other space without charging Jesse the fee. Although it wouldn't address her loneliness, it would enable her to feel safe on campus.

What should Carson do?

HOW "FREE" IS FREE SPEECH?
STEVEN MARKS

Robert is a resident coordinator at Horizon State University (HSU), which is in the mid-Atlantic region. The university has a predominantly White, middle-class student population of approximately three thousand students. The institution's Office of Diversity and Social Initiatives works with the Residence Life Office (RLO), which houses eight hundred residents, to promote a welcoming and affirming environment for minority students whose families and who themselves would have the potential to be negatively impacted by policies that politicians and conservative-leaning activists stand behind. Before the start of the school year, the office developed a poster, which is displayed at the Residence Life front desk, that reads:

> *Dear ALL students,*
> *We are here to support and learn from one another.*
> *Dear Black students,*
> *Your lives matter.*
> *Dear Female students,*
> *You are valued and respected here.*
> *Dear International students,*
> *You are welcome here.*
> *Dear Latino students,*
> *You will not find walls here.*
> *Dear LGBTQ+ students,*
> *You are supported here.*
> *Dear Muslim students,*
> *Your beliefs are respected here.*
> *Each and every one of you . . .*
> *YOU BELONG HERE*

During a night on duty, Robert arrives at the RLO to begin his expected duty responsibilities when Annie, a resident assistant, approaches him and asks whether he saw a post from another student on the HSU Student Facebook page regarding a poster on display at the front desk of the residence hall.

Robert begins to look through the page and discovers that Jim, a student who works at the front desk in the RLO, posted about his frustration with what he refers to as HSU pandering to minority students while not taking care of the White students, who make up 86 percent of the student population. In the post, Jim demands a response from the university president and states that the flyer should be destroyed. Immediately after Jim's post appears, students begin commenting with various opinions on the page.

Robert later discovers that the flyer was removed from the front desk but is unsure where it went. Robert contacts Aynur, the resident assistant on duty, and asks if he is aware that the flyer was removed. Aynur tells Robert that he saw Jim take a picture of the flyer and he believes Jim returned to his room with the picture. He did not know who removed the flyer, however. Robert emails his supervisor about the post and the missing flyer before heading back to his apartment.

The following morning, Robert, along with all the members of the student affairs staff, receives an e-mail from the dean of student affairs instructing them not to discuss the post with students and not to confront Jim about it. Just then, Crystal, a student leader from Latino Students United For Change who lives in the building, enters Robert's office and looks visibly upset. She asks Robert why the post is not being taken down. "This is hate speech, not free speech! Jim needs to be penalized for his hateful actions," she says.

What should Robert do?

Chapter Seven

Student Involvement

LIMITLESS ABILITY: ADVOCACY, ANGER, AND DEMANDS
MICHAEL KAVULIC AND BRENDA L. MCKENZIE

Aaron is completing his third year as a new professional at Northeastern State University (NSU) in the Office of Student Activities. NSU is a four-year, public, research-intensive institution located in the Northeast, fifty miles from the nearest urban center. The total student enrollment is twenty-five thousand with seventeen thousand undergraduates and eight thousand graduate students. NSU also has more than five hundred student organizations, including nearly one hundred identity-based groups in any given academic year.

In his role at NSU, Aaron oversees several student organizations and coordinates a year-long leadership training curriculum for members of student organizations. During his three years at NSU, Aaron has gained a reputation as an advocate for the needs of the students and they have grown very comfortable coming to Aaron for advice and guidance. One of the organizations that Aaron oversees is Limitless Ability (LA) which was founded two years ago and whose aim is to advocate for students with disabilities and to provide educational programming for the campus. Students with disabilities currently comprise approximately 5 percent of the total student population, based on students registered with the Disability Services Office.

Over the past year, LA has become aware of an increasing number of curricular and co-curricular challenges facing students with disabilities on campus. For instance, with some support from Aaron, members of LA have pointed out to individual faculty and to academic leadership, including the provost, that at least one general education course that serves up to 300 students each semester included documents in the course management system that were not accessible by screen reader. Additionally, a recent campus-wide survey included a non-mandatory item that allowed respondents to self-select a disability with which they identified. However, the survey defined disability as only relating to physical impairments and made no reference to the range of invisible disabilities individuals may claim. Individuals who identify as being on the autism spectrum, having learning disabilities, or having psychological disabilities including depression all left survey responses indicating frustration that their perspectives were not included in the design of the survey. Finally, several attendees at last year's commencement provided feedback to the university noting that the ceremony, held at the university football stadium, did not have real-time captioning and that the American Sign Language interpreters were obstructed by a banner. Despite feedback from students and external stakeholders to university administration, LA members believe that the university has not responded appropriately to the issues raised. In light of persistent climate issues that are not being addressed and which have not been publicly acknowledged by the provost or other university leadership, LA members feel there is an institutional culture that does not understand or care about their needs.

Over the past ten months, a campus-wide committee has worked with the provost to develop a new three-year academic strategic plan. A town hall was held at the end of February where the provost and the committee rolled out specific aspects of the strategic plan. Students in LA, as well as other students with disabilities, expressed concern with a statement made by the provost at the town hall and in a media release stating that NSU has worked to "remove all barriers to student success." When asked by the student newspaper about her reaction to the concerns expressed by the disability community on campus, the provost again broadly stated that the strategic planning committee addressed barriers to student success for all students.

Following the town hall and after seeing a social media posting from the student newspaper about the provost's response, Aaron set up a meeting with his supervisor Beth, the director of student activities, to address the situation. During this meeting, Aaron summarized the LA students' concerns and answered Beth's questions about the group and their recent activity. At the end of the meeting, Beth shared she had heard from the director of the Disability Services Office that the group might be planning a protest. Beth also mentioned that the provost and the dean of students, her supervisor, both expressed to her some concern about the activity of the group. Beth strongly encouraged Aaron to reach out to the Disability Services Office for any additional insights they might provide. Aaron agreed to reach out to the Disability Services Office but also shared that he was beginning to struggle with this situation because he agreed with much of LA's argument. Beth recommended Aaron advise the students about the consequences of unsanctioned and disruptive activity: "If Limitless Ability chooses to not follow university policy, we will have to hold them accountable for their actions. I know this is an emotional topic, but we must help the group find constructive ways to work through this. Remind them about our policies and the need to register a demonstration. They can absolutely share their perspectives, but I don't want this to get out of hand." Aaron understood the Beth's point and agreed to speak with LA's president.

When Aaron checks his email, he sees a message from LA's president, Courtney, calling an "emergency meeting" of the group that evening. Aaron is not sure of the purpose of the meeting but thinks it will give him a good opportunity to speak with the whole group about his conversation with his director. When Aaron arrives at the meeting, Courtney, who seems agitated and very eager to get started, opens the meeting with a stern statement outlining how the Limitless Ability student leaders, further frustrated by the provost's recent response regarding the strategic plan, has begun drafting a list of demands for the administration. As she passes around copies of the draft demands, Courtney explains how campus protests at other institutions have been effective at fostering change and that the LA leadership believes these demands will let the university administration know they were serious about their cause.

Before opening the floor for discussion to finalize their demands, Courtney states, "This is not the first time that the provost and the university have ignored the issues related to the climate around disability. To say that the strategic planning committee worked hard may be true but does not acknowledge that there is still work to be done. Now is the time for us to use our collective voices and make the administration understand that we are here and are not going to be ignored!" Those in attendance have a lively debate, ultimately coming to consensus that they should march through the campus to the provost's office and insist upon a meeting to express their frustrations and share their list of demands. Throughout the meeting, Aaron interjects to raise some questions and concerns and to clarify university policy regarding marches. It had been Aaron's initial intention to steer the group away from the idea of the list of demands and the march, but the responses from the LA membership to his suggestions shows him that they are set on this course of action. After the meeting, Aaron pulls Courtney aside for a quick chat.

In an effort to guide Courtney in considering the implications of the group's actions, Aaron shares, "I am really supportive of your concerns and agree that some changes would make a big difference, but I am concerned that your approach might not yield the best results."

Courtney responds, "Thank you for your support and concern, but we have decided we are going to do this. We need to act."

Aaron continues, "I am not telling you not to act. I am just trying to suggest actions that will not put the provost and the dean of students on the defensive. The director of student activities really wanted me to make sure you and the group know about the consequences of disruptive actions like the unregistered march you are talking about. Please know that I want to do everything I can for you because I agree with your concerns."

Courtney is unwilling to back down, but is happy to hear that Aaron is supportive. "I am not afraid of the consequences. I am afraid of what will happen to our community if we do nothing and that is exactly what it sounds like you and the director are trying to get us to do. Again, Aaron, I appreciate that you are supportive here and am thankful that you are on our side but I need to get going. Good night."

As soon as he gets home that evening, Aaron writes an email to Beth and the dean of students summarizing what happened at the meeting. The next day, word of Limitless Ability's plan for the march and sit-in at the provost's office is already spreading across campus. Several members of LA had posted an announcement on social media as a way to garner more participation and one post from Courtney thanked Aaron for supporting the group in their decision to march. By noon that day, Aaron has received several text messages from colleagues across campus indicating that they had heard he was encouraging the students to take action. Aaron also receives a phone call from Beth who tells him that the situation is starting to "get out of control." She also informs Aaron that the dean of students wants to meet with them for an update and to discuss concerns about the appropriateness of Aaron's support of the group and its actions. As Aaron is preparing for the conversation with the dean, he starts thinking about what had happened thus far. He wonders if he has done anything wrong, especially considering his internal struggle between supporting students and enforcing university policy. Aaron knows, however, that regardless of what had happened to this point, he will be dealing with this issue for some time.

What should Aaron do?

TWO SIDES OF THE STORY
TAYLOR PERKINS AND KIPP VAN DYKE

Tara is a first-year assistant director for orientation and transition at Northeastern Metro University, a mid-sized, public, four-year institution in the southeastern United States. Tara is one month into her first summer of orientation programs at the university. Northeastern Metro University's orientation program spans from the beginning of May to the end of July. In her position, Tara works with the director of orientation and transition, Maria, and one student coordinator (SC), Carolina, to supervise twenty-five orientation leaders (OLs). The OL role is a paid leadership position on campus. The director, assistant director, and the SC make up the Leadership Team.

It is halfway through the summer and the Leadership Team is starting to notice that OLs are not listening to instruction, challenging supervisors, and missing duties. The Leadership Team has documented several occasions where OLs have slept in past their morning job assignments, given inaccurate information to students/families, and failed to follow outlined lesson plans for small group discussions with prospective students. The Leadership Team addresses these concerns in an all-staff meeting, making a clear statement that the OLs' performance needs to improve. Following the meeting, they notice a few positive changes, but are unsure if their message was received by everyone. There is one OL that is particularly concerning; Craig has overtly ignored Leadership Team's expectations.

Since the summer orientation sessions started in May, the Leadership Team has documented five different occasions when Craig was confronted for failure to meet expectations of the position. It is now the end of June and the Leadership Team has seen little improvement; Craig has shown up five minutes late to several meetings in the past few weeks. The Leadership Team has also been notified that Craig continues to tell family members that "meal plans aren't necessary" and defends this claim to the Leadership Team by saying, "but, it's what the families want to hear." Additionally, it has also been noted that Craig is frequently browsing his phone while he is supposed to be co-facilitating small group discussions for prospective students. Though the Leadership Team has confronted him on multiple occasions for these behaviors, he is a leader among his peers, which is starting to influence behavior of other OLs. Regardless of the countless conversations with Craig, he still ignores the Leadership Team's instruction and supervision.

The Leadership Team holds a meeting to discuss Craig's performance. They decide the best action to take is to terminate Craig from the position. Because of his disregard for team rules and Leadership Team supervision, they decide the best route is to let him know as soon as possible. Tara contacts him right away and asks to meet with him later that afternoon. The

Leadership Team plans to inform the rest of the team that Craig is no longer on staff during their morning staff meeting the next day.

When Tara meets with Craig, he seems receptive to the feedback and understanding of the decision. He even apologizes on several occasions for the impact his actions had on the team. She tells him that his termination is effective immediately. Before leaving the meeting, Craig asks Tara if they planned to let the team know of the details of his firing. She assures him that while no details would be shared, the team would know that he was no longer on the team.

Before the team meeting the next morning, Carolina approaches Tara and shows her a lengthy message that Craig sent in the OL GroupMe chat the night before. GroupMe is a group chat that the Leadership Team does not have access to, but that all the student staff participate in. In his message, Craig explains in detail that he is *quitting* the position because he does not feel welcomed or respected by the Leadership Team. He expresses his frustration with the Leadership Team for displaying favoritism for a select few OLs on the team; in his words, "I cannot work for people who do not value who I am or what I do. Some of us have not been treated fairly or given the same opportunities as others. You all can stay if you want to, but I'm done." He concludes his message by encouraging other OLs who are feeling undervalued to quit the position, as there were "better" leadership positions on campus that they could pursue. Several OLs respond with messages similar to "you're right, I'm sick of this!" Not only surprised that Craig clearly lied about *quitting* the position when he was *fired*, Tara is also shocked to see that other OLs are affirming his message. Assuming that the message came from a place of frustration in an effort to retaliate against the Leadership Team, Tara does not know how to address this message. She wants to ask Maria for guidance on how to respond, but Maria is out sick for the day and not answering her phone.

Tara has fifteen minutes until the start of the team meeting. The Leadership Team's original plan was to notify the OLs at this meeting that Craig is no longer on staff without details about why. Knowing that the team has seen and responded to Craig's message in the group chat, Tara must figure out how to address this situation and is more inclined to indicate that Craig was let go. Tara is concerned that if she does not address the claims she will lose credibility with the rest of the team. She is also unsure about how much she can actually share with the team, and is concerned about how her students will react knowing she has seen the group messages.

What should Tara do?

STUDENT ORGANIZATIONS AND DUE PROCESS:
A SETTLED ISSUE?
LAURA BOEHME AND LOUISE MICHELLE VITAL

Commonwealth Community College (CCC) is a public community college in the rural Northwest serving approximately thirteen thousand full- and part-time students each year. Consistent with other higher education institutions, CCC has robust student activities and information technology (IT) units. One of the fundamental functions of the IT unit is to create and maintain student and employee email accounts, document storage, and access to educational systems needed for coursework. Commonwealth has a variety of student activity organizations that periodically request email accounts and document storage to support their function at the college. Lisa is the student activities adviser at CCC and adviser to the Associated Students of Commonwealth (ASC). Additionally, Lisa serves as her office's liaison with IT.

Kirsteen, the president of the Associated Students of Commonwealth, asked IT to create a generic email account, ASC@ccc.edu, for the four student government officials to use for official student government business. Although this practice was not typical, IT security vetted and determined it was a valid and reasonable request to have student government officers conduct business from this generic email rather than their own personal, school-issued email account. As such, Lisa, in her role as the student activities adviser/supervisor of ASC and liaison with the IT unit, was provided the email account login information to share with the students. She was required to sign a student privacy agreement that asked her to acknowledge she would maintain student privacy and ensure the security of account access and usage.

Within a few months of the new ASC email account being used, the Community Relations department received student complaints. Someone using the ASC@ccc.edu account was posting inflammatory gender-based and culturally insensitive comments to Facebook and Twitter. The complaints were reported to the Campus Public Safety (CPS) Department and the CPS director, Seth, who immediately began investigating the situation. He scoured the four ASC students' personal Facebook and Twitter accounts for information. Seth found posts by one student that raised considerable concern about the student's behavior and the personal safety of other students at CCC. No direct threats to students occurred, but the posts included links to White nationalist websites and references to violence against women and other ethnicities. First thing on Monday, Seth contacts Lisa as the adviser, asking for login access to ASC@ccc.edu and the offending student's CCC issued email account and document storage.

The college abides by FERPA and HIPAA policies, but does not have a formal policy regarding protection of CCC email and document storage accounts. Prior instances of student and employee email privacy have been brought to the attention of the IT chief information officer (CIO), Donna. Unfortunately, the CIO had not taken the concerns to the president or other policy committees seriously. Instead, Donna developed a written protocol regarding access to CCC email and data accounts. The protocol indicates that no party within or outside the college would be granted direct access to CCC student or employee email and data accounts without prior risk management and legal counsel review. This protocol has been shared with the college president and the heads of major units in the college, including CPS, student services (and the Student Activities Office), and IT without any resistance or apprehension. Thus, when Seth requests direct access to the email and data accounts, he should be aware that this request violates protocol. State-mandated open records requests require a form to be submitted from the requestor to the institution to obtain access to public institution-related email content but provides no ability for direct login access by college personnel to public email accounts.

Lisa likes Seth and does not want to frustrate the investigation but is concerned that direct access to a student's or a student organization's email accounts without prior legal review by CCC's risk management team may result in student privacy violations. Lisa is especially concerned because in her mind, students, and student organizations should have a reasonable expectation of due process and privacy from their higher education institution. Even if a student has potentially done something unethical or wrong, Lisa does not feel it is in her purview to allow access to account information without proper authority and approval. Lisa follows the IT protocol and tells the CPS director, Seth, that his requests for access are denied due to CCC student and data privacy practices until a legal review is conducted, which could take up to twenty-four hours. Seth indicates the investigation is at a critical stage and information contained in the emails and documents is imperative in determining who is posting from the account, and potentially making a case against the offending student. Additionally, he states the material found on the student's social media accounts is cause for granting immediate access due to the inflammatory nature of the content. He appeals to Lisa's duty as a college employee and student organization adviser to provide access to facilitate the work of CPS in resolving complaints against the college and protecting students. Again, Lisa explains the legal review protocol and refers Seth to her supervisor, Stephen, the vice president of student services, expecting Stephen's support. Seth becomes extremely angry, yells vehemently at Lisa, and threatens to escalate the request to his supervisor, the vice president of administration, and the president of the college. Lisa tells Seth she understands and follows the legal review protocol.

Seth immediately contacts Stephen, the vice president of student services, to lodge a complaint about ASC and Lisa. Seth asks Stephen for his support in obtaining immediate access to the email accounts to further his investigation. Stephen, unbeknownst to Lisa, concurs with Seth's rationale and agrees Lisa should provide Seth instantaneous access to the accounts. Stephen believes that ASC's use of a generic college issued email address is a privilege granted on behalf of the college and therefore should not fall under the same due process rules as email addresses issued to individual members of the college community. Because the student organization falls under the purview of his division, and Lisa as the adviser, Stephen sends an email in support of Seth's request to both Lisa and Donna, the CIO.

Mid-day Monday, Lisa, frustrated by Stephen's email, receives another call from Seth who states that the president is out of town, and Seth's supervisor, the vice president of administration, has given Seth verbal permission to access the student's and ASC accounts as part of his investigation. Lisa, concerned for her job, talks to the CIO, Donna, about the dilemma of ensuring student privacy while being pressured by college leaders to acquiesce to their authority. Donna validates that the vice president of student services has no authority to override IT's practices with regard to students/student organizations. The vice president of administration's verbal approval is also insufficient in light of the protocol, as the vice president of instruction, not the vice president of administration, has authority to act in the absence of the president. Lisa again informs Seth his request is denied until legal review concludes, which has not even been requested yet. Later on Monday, Lisa gets a call from the IT account management team who shares that Seth is standing in their offices and refuses to leave the premises until he is given direct access to the four ASC student accounts as well as the ASC generic email account. Per protocol, the IT staff are notifying Lisa as the adviser.

What should Lisa do?

NO ONE WOULD STEAL FROM A FUNDRAISER, RIGHT?
PAIGE MATZERATH

Lily is the director of student leadership and engagement at Shore University, a private institution with under two thousand students in New Jersey. Her position allows her to develop leadership programs, hold various fundraising events, and supervise Charlotte, who is the assistant director of student leadership and engagement. Charlotte has been the assistant director for over a year and absolutely loves her position. Her main priority is assisting Lily with various leadership development and fundraising programs, as well as overseeing the department's student workers. Charlotte is thankful that she has a great relationship with her boss; they collaborate equally on events, are constantly bouncing ideas off one another, and disclose personal information when necessary. Recently, Lily has expressed to Charlotte that there is tension in her personal life at home. Her husband was just laid off from his job and they are about to send their third child off to college. Lately, Lily has been acting differently, presumably due to the situation she has been dealing with at home. Typically Lily invites collaboration with Charlotte, however, lately Lily is quick to snap at Charlotte and is not asking for input when making final decisions. Charlotte feels horrible for everything Lily is going through. Charlotte plans to help her in any way possible since Lily has been so supportive of her since she started working in this position.

Currently, Lily and Charlotte are working together on a new type of fundraiser for the month of October to raise money for breast cancer research. The event will take place on a Friday where students will be able to come to the gymnasium for a night full of fun activities. There will be a performance by a local band who is donating their time, multiple bounce houses, different types of giveaways from free food to t-shirts, and various hands on crafts. Both Charlotte and Lily have been working hard to make this event possible.

The day before the fundraiser, Lily and Charlotte have a meeting to finalize the details. They realize that all the stations are covered by their student workers except the donation table where students give their donations in order to gain access to the event. Charlotte offers to help with the donation table since Lily needs to take care of a few last-minute requests. Charlotte is shocked when Lily snaps at her by saying she can handle the donation table on her own. Charlotte decides to brush off Lily's aggressive attitude, assuming Lily is overwhelmed with all the event logistics. On the bright side, Charlotte hopes that she will be able to gain more experience using her problem-solving skills during the actual event because she is typically assigned simple tasks.

The night of the event, Charlotte is thrilled about having more than a quarter of the school attend. Students continue to tell her that they are having a great time and would like more events like this on campus. After the night is over, Charlotte checks the tally of attendees at the registration table to see how many students attended. There was a total of 602 students, which means that if each student gave the minimum of the suggested two dollar donation then there should be at least $1,200. Since this was the first year they planned this event, Charlotte is overcome with joy because of the successful turnout. In addition, Charlotte is ecstatic with the anticipated amount raised, especially because her grandmother passed away from breast cancer two years ago.

After both Lily and Charlotte finished cleaning up, Charlotte makes a comment to Lily about how impressed she is with the number of attendees and how much more money they raised than expected. Lily brushes it off and says that they have not yet calculated the final total and should not jump to conclusions. "They didn't *have to* give the suggested amount, and not all of them did, so let's not get too excited," Lily says, sounding a bit irritated. Charlotte is taken aback by Lily's tone but decides to drop it, hoping that she will be in a better mood at work Monday morning.

On Monday, Lily and Charlotte meet to debrief the event. When discussing finances, Lily mentions that the total amount of money raised was $320 with the total number of attendees being 602. Charlotte is surprised that the amount is so low given the attendance. That means that almost half the students did not donate any money or participate in any of the raffles. According to Charlotte's calculations, the total should have been at least $800 higher than what Lily reported. At the end of the meeting, Charlotte goes back to her office and contemplates the situation. She knows that there was only one way to get into the event which meant students were obligated to enter through the registration table. In order to track students, they swiped their school ID card so she knows the attendance numbers are accurate. All things considered, the only plausible answer Charlotte can come to is that money was taken from the fundraiser total. Charlotte is disappointed in the outcome, especially since the event benefited a cause close to her heart. She cannot move forward without discussing the outcome of the event and figuring out who might have taken money from the amount raised. She wants to say something to Lily but she can't help wondering—what if Lily was the one to have taken the money considering her financial troubles at home?

What should Charlotte do?

CHALKBOARD CONTROVERSIES
REBECCA M. TAYLOR AND PAUL ROOT WOLPE

As a new fall semester began, Middle University launched a new program aimed at fostering a culture of integrity on campus. Middle University is a private residential institution that has encoded into its policies strong protections for free speech on campus. The integrity program was implemented by a collaborative cross-campus team with representatives from the faculty and various student affairs departments including residence life, orientation, and leadership programs as well as from a multidisciplinary academic center. Desiring to get the program started in a highly visible way that would spark robust dialogue on campus, the team decided to install large chalkboards across campus. They planned to pose a new prompt on some aspect of ethics and integrity each week, with the hope that they would solicit written responses and get the entire campus community thinking and talking about integrity.

A student affairs program coordinator, Lauren, took the lead on implementing this endeavor. She began by procuring free-standing chalkboards and the requisite permissions to have them placed around campus. She worked with other members of the team, including faculty, to develop a list of weekly prompts and guidelines for contributing to the chalkboards that aligned with the campus's open expression policies. Finally, she trained a team of undergraduate interns to help maintain the chalkboards and record their contents.

The chalkboards were installed over the summer prior to the start of the fall semester during a presidential election year. When students arrived on campus in August, they encountered the large chalkboards situated in numerous locations around campus, including residence and dining halls and highly trafficked pathways. Some prompts asked generally about community values, whereas others addressed controversial recent events that raised serious questions about how individuals should live together as a diverse and inclusive community. Examples included:

- Integrity at Middle University looks like . . .
- An obstacle to respectful dialogue at Middle University is . . .
- College students are impacting this election by . . .

The team decided to use the university's open expression policy, which strongly supports rights to free speech on campus, as a guide for monitoring the comments on the boards. Consequently, they regularly reviewed the boards for comments that violated university policies regarding conduct, discrimination, and harassment. Other than the responses that violated university policy, they allowed the boards to function as spaces for open expression. A sign next to each chalkboard noted that the boards would be erased on a weekly basis in order to add new prompts and that all comments would be archived before erasure.

Thousands of students, faculty, staff, and university visitors passed by these boards each day during the fall semester. They contributed to and saw a wide variety of responses to the prompts. Some responses were serious comments about ethical challenges on campus and how the university community could improve. Others contained political statements about the presidential candidates. Some expressed views about the campus values, whereas others offered criticisms of the university. And finally, many memorialized the recently killed captive gorilla Harambe (a popular meme at the time), whereas others asked that people stop with Harambe already.

Many of the contributions to the chalkboards were responsive to the national political climate at the time. That fall, the atmosphere surrounding the presidential election was particularly divisive both across the country and at Middle University. One of the candidates regularly called for the other candidate to be imprisoned, and popular political memes pitted groups against one another in ways that often questioned the humanity of the opposition. Many of the comments on the chalkboards reflected the exceedingly polarized political discourse at the time and included memes drawn from the political movements that were offensive to many members of the diverse campus community.

Seeking to remain consistent with their policy of respecting speech and erasing the boards in a content-neutral way only when adding new prompts (except in cases of speech that violated other campus policies regarding conduct, discrimination, and harassment), Lauren and her colleagues tried to manage these spaces on campus with the aims of respecting speech and fostering conversation about integrity on campus. When they saw that one prompt seemed to lead to more polarized or off-topic speech, they took a new tactic the subsequent week, all the while recognizing that the national political context was so present on campus that fostering meaningful discourse would be challenging.

Although the chalkboards were originally intended to spark conversations about ethics and integrity on campus, the nature of the contributions to the boards in the political context at the time created challenges. Given the extent of controversial, profane, and simply irrelevant comments on the boards, their visible presence began to raise questions about the relationship between open expression on campus and a shared responsibility to create a respectful community of care. The new integrity program aimed to value students' contributions but also to be a positive force for respectful engagement with difference on campus. These two goals seemed to be coming into conflict.

Partway through the fall semester, Lauren became increasingly aware that the chalkboards were becoming controversial on campus. One day, the situation escalated as she received two alarming reports. First, a member of the university's board of trustees had seen some alarming political content on the chalkboards and had called the university's president to express concern that these displays did not represent the university well. Second, she received an email from a student who was offended by a drawing of a contentious political cartoon on one of the chalkboards and wanted to report it as a bias incident. The email made it clear that because of the chalkboard contents, the student who reported it was not feeling safe or welcome on campus. After consultation with the concerned parties as well as internal deliberation with the committee, Lauren and her team decided to remove the chalkboards from campus in order to avoid any further controversial, offensive incidents.

However, after the chalkboards were removed, faculty and students concerned that open expression was being quashed on campus demanded their return. A group of student activists wrote an open letter claiming that their right to express their political views on campus, even if those views are offensive to others, was being diminished. This letter garnered national media attention, Middle University found itself under intense scrutiny, and Lauren and her team faced heated demands from across the university that the chalkboards be returned.

What should Lauren do?

WHAT HAVE I GOTTEN MYSELF INTO?
CHRISTINE PAJEWSKI AND MICHELLE J. BOETTCHER

Jessie—a White, cisgender woman, and a legacy in her sorority—recently completed her master's degree in student affairs at Omega State University and has accepted a full-time program coordinator position in Fraternity and Sorority Life (FSL) at Alpha State University (ASU). ASU is a predominantly White, mid-sized, public institution located in the Southeast. The total enrollment at ASU is about twenty thousand students and nearly 35 percent of the undergraduate student body is Greek affiliated. Additionally, some of the major donors to the institution pride themselves on their Greek affiliations. Though the Interfraternity Council and Panhellenic Council are the two larger Greek councils, ASU also has eight of the nine National Pan-Hellenic Council chapters and a Multicultural Greek Council. The NPHC and MGC organizations have each won national awards in the past two years for the dynamic ways they engage in community service and campus events as well as for the significant growth of these chapters as a means of fostering student engagement.

In the first semester, Jessie acclimated to her position as a program coordinator in the Office of Fraternity and Sorority Life. She met with current chapter leaders, advisors, and potential new members as ASU has deferred recruitment until the spring semester for all Greek organizations. In January, recruitment for both the Interfraternity Council and Panhellenic Council was held and Bid Day events for both larger councils occurred with no significant issues as new members joined the various organizations.

Jessie's nascent confidence from successful recruitment events is shattered when, at the beginning of March, news breaks that a Greek male first-year student unexpectedly died. She is brought into a number of meetings and given select details including that this occurred during a suspected hazing incident. A few days later, the student's name is released and the local media shares that he was a new member of Alpha Alpha Delta fraternity, an Interfraternity Council organization. Rumors begin to swirl that the student was forced to drink an entire bottle of hot sauce and consume other substances before his death. National media outlets descend on the ASU campus, looking for any individual willing to provide information regarding the tragic death of the student.

In reaction, Dr. Gray, the vice president for student affairs (who is not a member of a Greek organization) suspends all Greek life activities effective immediately. New member orientation activities are halted, and no organization is permitted to gather or host events. This is a shift from a previous VPSA (who was FSL-affiliated) regarding incidents on campus involving this same organization. In the previous incident, the organization was investigated due to a hazing report where the current members forced new members to stay up all night and recite facts about current members. The organization was allowed to continue activities during the time that the incident was being investigated because the nature of the incident was not as serious.

After the suspension of Greek life activities, Jessie is confused and in shock. She is horrified that a hazing-related death took place on her watch. To her knowledge, the FSL communities with whom she worked have abided by the strict no hazing policies, which she supported wholeheartedly. She has facilitated hazing prevention programming and is seen as a resource for students with concerns about potential hazing activities. She also provides workshops leading up to recruitment activities to provide approval for events and to ensure no hazing takes place during that time when potential new members are particularly vulnerable.

Further, while she understands the need, Jessie is frustrated that the focus on hazing this year has taken her attention away from her leadership development plan, which she believes will benefit the Greek system more. She has little time to focus on the assets of developing students because she is instead inundated in person, via email, on social media and over the phone with questions about the crisis. However, she tries to continue to forge ahead to provide leadership to members of the FSL community who are also struggling and confused. Together they work to plan new member intake events for the fall semester. However, the vice president for student affairs releases a new statement two days later: ASU's Board of Trustees will convene and vote on whether to disband the Greek system altogether. Jessie is blindsided by this information. Her supervisor provided her no information that this announcement was coming, rather she was told to direct all inquiries about the Greek system to the president's office. She is also instructed not to give any definitive answers to concerned constituents regarding the future of the Greek system at ASU. The announcement sends the already grieving students into crisis. Jessie too is reeling as, in addition to all the pressure and scrutiny she is facing, she suddenly also has worries about her job.

In reflecting on the past few days, Jessie decides to call a faculty member from her graduate program to discuss the situation. If Greek life at ASU is disbanded, Jessie's position will be terminated effective immediately. However, her experience as an affiliated member of a Greek organization and as a graduate assistant in the Office of Fraternity and Sorority Life in graduate school really fostered her passion for Greek life. In talking with the faculty member, he encourages Jessie to think about sharing her unique expertise as a Greek-affiliated person and insider to the situation. He suggests that it might make Jessie feel less helpless and like she has more agency over the situation. He also indicates that, if Jessie's job is terminated, having a thoughtful piece in the public domain would do a lot to help her chances of getting hired elsewhere. Jessie is confused; she's ordered not to speak publicly about the incident but wants to defend Greek life as a whole. Incidents like this are terrible but also rare; one incident does not define a group of organizations or the people in them as there are so many positive aspects to Greek life—from philanthropy to personal development.

What should Jessie do?

ADVISOR'S ANGUISH OVER ANONYMITY
JAMES JACKSON AND LAURA KANE

After completing her master's degree in college student personnel, Erica (she/her/hers) was excited to accept her first professional position serving as coordinator in the Office of Sorority and Fraternity Life at Southern State University (SSU). SSU is a predominantly White, public institution with an enrollment of 15,000 undergraduate students and a vibrant international sorority and fraternity community. The community consists of four councils: Interfraternity Council (IFC), Multicultural Greek Council (MCGC), National Pan-Hellenic Council (NPHC), and Panhellenic Association (PHA).

Erica's position involved serving as advisor to the PHA. Her role includes meeting regularly with the Panhellenic and sorority chapter leadership and advising on all areas of chapter management, including recruitment and new member education practices. Additionally, Erica works with other members of the Office of Sorority and Fraternity Life to develop hazing prevention programs. In her previous role as a graduate assistant in fraternity and sorority life at a different institution with all international organizations, Erica worked hard to overcome her apprehension and sense of inadequacy regarding her local sorority affiliation of not being "Greek enough" by becoming a great mentor and supporter of the sorority women on campus. At SSU, Erica's interaction with the members of PHA got off to a great start with a successful retreat, and the trust the students showed Erica as their advisor continued to grow throughout the fall semester.

In October, Erica received an anonymous letter alleging hazing within one of the PHA sororities. The vice president of student affairs, director of sorority and fraternity life, and director of student conduct also received the letter. The letter did not identify the organization but informed that, along with forced drinking of alcohol, new members of the sorority were branded by current members who performed a ritual on these new members and burned sorority letters into their skin. The language in the letter suggested it was written by an active member of the organization allegedly engaging in this dangerous behavior.

A meeting of university administration, legal counsel, and PHA chapter presidents was convened to make chapter leadership aware of the allegations. During the meeting, chapter presidents were reminded of the disciplinary and legal ramifications of hazing as well as their reporting obligations, and were encouraged to identify the organization. The vice president of student affairs advised the chapter presidents that if the responsible chapter came forward in forty-eight hours, the university would see that action as mitigation. Forty-eight hours passed without anyone stepping forward.

In the following days, Zoe, a sophomore member of the sorority Rho Eta Lambda, approached Erica regarding her concerns about the sorority, Sigma

Beta Mu, engaging in dangerous hazing practices. She claimed to have seen a brand on the lower back of her roommate, Megan, a sophomore member of Sigma, in the shape of a Greek letter "Sigma." Additionally, she had witnessed poor treatment of the organization's new members when walking across campus one night last year during "Hell Week." The poor treatment was described as active members screaming at new members and the new members being forced to perform exercises. Zoe felt obligated to report this information given the recent rumors surrounding the anonymous letter. Given the fact that PHA sororities were very competitive with one another, and that she obtained this information from her roommate, Zoe was quite fearful of being discovered as the source. She stated while she felt compelled to report this information, she only was comfortable with this information being used in an investigation on the condition that she could remain anonymous.

Through the conversation, Zoe also informed Erica that she was fairly confident that Megan authored the anonymous letter. Megan and Zoe became friends as first-year students; Megan encouraged Zoe to participate in recruitment in the first place. While both joined different sororities at the end of the process, Megan never told anyone that she had listed Rho as her first choice and was disappointed to be matched with Sigma in the end. From the beginning of the new member process, she never felt like she fully belonged in the chapter and was ashamed of the hazing she endured as a new member. Recently, Megan had confided in Zoe that she was questioning her involvement with the sorority and disclosed her desire to end the hazing practices of the new members now that she was a sophomore.

Sigma Beta Mu was the first sorority founded at Southern State University in 1939 followed shortly by the second sorority, Rho Alpha Phi, in 1941. Sigma and Rho were highly competitive with one another; much of the sorority and fraternity community culture was driven by these two organizations, as they were the center of the social scene. Members of both organizations often competed for prominent campus leadership positions and regularly faced off in intramural competition championships. During formal recruitment, they compete for the same new members and the chapters often submit petty recruitment violation complaints against one another.

The Sigma chapter leadership went out of their way to make Erica feel sincerely welcomed when she first started her role at Southern State. The women fully participated in all regularly scheduled meetings and even sought out her advice on many occasions. On the other hand, the Rho chapter leadership was hesitant to trust Erica, only ever meeting the basic expectations of the Office of Sorority and Fraternity Life.

Erica informed her supervisor of the information provided by Zoe, but withheld Zoe's name to maintain her trust. Based on the information provided by Erica, the Office of Student Conduct and Campus Police investigated the Sigma sorority by interviewing each of the current members, new members, and potential new members that left the recruitment process prior to initiation the previous year. The investigation, while thorough, failed to uncover any additional information as each student interviewed denied all the allegations and reported their experiences as positive.

Following the fruitless initial investigation, the director of student conduct approached Erica requesting that she provide the names of the students that provided her with information. Erica was informed that the student handbook required that allegations against student or student organizations be proven by a preponderance of evidence. Staff members were able to serve as witnesses during a hearing only if they had firsthand knowledge of an incident. The student handbook prohibited witnesses from relaying information of other individuals if that individual with firsthand knowledge was available to participate in the hearing.

Erica approaches Zoe to encourage her to come forward and report what she knows, explaining the student handbook policy does not allow Erica to provide a statement on her behalf during a hearing. Zoe refuses. Erica knows that the investigation is doomed without Zoe's report.

What should Erica do?

CHOOSING SOCIAL JUSTICE OR CONCERNS OF
THE BOARD OF TRUSTEES AND THE LEGISLATURE
JESSE BENNETT

Angelina Grey, a recent graduate with a master's degree in student affairs administration, has taken a job as the assistant director for civic engagement in the student life office at Peachtree Community College, a large, urban community college in the heart of downtown Atlanta. The college's total enrollment is over twenty thousand students. The mission of the community college is to meet students wherever they are in their educational goals, so inevitably it is a gateway to a diverse population of international, minority, low-income, and first-generation students. More than 55 percent of the total enrollment identify as persons of color. Therefore, Angelina places a strong emphasis on the Social Change Model of Leadership Development and cultural competence. Ultimately, her belief and professional philosophy is that building students' awareness of positionality, privilege, and inequality will enhance students' learning and development of self-awareness and will facilitate positive social change at the institution and in the community.

Students at Peachtree Community College are used to participating in programming that celebrates differences, educates them about privilege and cultural norms, and fosters an environment where they feel like they are a part of a community. Recently, Angelina held a discussion panel series that explored diverse perspectives and issues based on religion, race, and sexuality. It was well received by students, and campus administrators have always been supportive of her creativity in program ideas and student development techniques.

Three days ago, Raymond Kadeem Jefferson, an unarmed African American man, was fatally shot by Gregory Williamson, an African American Atlanta city police officer. Over the past few days, the shooting has been generating both peaceful protests, including a "lay-in" at nearby Atlanta State University, and violent riots in downtown areas very close to Peachtree Community College. The college has not sent out any formal statements to students about the shooting or the riots that are occurring right up the street from the campus.

Angelina is thinking about inviting the local police department to campus to have a discussion with students about society's view of the police and interacting with law enforcement officials. She discussed the idea with several student leaders from a variety of student groups. The president of the Black Student Association hears about the event and wants to bring in leaders from the NAACP and activists from the Black Lives Matter movement. Students propose that the discussion be in the format of a forum to discuss police brutality. They also want to invite participants outside of the Peachtree Community College community and the media. Angelina thinks this is a great idea that will be well received by the community, like the peaceful "lay-in" that occurred at Atlanta State University.

A day before the event, the vice president of student affairs asks to meet with Angelina about the program. He indicates that several members of the college's board of trustees and the state legislature are unhappy about students being exposed to ideas by the members of the Black Lives Matter movement, and they feel that this group has been influencing the city riots. The state legislature is threatening to cut funding. The vice president thinks that the program is a good idea but wants Angelina to figure out how to make it happen without upsetting the board of trustees. They indicate that they do not want the media, representatives from the Black Lives Matter movement, or non–Peachtree Community College members on campus for the event. Angelina knows that most of the college's board of trustees are White men and may not understand the importance of this event for the institution's students of color.

Angelina leaves the meeting and thinks about seeking advice from her supervisor, the director of student life, about how to best support the students with their program and still comply with the request of the vice president for student affairs, board of trustees, and state legislature. She decides not to, because she believes her supervisor will want to appease these higher powers. Angelina feels like no one is advocating for the students' desires and that her position exists to support the students' goals for social change and not the interests of the board or the state. Angelina also knows of a loophole in the college's policy on free speech and public assembly, and is considering recommending that the students have the activists from the Black Lives Matter movement register to use this space, since the college recognizes the right to assemble and to petition the government by outside organizations and agencies. As a new professional at Peachtree Community College, Angelina feels torn about whether or not she should try harder to reassure her vice president and supervisor that the students' event will not have negative consequences for the college or if she should help the students work around the system.

What should Angelina do?

BUT I WAS SUCH A CHILD
KEVIN J. BAZNER AND GREGORY FINK

After a few years working in student affairs at Hawthorne State University (HSU), Alex was recently promoted to a position advising the student government association (SGA). The SGA is one of the largest and most prominent organizations on campus. HSU is a large institution with a predominantly White student enrollment and often characterized as socially conservative. Over the past few years, both the SGA and HSU have had several high-profile incidents attracting local and national media attention on issues of diversity, race, and inclusion. After a series of racial incidents on campus, an anti-racism student group called "No Hate @ Hawthorne State" emerged to engage in deeper conversations and demand action of the university regarding the racial climate. The organization would regularly hold campus rallies, meet with HSU administrators, or post about race-related issues on campus.

Alex has been at HSU for five years and is aware of the racial climate issues within the SGA and the university from his prior organizational advising roles. Through programming and ongoing advising conversations, Alex has worked to address what he perceives as a sometimes-unwelcoming climate within previous organizations and areas he advised. Now, working with the broad scope of SGA, Alex is anxious to work with an organization that could make a broader impact on campus education. He is particularly excited to work with the current student body president, Jessica, who ran on a platform of diversity and inclusion. Jessica has had a long history as a top HSU student leader, preparing her to fill the role as voice of the student body. Due to her previous student leadership roles, she also gained the admiration of many senior university administrators over the years, including David, the director of public relations for the university.

As Alex walked into his office one morning, he was met by one of his coworkers, Destiny. "Alex, have you heard about this Facebook screenshot circulating about something Jessica posted a few years ago?" Destiny asked. Immediately, Alex remembered how No Hate @ Hawthorne State posted a screenshot of another student during the previous year involved in a campus leadership role using a racial slur, leading the student leader to issue an apology and resign from their leadership position. Surprised to hear about any negative connotation regarding Jessica, Destiny showed Alex a Facebook screenshot of a fourteen-year old Jessica using the N-word in a social media conversation with a schoolmate. Adding to Alex's surprise, there were rumors the No Hate group would unveil this information during an upcoming public forum.

Alex immediately texted Jessica to meet with him. When she arrived at his office, Alex informed her of what he had just learned. Jessica began to cry, "But, I've learned so much since then. I was such a child," she stated. Alex shared his viewpoint that the high-profile nature of her student leadership position and her diversity and inclusion platform could cause a lot of confusion on campus and that her actions moving forward could greatly impact how others perceive her dedication to diversity and inclusion. He also encouraged Jessica to be mindful of the impact her words, even from the past, and the impact her identity as a White woman had on the racial climate of the university. Jessica asked Alex, "Do you think I should resign?" Alex did not think a resignation was necessarily the best course of action for this scenario. Instead, he advised Jessica to use her platform to engage the broader HSU campus community in a conversation about her personal growth, learning about issues of racism and becoming more committed to social change.

Jessica and Alex began to identify which university leadership could provide the most helpful guidance to make meaning of the scenario. As Alex worked to inform his fellow colleagues within student affairs administration, Jessica contacted the person who might need to know the scenario the most and could provide the most support in communication efforts—David. He functioned as the chief communications officer of the university and a primary consultant to the university president for media relations. His relationship with Jessica was strong since the beginning of her term as SGA president. David's prior experience with campus incidents would provide additional guidance and support.

The next day Jessica met with Alex to discuss what she and David talked about. "David and I developed a plan. I am going to directly contact the person who sent the screenshot. I know she is one of the leaders of No Hate @ Hawthorne State. I want to go straight to the source and apologize. David thinks that just a sincere apology from me should help clear the air. I want to talk about my journey of how I got to who I am today and emphasize that I am committed to creating an inclusive campus community. We really think it will help. What do you think about our plan?"

This was quite a different plan than he expected. It was difficult for Alex to respond. Alex thought to himself, "Where was the ownership of her actions? What about the discussion they had had about her Whiteness and other identities? Where was the rebuilding of damage to those hurt other than the person with the screenshot?" It seemed like David and Jessica were trying to keep conversations as isolated as possible to save HSU from grabbing more media headlines about the campus racial climate. Alex responded to Jessica, "Yesterday, we talked about using your leadership platform to have a larger discussion about racism and your commitment to diversity on campus. I don't know if this plan takes into consideration all of what we discussed and incorporates the foundation of your leadership campaign. Was that intentional?"

Alex trusted David and Jessica, but it seemed like there were too many gaps in this plan. Continuing his processing, Alex thought, "Maybe Jessica explained the scenario to David differently?" Alex debated contacting David directly to explain the situation and advocate for a more educational approach to the situation. Yet, he knew David would prioritize his public relations lens, not student development. Alex understood that Jessica being vulnerable and taking ownership of her actions would be difficult, but Alex saw this as a larger educational opportunity for Jessica and the entire university community. It could be a platform for larger conversations about diversity and inclusion, and particularly impactful coming from a campus leader like Jessica. He wished more could be done.

What should Alex do?

VOLUNTOURISM
JESSE SIMMONS AND MICHELLE J. BOETTCHER

The excitement of being in their first full-time role at the University of Faithful Service (UFS) consumed Doug (they/them/theirs) on their first day of work in June. Doug just graduated with their master's in a student affairs program and had accepted a job in service learning at this small, private, Jesuit institution in the Northeast. Doug has been dedicated to this work since they were a high school student and is excited to have the chance to do this work at UFS. Doug's philosophy of service learning centers on the communities being served even though they have seen a number of programs that focus more on the students participating in service projects instead.

UFS is very proud of its alternative breaks program, and frequently boasts that over a third of the student body participates in the program during their time at the institution. The program is funded through student fees, a contribution from the vice president for student affairs' office, and by private donors that sponsor specific experiences. The vice president for student affairs (VPSA), an alumnus of UFS, often recalls her experience with the alternative breaks program when she speaks to students at events.

Part of Doug's new job responsibilities are to coordinate, implement, and assess the alternative breaks program at UFS which mostly occur during the winter and spring breaks. In a meeting with their supervisor, Doug asks what has been done in the past with these programs, and Layla, their supervisor, explains that historically, the "success" of these programs as defined by the institution has focused on the number of students who go on the trips and the number of hours of service completed. Additionally, students determine their own learning outcomes and journal during their travel to provide a forum for documenting and reflecting on how they are working to achieve the outcomes they have chosen for themselves. Finally, the service learning coordinator has always done a follow-up interview with the site host(s) about their perceptions of the program. This feedback is almost exclusively satisfaction-based in terms of work completed and the relationships developed during the break trips.

The VPSA also spends a lot of time with Doug's supervisor talking about where the trips are going this year. The trips go to a different location each semester. Past locations have included New Orleans, Los Angeles, New York City, the Bahamas, Chicago, and Seattle. The program has developed a reputation for choosing tourist destinations when identifying service sites. Students sometimes go to the cities a few days early or stay a few days after the trip for additional sightseeing at their own expense.

In addition to being focused on the student participant experience rather than community impact, there is very little preparation and education in advance of travel, and there are no concerted debriefing efforts following the trip other than two evening conversations during the trip itself. Students talk about their lives being "transformed" as a result of the trip, but there is no follow up or assessment done in any formal sort of way to see what lasting impact the experience has on student participants. Similarly, there is no follow up with communities served or organizations with which UFS has partnered to see what the longer-term impact (positive or negative) is for the service site.

When they interviewed, Doug shared they would like to build deeper and more sustained relationships with specific communities rather than planning trips based on where students want to travel. Ideally, Doug would like to develop ongoing partnerships with two or three specific communities and provide recurring service to those sites. Eventually they even hope that there might be additional partnerships with academic programs—education, engineering, city and regional planning, and so forth—depending on the needs of each site. In this way a collaborative partnership can be developed to engage with residents as experts and partners in order to pursue solutions they themselves provide for issues and areas of concern.

Doug's assistantship in their master's program was in an office that had a national reputation for excelling in this work. Informed by that experience, Doug would like to build a course for the term of the travel that engages participants in issues of privilege and an examination of socially just models of service as well as formal debriefing and student presentations following the travel. They have identified a location in an impoverished community in a rural setting. Doug's hope is to return to this site for several years to partner with a county organization working to provide support to LGBTQ+ youth in the area. There have been several suicides/suicide attempts by LGBTQ+ junior and senior high school students in the past six months, so there is clearly a need for this support.

When the VPSA sees Doug at a campus event and asks about this year's trip, Doug shares their hopes and how excited they are to build a more sustained relationship with the county organization and the specific community and students. The VPSA says, "I like the idea of serving the youth, but the location isn't very exciting. Maybe you could find something similar in a place more people would like to go." Another colleague walks up and starts another conversation with the VPSA, who excuses herself to talk to the other person.

What should Doug do?

LADY LUCK
CHRISTOPHER L. GIROIR

Danielle is excited to embark on her second year as the coordinator of student activities at her alma mater. The small, public, liberal arts institution where Danielle works is known for its strong academic programs and even stronger co-curricular experience for students. In her role, Danielle is working with some amazing student organizations and oversees the fraternities and sororities on campus. One of the first events Danielle's office sponsors before the fall semester begins is the campus involvement fair, where mostly first-year students get an opportunity to learn more about what the college has to offer outside of the classroom. During the event, Danielle and several juniors and seniors meet and interact with lots of new students and hear about many of the typical questions, concerns, and excitement these students are experiencing.

Allison, Danielle's cousin, is a first-year student from a small, rural community and is excited about starting her collegiate career. As an only child, Allison is very close to her family and is thrilled to be accepted into the college where Danielle works. A bonus is her proximity to her hometown. She feels fortunate to have received one of the state's tuition scholarships generated from the state-managed casino and lottery program. Being from a single-parent home, receiving the scholarship allows Allison to pay her tuition and fees and not put her family in financial distress. Money always has been very limited for Allison, but she appears to have found a way with the scholarship and student loans to pay her expenses in school, plus keep some money for an occasional fun weekend.

Throughout her life, Allison dealt with judgmental glances from others and had to make excuses for why she did not always have the money to participate in school activities. Now in college, she is concerned that people will continue to judge her for being from a small, rural community and not having the financial means that she sees in her peers. Danielle assured her this college was very welcoming and shared with her that many of the student organizations on campus are free or low cost to join. Pride overtook Danielle as Allison shared with her that she was interested in joining the same sorority as Danielle, who now serves as an active sorority alumna. Danielle introduced Allison to Brittany, who served as the fundraising co-chair for her sorority, and the two women talked about the college and ways to get involved on campus. Over the next few weeks, the two women kept in touch and really began to form a friendship that eventually led to the women becoming roommates. Brittany is from an affluent family and she has full financial support from her parents. A second-year student who is popular with her classmates, Brittany welcomes a connection with Allison as a way to escape from her sometimes dramatic friendship circle. Allison, shy and quiet, enjoys how Brittany encourages her to put herself out there.

Danielle is hopeful living on campus and living with Brittany will help Allison "break out of her shell." Additionally, Danielle and Brittany would love to see Allison join their sorority, so they invited her to attend a fundraising event that also focused on new member recruitment. Although Allison had a great time at the event, she soon realized the financial commitment associated with being a sorority member, which dashed her dreams of joining the sorority. Allison was embarrassed to tell Danielle and Brittany she did not have the money to join a sorority, so she was determined to find a way to be part of the Greek community on her own.

The following week, Allison stopped by Danielle's office to talk about sorority recruitment—how she was interested in possibly participating in the selection process but fearful she may not have the funds to pay the recruitment fee. Allison asked Danielle if there was a way to get around the sorority "recruitment" fees. Danielle told Allison that although she could not remove the fee, she would make a special exception and allow the payment to be made in two installments, with the first payment due forty-eight hours from the time she signed up for recruitment and the balance due the following week. Allison was appreciative and left the office stating she had a way to pay the first installment by the deadline to participate in the recruitment process.

Later that week, Brittany meets with Danielle to discuss a situation with the sorority. Brittany shares how some of the money collected from the fundraising event, which was being stored in her residence hall room, was missing and she had suspicions Allison may have taken it and used it at a casino. Danielle asks Brittany to explain, and Brittany shares that she thinks Allison may have gambling issues because she often sees used lottery tickets on her dresser and overhears frequent conversations about casino trips. Brittany also witnessed Allison bringing back large casino winnings to their room from different gambling adventures, and it seemed as though her roommate quickly turned to gambling as a fast way to earn cash. One night after the fundraising event, as Allison was leaving the room, Allison shared with Brittany she felt "lady luck" was on her side and hoped to score a big cash jackpot at the casino to pay off a bill that was coming due. Unfortunately, it was not a good trip to the casino and Allison lost all her money. Brittany further states Allison went back to the casino the next day because she told her she "borrowed" some money. Upon hearing this statement, Brittany became suspicious and assumed her roommate may have "borrowed" some money from her or from the money that was collected from the fundraiser. Brittany and the fundraising co-chair decided to count the money collected and discovered the amount of money in the fundraising jar did not match the amount they believed was collected at the event. Brittany assumed Allison had taken the missing money and gambled with it. Brittany, who is scared and angry that something like this could happen, takes a deep breath and tells Danielle she believes Allison was involved with the missing money. She says, "I know I should report this to the police, but I came to you first. Do you think I should call the police?"

Danielle thanks Brittany for coming to see her and encourages Brittany to talk to Allison about the missing money before taking any additional steps. Danielle shares that she also feels the need to act, especially because she is worried about her cousin. She asks if Brittany would be okay if Danielle discussed the situation with colleagues to get some perspective. Brittany indicates that she is fine with whatever Danielle needs to do with the information. Brittany assures Danielle that she will keep Danielle appraised of any developments.

In her office, Danielle is left trying to decide what to do because she does not want to put her cousin, Allison, into an awkward situation, yet she also knows she cannot let this situation go unaddressed. Typically, Danielle would have referred this type of issue to the dean of students, but she's concerned about the embarrassment that this situation might cause her cousin, and quite frankly, she's concerned about how it may reflect on her. Before she leaves that day, Danielle reviews her notes and reflects upon past conversations with both Brittany and Allison as she starts to decide how to proceed to the next step.

What should Danielle do?

NAVIGATING ROLES: ADMINISTRATOR, EDUCATOR, AND ADVOCATE
JON DOOLEY

Activate, a student group affiliated with one of the social identity centers at Prominent University (a private, nonprofit, nationally renowned university) has been having robust conversations about national issues surrounding their lives as students, their focus as a student organization, and the work of the office to support students with historically marginalized identities. Over the past few weeks the group has been talking about what they can do to raise awareness on campus and how the office can support them. Although the politicians for state and national elections have talked about similar issues—and there are clear partisan dividing lines—the students haven't been overtly partisan in their conversations and they seem more interested in advocacy and awareness than involvement in political campaigns. James, the assistant director who co-advises the organization with a faculty member, has been involved in the conversations and is supportive of the group. The issues of concern to Activate are also a passionate interest of James's as well.

In the past week, as Activate planned its awareness efforts, the students started talking about decisions, policies, and practices on campus that are related to students with marginalized identities. After their most recent organization meeting, a group of students stayed after and were talking with James and their faculty advisor, Dr. Jordan, about the things happening on campus. During the conversation, the tone shifted from interest in the national issues to frustration that the university isn't doing more. They questioned the university leadership and pointed to specific university actions (and inaction) that they believe exacerbate the concerns on campus. They talked about shifting the upcoming events from merely an awareness campaign to a campus demonstration against the university practices. The students asked Dr. Jordan and James if they support the work of Activate and if they can trust them to be advocates with the university administration. Both Dr. Jordan and James respond that they are supportive advocates and the students know that Dr. Jordan has been active with demonstration and protest movements throughout his career. James participated in a few demonstrations/rallies as a student, but as he responded to the students that they can trust him as an advocate, he privately wondered to himself about his role with students in a campus demonstration.

Since that meeting, the debate among the students has erupted and they are becoming increasingly energized in their rhetoric and tone. Discussion about what needs to be done has become more heated, with differences of opinion among the students about whether the organization should work with the administration or take a stronger stance of protest against the administration. The students don't exactly have accurate information about the university decisions and campus administrators they are most upset about, but James isn't sure if he knows all the details either, nor how much information he can share. James is still relatively new to the institution and has been working hard to develop positive relationships and earn the students' trust, and he isn't sure whether or not to tell the students that some of the things they are most energized about may be wrong for fear of getting too involved in their internal conflict and alienating some of the students.

The student voices calling for protest are growing louder and gaining support. Some of the students in Activate are also involved in one of the campus political organizations and they see this as an opportunity to help university students become more politically active, take stronger positions, and practice the civic engagement that the university seems to promote. They want to link Activate's official awareness events and unofficial protest activities to the campus campaigns for political candidates speaking out on these issues at the state and national level. Some students in the group disagree with these approaches, but they seem to be in the minority. The students who disagree with what is unfolding ask James to help intervene with the other members. Although James isn't sure the protest strategy will be effective, the executive officers seem resolute in their decision to proceed in that direction.

As the conversations among the students around the office are becoming more heated, political, and partisan, it seems that most of the people who drop by the office and get involved in the discussion agree strongly with the positions, if not the approach, being taken by the majority. As usual, Chris, the administrative assistant, hears most of the conversations and is very aware of what is going on. Sometimes the students involve Chris in the conversations, asking for his thoughts, but Chris isn't sure how to respond. Although he really likes the students and is supportive of them, Chris believes their limited life experiences suggest some holes in their thinking and wonders whether the students have thought about the consequences of their decisions to protest. Furthermore, James seems to be managing the situation and Chris is concerned about how raising a contradictory perspective within the office will be received. In addition, Chris's personal political viewpoints don't align with the party and candidates the students (and it seems like the rest of the staff) want to support. In general, the office doesn't really feel like the place to talk politics and Chris is concerned about raising an opposing viewpoint because of how students and colleagues might respond as the rhetoric has been heating up. In general, he has become more uncomfortable with the work environment as a result of all the activity over the past few weeks.

Meanwhile, it has become increasingly clear that Activate intends to protest Fall Fury, an event planned in conjunction with the upcoming launch of the university's new comprehensive fundraising campaign. This jointly planned event by student government, student activities, and university advancement will be a high-profile university activity, attended by students, faculty and staff, senior staff, trustees, and donors. The students planning the protest are using Activate's GroupMe and listserv accounts to spread the news. They have prepared a list of demands for the university and have drafted a petition about the national issues involved. They have asked James and Dr. Jordan to support them by signing the petition. James is hesitant to do so, but the students have indicated strongly that if he supports the students and the conversations they've had to this point, the decision to sign the petition should be an easy one. They point to Dr. Jordan and the dozens of other faculty members who have already agreed to sign.

During today's office staff meeting, Activate's official awareness campaign and the unofficial protest, petition, and list of demands is first on the agenda. Michele, the director of the office, has been aware of the official organization activities and is supportive of the students and James, but is not aware of the unofficial protest, political rally, and list of demands. During the meeting Michele shares that the assistant vice president who oversees student life called her asking about rumors that students affiliated with Michele's office are planning to disrupt the student campaign launch event they have been working for months to plan. And, earlier this morning, the Office of Community Relations sent Michele an email indicating they got a report from an official with a local political party that there will be a rally on campus on behalf of candidates for office, asking for the location to include with a press release they are sending. In between meetings, Michele's supervisor asked about the situation and requested an update for the vice president for student affairs, since they had been asked by members of the president's cabinet about rumors that students are planning a demonstration. Feeling overwhelmed and in the dark by all these requests, during the staff meeting Michele asks the staff to talk about what they know about the situation and how they should respond. James and Chris aren't exactly sure what to say and Michele wonders how to simultaneously support the students, staff, and their colleagues on campus. Political and civic engagement is a value of the institution, but this seems to be getting really messy, and Michele increasingly feels like this is becoming a high-stakes situation.

What should James do?

LADIES' NIGHT
KEVIN M. COOK

For three years, Greg has been the student activities advisor at Mehlville College, a private, liberal arts college in the Pacific Northwest with 1,800 students. Working in student activities at the University Center is his first full-time job after completing graduate school. As a part of his responsibilities, he advises the "Late Nite at the UC" events. These are events that are designed to provide involvement and programming opportunities to students during the weekends as a substance-free option. The Late Nite at the UC events are planned by a subcommittee of the Student Activities Board.

The Student Activities Board (SAB) is a relatively diverse group of student leaders, including students from underrepresented racial identities, international students, and various gender and sexual identities. This diversity is reflective of the population of Mehlville as a whole due to the administration's extensive diversity recruitment strategies. Once a month, the entire SAB comes together to share ideas and upcoming events. This meeting is led by the two SAB co-chairs, one of who is Olivia. Greg and his supervisor, Karen, also attend the meetings as advisors to the group. Karen serves as the director of student involvement at Mehlville and has been in that role for seventeen years. Individually, Greg and Karen also divide advising responsibilities for each subcommittee of the SAB.

At the monthly meeting, the chairs of the Late Nite committee, Stephen and Jessica, share a new program idea they call "Ladies' Night." They explain that the group would host manicures and pedicures in collaboration with the local cosmetology school, chair massages, and a variety of crafts. They would also like to show the movie *Bridesmaids*. Many students on the board were very excited about this idea. Olivia, one of the co-chairs for SAB, was so excited that she suggested adding mocktails to the event and making it even bigger.

As Greg looks around the room he notices that a few of the students are silent, particularly those who identify as male. Sarah, one of the co-chairs of the diversity programming subcommittee, asks, "Do you think that this program is representative of all of our students or would appeal to most students?"

Jessica quickly dismisses Sarah's comment by saying, "If we try to please everyone, we will never do any programs."

Sarah continues to challenge Jessica and the program proposal. "We get our money from student fees, all students! It doesn't seem right to intentionally exclude students from the programs."

At this point Karen steps in. She is the subcommittee advisor for Late Nite. She says, "This type of program has happened in the past and there didn't seem to be an issue, but maybe the Late Nite committee could take some time to consider how they want to move forward."

Greg notices that Sarah continues to seem frustrated. Greg also feels somewhat uneasy about Karen's response but doesn't want to undermine her authority in front of the students. The meeting proceeds with other subcommittees making their reports with little incident.

The next day, Greg continues to feel conflicted about the events of the night before. Greg has seldom disagreed with Karen. He appreciates her supervisory style, years of experience, and connection to the students. He considers her a mentor. He decides that he needs to talk to Karen about the issues the students raised and his own thoughts. He pops into Karen's office and asks her if she has time to talk about last night's meeting. Karen says, "Sure."

Greg starts the conversation by explaining to Karen, "I see where Sarah is coming from with her concerns about the event." He then says, "I also feel like this event might not be as inclusive as it could be and I want to encourage the students to reconsider."

Karen quickly responds, "I have advised this group for many years and as the subcommittee advisor for Late Nite, it is my role to provide them guidance. I see no major issues with this event. The last time a similar event was done, more than two hundred students attended, and no one raised any concerns. That is a success in my book. As advisors, it is not our job to tell the students what to do. This is their organization and it is ultimately their decision."

Greg is taken aback by Karen's response. Somewhat at a loss for words, he thanks Karen for her time and returns to his office.

Later that day as Greg is working in his office, Sarah knocks on the door and asks if he has time to chat. Greg invites her in. Sarah proceeds to share her frustrations with the events of the previous evening's SAB meeting. She says, "I don't feel like Jessica was listening to me. She was defensive and didn't take my concerns seriously. I also didn't appreciate Karen supporting her position. I think that Karen is part of the problem. She dismissed me just like Jessica did, and because she's the advisor she gave them an excuse to continue the program even though I had concerns." Sarah indicates that she is considering ways to get Karen removed as the advisor of Student Activities Board, maybe by starting a social media campaign to call her out on her "old-school and exclusive views." Sarah indicates that if Karen had a "wake-up call" maybe she would realize that times have changed.

What should Greg do?

WHERE DO YOU LIVE?
AMBER N. RACCHINI

Mike is an assistant director in the Student Leadership and Engagement Office (SLEO) at Sherman State University (SSU). SSU is a mid-sized, public, urban institution located in the Midwest. Among Mike's responsibilities are to oversee the Student Government Association (SGA) and Student Activities Committee (SAC). The SLEO is in the Student Union building which is situated in the center of campus. The Student Union is open from 6:00 am to 11:00 pm while classes are in session. The Student Union includes office space for the SLEO staff, office space for SGA and SAC, campus programming space, dining facilities, a fitness center, and locker rooms.

Mike is also responsible for working with SAC to design and facilitate campus-wide events; thus, he is often in his office late at night. The SAC has five executive board members and Mike serves as their advisor. He meets weekly with the board to provide logistical support and guidance for the campus programs they want to implement. Since Mike's office is beside the SAC office, it is common for him to see the executive board members several times a week; therefore, he has developed a strong rapport with these students. Members of the executive board have a key to the SAC office and can use it whenever the Student Union is open.

Brad is the vice president of SAC and has been serving on the executive board for the past year. Brad lives in an off-campus apartment and his mother helps him pay rent. Earlier this year, Brad's mother lost her job and is no longer able to help with his rent. After a few months of struggling to make ends meet, Brad was evicted from his apartment. Brad was too embarrassed to talk to his friends about his situation and did not know where to turn for help. He knew there was a homeless shelter a few miles from campus but wasn't sure how to access their services or how he would make it to and from campus. Since there were only a few weeks before the end of the semester, Brad decided to move into the SAC office. He utilized his key to enter the office before the building closed at night. He was able to use the locker room to shower and get ready for the day. Although the other executive board members were giving Brad a hard time about spending so much time at the office, they were unaware that he was living there.

One night after the Student Union closed, Mike had to enter the building to grab a file for a report he was preparing for the dean of students. When he walked down the hallway to his office, he thought he heard noises coming from the SAC office. He opened the door and was surprised to see Brad laying on the floor in a sleeping bag listening to music. Brad was startled by Mike's entry into the office. He jumped up and immediately started to explain his situation. After sharing his story, he asked Mike to forget this ever happened, reminding Mike that the semester was almost over.

What should Mike do?

INAPPROPRIATE USE OF INFLUENCE
EMELIA DUNSTON AND LAURA PETRUS

Taylor just completed her first year as a new professional within the Office of Student Involvement at a mid-sized public university in the Southeast with approximately thirteen thousand students. A vacancy recently opened on the university's Programming Fee Allocation Committee and her supervisor nominated her to serve as a voting member on behalf of the office. Since she has been looking for additional ways to expand her reach on campus and form new connections, Taylor eagerly accepted the role.

This committee has been led by Toni Robins, the associate vice president for student affairs. It is composed of representatives from Residence Life, Campus Recreation, Intercultural Affairs, Student Government Association, Student Involvement, Wildcat Programming Board, Graduate Student Association, Student Athlete Advisory Council, and Faculty Senate. All members of the committee have voting privileges except for the chair. This individual is only allowed to vote in the event of a tie. Each semester, every enrolled student pays an activity fee of $110 that is earmarked for programs designed to enhance and enrich campus life. This committee is tasked with allocating the full amount collected, approximately $2,860,000 annually. All registered student organizations and student affairs departments supported by this fee are required to submit a funding request and present their proposed operating budget for the next fiscal year to the Allocation Committee every April. Funding is not guaranteed, because every year the amount requested exceeds the amount of funding available. The committee typically reviews requests from thirty registered student organizations and student affairs departments. Presentations take place across three days toward the end of April. Each area is allotted twenty minutes to complete their presentation before the committee. The committee discusses and votes on the proposed funding request after each presentation.

On the second day of presentations, the university's Spirit Group presented their proposed budget. The purpose of the Spirit Group is to support university athletics and represent the university in the community. For the upcoming year, the group has requested an increase in funding—approximately $1,000—to cover the cost of organization t-shirts, to be distributed at events to entice students to attend more basketball games. The group was created by the Division of Student Affairs but moved to the Athletic Department five years ago. This group does not receive any financial support from the Athletic Department and relies on funding from the Programming Fee to operate, which has been a point of contention for the AVP since the transition was completed back in 2013. Toni argued for Athletics to take full financial ownership of the program if it were to leave the division, but the athletic director was able to convince the university president that funding should continue to come from the Programming Fee.

During their presentation, Taylor noticed atypical behavior from Toni—sitting with arms folded and rolling her eyes during portions of the presentation. Toni did not reference the application materials when asking questions and seemed more critical of these students than she was with any of the other organizations that presented previously. During deliberations, Toni was also more vocal than normal about this group's request, deeming some expenditures as unnecessary and wasteful. Yet, other organizations had requested the same items and she made no objections to giving them the funds. Taylor and the other committee members were leaning toward approving the request but once Toni shared her opinion, it caused several members to reconsider their decision. The committee became deadlocked on the funding vote, which forced Toni to cast the final vote, in which she voted to deny the funding increase.

The next day, Taylor contacted her colleague in Campus Recreation who was a returning member of the committee to gauge his impression of the chair's affinity toward the Spirit Group. He shared, "Toni does not hide her dislike of the Spirit Group and this has been going on for some time. The last person who tried to push back against Toni on behalf of the Spirit Group was not asked to be on the committee the next year. I've learned that life is easier on this committee if you go along with what Toni wants and don't rock the boat." Taylor is concerned that Toni has used her influence inappropriately to sway the committee's decision and has compromised the integrity of this process by unfairly penalizing the Spirit Group.

What should Taylor do?

DISCLOSURE OR DISMISSAL
ANN E. WENDLE AND RICHARD A. STEVENS

Middle States University is a mid-sized liberal arts institution enrolling seven thousand undergraduate students and one thousand graduate students. The university is in the suburbs of Washington, DC, and regularly uses the city for programs and services for students. MSU is known for their commitment to diversity and social justice and has won state awards for their comprehensive programs and services around sexual orientation and race initiatives.

Morgan Sattlemyer is the assistant director of the Disability and Equity Resource Center at MSU. She processes evaluations and requests for accommodations for all students who register with the office. Morgan builds strong relationships with these students as they rely heavily on Morgan and the Disability and Equity Resource Center staff for ongoing support while attending MSU.

Gary Elias is a graduate student in economics and a graduate assistant in student activities. He requires accommodations that include a waiver from interpersonal communication in certain circumstances and additional time on assignments and exams because he processes differently. Often when Gary has personal and/or public interactions, they trigger anxiety for him. Gary needs additional time to work through this anxiety before he can respond or complete assignments. His self-disclosed diagnosis includes neurodivergence, anxiety, and depression. Stress exacerbates his symptoms which display as anti-social and slow to respond with poor word choices.

Gary's academic year begins with enthusiasm and a sense of achievement as he has struggled as an undergraduate and is excited about his new possibilities as a graduate student. As the semester progresses, Morgan notices that Gary has lost some of his passion and seems a little down. He is less social and articulate and seems to have a flat affect most times that she encounters him. This behavior and appearance are contrary to how Gary presented himself at the beginning of the semester. Morgan speaks with Gary about the change and he explains how he feels like he wasn't such a good fit with his graduate assistantship. He isn't sure why the fit doesn't feel the same but declines to discuss it further with Morgan.

Both the Disability and Equity Resource Center and Student Activities Office fall under the Division of Student Affairs at MSU. During a programmers' meeting with several other full-time team members, Tyler Mathews, student activities coordinator and Gary's direct supervisor, shares with the group that he has concerns about Gary's performance and communication style. He states that Gary "acts like he doesn't hear when people speak to him, and doesn't respond in a friendly manner when he finally responds." Tyler continues to explain that Gary's affect doesn't change, and he has called out sick from work a little too frequently. Lately Gary has missed some deadlines and doesn't seem responsive to feedback from Tyler. Gary is labeled as "odd" by Tyler and he is considering removing Gary from his GA position. During a break in the meeting, Morgan speaks with Tyler privately about the inappropriateness of those comments, including discussing employee performance in a public space and specifically his use of the word "odd" as an inappropriate descriptor, but due to confidentiality does not address Gary's accommodations.

Morgan has knowledge that Gary's affect and communication strategies were directly related to his diagnosis and accommodations, but the American Disabilities Act (ADA) and 504C compliance does not permit Morgan to disclose her knowledge of Gary's registration with the Disability and Equity Resource Center or the circumstances of his registration. Tyler's complaints are about the symptoms of Gary's diagnosis. Morgan reaches out to Gary and asks him how things are going with his graduate assistantship. He indicates that he senses his coworkers don't understand him, and he doesn't fit in. Morgan asks if he would like to register his accommodations with Student Employment, which would allow Gary's supervisor to have specific information that might help him understand how to best support Gary as a student employee. Gary declines and insists that he can manage the situation.

Throughout the semester, Morgan schedules check-in appointments with Gary, who shares he is struggling more than he expected in his graduate assistantship and notices that it is also having an impact on his academic performance. Gary confides in Morgan that he is seeking additional support outside of the Disability and Equity Resource Center office but still maintains that he does not need to register his accommodations with the Student Employment Office. Tyler continues to express frustration to Morgan, who is a confidant and sounding board, regarding Gary's performance and unsuccessful communication with Gary about these issues. Tyler also confides with Morgan that he is planning to release Gary from his graduate assistantship. It is clear to Morgan that Tyler is not viewing Gary's performance as related to a disability, otherwise Tyler would ask for her for advice. Further, Morgan now has knowledge that Gary is going to lose his position and that his behaviors exhibited in his graduate assistantship are directly related to his diagnosis and needed accommodations. Morgan is aware that the Americans with Disabilities Act and the 2009 amendments would protect Gary from this dismissal if he chooses to share his situation with Student Employment.

What should Morgan do?

Chapter Eight

Student Conduct Cases

MORE THAN A VIOLATION OF THE CODE OF CONDUCT
MATTHEW R. SHUPP

Keating University is a mid-sized public state institution with an enrollment of 9,000 undergraduate students and 1,500 graduate students. When classes are in session, the town's population, where Keating University is located, doubles in size. As a result, the institution and its student enrollment are a major economic engine for the small, rural, working-class town. Although the town's population is fairly homogenous, Keating University's student population is rather diverse, proudly boasting an international student population of over 10 percent of the entire student body, with large cohorts from the Middle East, China, and South Africa. Until recently, Keating University was able to keep its tuition relatively stable, only increasing 3 percent over the last five years, a result of support from state funding and generous alumni donors. A new governor was recently elected, and she made it known that she was not a supporter of public higher education. As a result, during this most recent academic year and without warning, 15 percent of the state funding was removed from the annual budget. Working within numerous union contracts, and attempting to not lay off faculty, staff, or administrators while still maintaining "business as usual," Keating University's president and Council of Trustees, in concert with the state's Board of Governors, decided to increase tuition a staggering 12 percent. This increase would keep up with annual inflation and help offset the loss of state funding. As a result, due to students' growing unmet financial need, enrollment of returning students dropped by 6 percent in one academic year. Likewise, new student enrollment dropped by 10 percent from the previous year's fall enrollment. Students simply could no longer afford to attend Keating University.

With the decrease in enrollment, the campus has been unable to maintain its current operational structure, even with the tuition increase. Campus leadership has been struggling with how to both increase and maintain enrollment. One solution was to relax the "zero tolerance policy" sanctions that currently exist within the Student Code of Conduct for alcohol and marijuana use deemed to be "high risk." Traditionally, students involved in gatherings consuming large amounts of alcohol or any amount of marijuana would be suspended for a minimum of one academic semester as indicated by the sanctioning guidelines in the student Code of Conduct. Keating University has the reputation for being a party school; there were ninety suspensions the previous academic year (1 percent of Keating's entire enrollment), the highest in the entire state.

Gabe is starting his third year as the assistant director of student conduct and, until recently, has only been tangentially involved in conversations with the Enrollment Management Team. Gabe's supervisor, Frank, the dean of students, is co-chair of the Enrollment Management Team and has kept Gabe informed of the proposed solutions for increasing enrollment. One solution directly involves a change in sanctioning adjudicated students. The dean of students instructs Gabe to immediately consider lowering the sanctioning threshold for first-time offenders of Keating University's drug and alcohol policy, whenever possible, thus providing opportunities to keep students enrolled who would have otherwise been suspended. Gabe recognizes the time, energy, and input required to enact such a decision, and wonders if this suggestion is a direct order. If so, it would change campus policy mid-year, certainly appearing arbitrary and unfair. Gabe also recognizes that this request would not be made if the institution was not facing its current financial difficulties.

Every Monday morning, Gabe receives reports on the previous weekend's activities from University Police, Township/Borough Police, and the Office of Housing and Residence Life. On this particular Monday morning, Gabe reads the following report from the Department of Housing and Residence Life:

> On Saturday morning, around 1:30 AM, Officer Fahey responded to a call from Residence Director (RD) Callahan. RD Callahan reported that she was contacted by Resident Assistants (RA) Walsh and Collins. During their last duty round of the evening, Walsh and Collins heard loud noise coming from room 243 Willingsbee Hall. RAs Walsh and Collins knocked on the door, promptly identified themselves, and asked for the occupants to open the door. RAs Walsh and Collins reported that a male "cracked" open the door, was slurring his speech, speaking incomprehensively, and promptly slammed the door shut. RAs Walsh and Collins knocked on the door a second time, identified themselves as staff, and requested that the occupants open the door. To

this request, the occupants in the room turned the music up louder and began to shout profanities. RAs Walsh and Collins contacted RD Callahan.

RD Callahan arrived on scene and similar requests were made with little response from the occupants in room 243 Willingsbee. RD Callahan contacted Keating University Police. Upon receipt of the call from RD Callahan, Officer Fahey arrived on scene, knocked on the door, and, with concern for the safety of the occupants in the room, asked the residence life staff to key into the room. Upon entering the room, the officer observed 5 individuals (identified as M. Woodland, 20, O. Halloran, 21, D. Winterhouse, 19, A. Defallon, 19, and L. Castlerigg, 18) in the room. A. Defallon and L. Castlerigg were later identified as residing in 241 Willingsbee. The residents of the room have been identified as O. Halloran and L. Starling, 22. L. Starling was not present and it was later revealed that he was away from campus during this incident.

During initial observation of the scene, Officer Fahey noticed 9 opened cans of beer, a half-full bottle of vodka, and two almost-empty bottles of whiskey. Upon questioning, M. Woodland became extremely belligerent, yelling profanities at the officer and specifically using threatening language toward RD Callahan. At this time, M. Woodland was taken into custody by University Police and removed from the situation. O. Halloran acknowledged that M. Woodland was his guest and that M. Woodland lived in 431 Marshall Hall. D. Winterhouse was a non-student visiting from O. Halloran's hometown. All individuals submitted to a field sobriety test and they all registered as follows:

M. Woodland, .24
O. Halloran, .08
D. Winterhouse, .19
Defallon, .06
L. Castlerigg, .00

A. Defallon and D. Winterhouse were cited for underage consumption and released. O. Halloran was cited for supplying to minors and released. In his initial statement to police, he indicated that L. Starling purchased the alcohol before leaving for the weekend. All other parties substantiated this statement. L. Castlerigg was not cited.

Residence Life staff asked the remaining four students in the room to gather up the alcohol and dump it in the nearest toilet. As the students were dumping the alcohol, A. Defallon was heard by RA Walsh saying that she "hated that (expletive) [RA Collins] and she will get what is coming to her."

Upon further investigation by residence life staff, it was found that neither M. Woodland nor D. Winterhouse were properly signed into the visitation log at the front desk of the residence hall.

End of Report.

Gabe recognizes both M. Woodland and A. Defallon as the children of generous donors to—and alumnae of—Keating University. For example, the Woodland and Defallon families provided a majority of the funding for Keating University's new Center for Service Learning, Cultural Immersion, and Character Education. Past experience makes Gabe confident the Judicial

Board will suspend M. Woodland, thus going against the dean's request to relax the conduct policy. A. Defallon's sanctions, if found in violation of making terroristic threats against a Keating University staff member, could be equally severe. Likewise, suspending M. Woodland will, undoubtedly, put Keating University in jeopardy of losing a very generous donor.

As Gabe contemplates these concerns, Frank calls and instructs Gabe to report to his office. When Gabe arrives, Frank informs him that the Woodlands and DeFallons have contacted the Board of Trustees, are on campus meeting with the president, and have threatened withholding gifts if the weekend's situation is not handled in a favorable manner.

What should Gabe do?

COMPLICATIONS WITH FERPA
JESSICA HENAULT

The Department for Sexual Assault and Domestic Violence: Advocacy, Response, and Education (ARE) provides any member of the Freedom State University community affected by sexual violence, dating violence, stalking, and sexual harassment with confidential, free, voluntary services and advocacy. Freedom State is a large, public land-grant research institution with over thirty-two thousand students. Freedom State is a predominantly White institution; 65 percent of students identify as White, 25 percent identify as African American, and 10 percent identify as Hispanic, Native American, or Asian American. Within the past year Freedom State has experienced a rise in hate crimes on campus. Black and LGBTQA+ students are the main victims of these hate crimes. There are three full-time advocates working within the ARE Department. These advocates work hard to participate in cross-campus collaboration, engaging in multiple leadership positions within organizations and committees.

Joni, a full-time professional advocate for the ARE Department, is currently representing the ARE Department in a Students of Concern (S.o.C.) meeting. S.o.C. meetings are held by the Center for Student Assistance and are designed to discuss information about students who are academically struggling at Freedom State. Academic advisors and faculty advisors who work primarily with students on academic warning or those who have recently been readmitted are invited to attend. Additionally, one representative from the Counseling Center, Health Center, Student Assistance Center, and ARE Department are invited to attend. During these meetings students of concern are discussed and S.o.C. members consult on what interventions, if any, should be used to best address the students' behavior and needs. Members attending these meetings must follow Federal Educational Right to Privacy Act (FERPA) guidelines and procedures to ensure information discussed remains confidential.

During this meeting, Dean, a, twenty-three-year-old student with no declared major, is discussed. Dean has been on and off Academic Warning for the past two years and recently began acquiring multiple absences with his courses. Within the past two months he stopped showing up to mandatory appointments with his academic coach, which he is required to attend because of his Academic Warning status. He is also unresponsive to email and phone calls. His academic advisor recently reached out to his coach informing the coach that Dean had just experienced the death of his father. His professors noted that the few times he has arrived at class he smelled of alcohol and seemed unmotivated to complete his work. It is clear that Dean is struggling with his mental health yet is resistant to receiving support and help. Last month, Dean had the cops called on him twice due to a physical altercation in which he was the aggressor. During the second altercation, which happened on campus, Dean physically assaulted another university student. Upon the arrest a handgun was found in the side of Dean's backpack without being properly stored in a holster. Three days prior to the S.o.C. meeting, Freedom State's Conduct Office contacted the S.o.C. members to inform them of the decision to dismiss Dean. A formal letter will be sent to Dean immediately notifying him of his dismissal.

When Joni hears the announcement, she is relieved, as she personally works with a client who named Dean as a violent perpetrator. The survivor remained anonymous, wanting their attacks to remain confidential, choosing not to press charges against Dean or notify Freedom State. Joni is not able to share this information with members of the S.o.C. board as Joni is bound by confidentiality policies determined by the ARE Department and in concordance with Title IX. Upon returning to the office, Joni notices Cade waiting in the sitting area. Cade is the client she worked with extensively last year who was assaulted by Dean. Cade is twenty years old, an agriculture major, and heavily involved with the Honors Program and LGBT Center. During their first meeting Cade mentioned that although their gender expression matched masculine characteristics, Cade was experimenting with their gender identity and used they/them/their pronouns and was also questioning their sexual orientation. Cade also mentioned they were not publicly out, so people still referred to them using he/him/his/himself pronouns.

Joni assisted Cade when they came to her last year about multiple violent sexual assaults they endured by Dean. Cade and Dean were previously close friends and before the first assault Cade felt comfortable confiding in Dean about their gender identity and sexual orientation. Although the sexual assault and physical violence occurred over the course of a couple months, Dean threatened and manipulated Cade to remain quiet, until Cade finally felt comfortable reaching out to the ARE Department. Uncomfortable with reporting the assaults or threats, Cade developed a safety plan, with Joni's help, that included blocking Dean on all technology. Cade had not heard from Dean since developing their safety plan and blocking him. The combination of Cade's unexpected arrival along with the distress they show alarms Joni. After spending some time calming down, Cade explains that Dean got a new cell phone number and created a new social media platform and began harassing Cade again. For the past month, Dean has demanded that Cade meet with him, threatening to publicly tell others about their gender identity and sexual orientation if Cade refused.

As Cade speaks to Joni, they state that they were planning on dropping out of Freedom State University. With Dean "always there" watching and threatening Cade, they feel extremely unsafe remaining on campus. Upon leaving Joni's office, Cade plans to go to the Registrar's Office and withdraw from the university. Cade also mentions that they are planning on meeting with Dean, with the hope that Dean will then leave them alone and keep Cade's personal information private. As an advocate, Joni sees her role as not to persuade Cade to remain enrolled, but rather to support Cade holistically on their healing journey as long as the steps they take support their safety and well-being. Joni understands that withdrawing from the university is what many survivors do because of fear of encountering their perpetrator on campus. It is common for survivors who report their assaults to see the perpetrator on campus, as the perpetrator is allowed to attend classes and social gatherings around campus while the case is being investigated.

Joni is worried about several aspects of Cade's situation. First and foremost, she is alarmed about Cade's plan to meet up with Dean. With Dean's increasing record of violence, his wavering mental health, and his possession and inappropriate handling of a gun, all signs point to Cade being in danger.

Although Joni is legally bound to keep Dean's academic and personal information private due to FERPA, she is torn. Telling Cade about Dean's dismissal from Freedom State would possibly help Cade feel safer, preventing them from dropping out. Joni also wants to inform Cade about Dean's recent physical altercations and possession of a firearm to stress the importance of Cade staying away from Dean. If Cade remains enrolled, it would also allow Joni the ability to continue working with Cade, supporting them in their healing and ensuring she gets them the correct resources.

What should Joni do?

LESSONS LEARNED?
CHELSEA JORDAN AND MICHELLE J. BOETTCHER

Jo is the new director of student conduct at a large, public research institution in the Midwest. She has worked in the office since finishing her master's degree three years ago. Currently, Jo is interviewing students to work in her office for the upcoming academic year. In addition to administrative tasks, the student staff member will help plan and present policy/conduct presentations across campus. This position requires the student to have access to FERPA-protected information and to be able to speak to the complexities of the student code of conduct.

The top candidate is Sarah. Sarah is a junior who has lived in the same building her first three years on campus. She has become increasingly involved in residence hall government and is popular among other residents on her floor. As part of the application process, students were required to submit an essay about why they would be good for the position. Sarah wrote about her first year of college and mistakes she made, but lessons she learned as a result of those issues. Sarah was documented and found responsible for policy violations on three occasions. First, she allowed her roommate to use her meal card to bring a non-student into the dining hall. Second, she was in a room documented for an alcohol and noise violation. While Sarah said she was not drinking and the other residents of the room where the violation took place also said she had not been drinking, she was found responsible for a noise violation. Finally, Sarah provided room numbers and building access to her older sorority sisters for the incoming pledge class, so they could prank the new members during initiation week.

Sarah acknowledges all these violations in her essay. She explains that she had a lot to learn about living in a community, reading policies, making sure to follow them, and that she has matured a lot as a result of her earlier experiences. Sarah has not had a violation since the spring of her first year on campus.

As part of her application to the position, Sarah obtained letters of support from her resident assistant and hall director. They felt comfortable providing letters of support for Sarah as every year, Sarah partnered with her RA to host a social for the floors to get to know custodial and maintenance staff. Sarah highlighted each custodian on a "get to know you" themed bulletin board each fall. Finally, Sarah coordinated a recognition week for custodians each spring including collecting thank you notes from residents and putting together candy and small gifts for each custodian in the building.

While all her letters of support are strong, Sarah remains on university probation from incidents during her first year. Because of the pattern of behavior involving multiple residence hall violations, she was placed on probation for the duration of her time living in the residence halls. She will be moving off campus for her senior year at which time she will no longer be on probation for the violations her first year.

Sarah did very well in her interviews with Jo's current team and the administrative staff with whom she would be working. The other two candidates for the job do not have any conduct history, but their materials and interviews were not as strong as Sarah's.

What should Jo do?

HORSING AROUND: WHEN PERSONAL AND
PROFESSIONAL ROLES OVERLAP
KRISTA BAILEY AND DARBY ROBERTS

College Town University (CTU) is a large, public research institution. The area surrounding College Town University has approximately 100,000 community members and the population grows significantly when the 40,000 students are on campus. College Town University is a Hispanic serving institution (HSI) in the Southwest that values community service and encourages faculty, staff, and students to volunteer. CTU provides many volunteer opportunities through courses with a service learning component, as well as through student organizations and department programs.

College Town University is the largest employer in town and has a large faculty, staff, and student population. CTU was recently awarded the designation of an HSI, a goal the institution had been working toward for several years. The Division of Student Affairs is a large division with ten departments, one being the Dean of Students Office, which includes multiple functional areas. The Dean of Students Office prides itself on having a strong relationship with the community and frequently partners with the town for community events.

One of the nice things about the town is the commitment to community service, volunteerism, and wellness, which aligns with the values of the institution. Thousands of students volunteer in the community through student organizations, courses, or on their own. It is common to see staff and faculty working next to students at community agencies such as food banks, animal shelters, and school programs. In addition, many students are employed in local businesses, so it is also common for students, staff, and faculty to interact, even if they do not know one another.

Brenda works in the Dean of Students Office as an assistant director overseeing orientation. She has been working at CTU for three years and completed her undergraduate and graduate degrees from College Town. Brenda frequently serves on student conduct panels and is very familiar with the student code of conduct. Her identity as an African American, first-generation student strongly influences her decision making and interactions with students. Last year she received the College Town University Student Support Award because she is loved by students across campus.

Brenda volunteers at the local equine shelter, tending to horses. She frequently interacts with students who are also volunteering at the agency. She sees some students more frequently than others, but most of the students do not know she works in the dean's office. A few of them know she works for CTU as a staff member doing something not related to classes. As a graduate of College Town, Brenda feels a lot of pride when she sees students serving the community. Similarly, when students make mistakes Brenda has been known to take it personally if her colleagues think poorly of the College Town students, especially if the colleagues are not alumni.

One day, Brenda overhears two first-year students talking. They are discussing the past weekend, where they both got drunk on the way to an on-campus event and damaged a campus parking gate. They talked about how relieved they were that no one saw them hit the parking gate. The students both had hangovers the next day and talked about how they really should have studied for their exams that Monday. One student mentioned that she was really relieved she was not caught because if she was expelled from the university she did not think she would be able to stay in the United States based on her undocumented status. Brenda seemed to recall reading something about the damage to the parking garage in the campus newspaper.

Brenda was disappointed and troubled as she listened to the students. Brenda was concerned about their behavior, health, and potential academic failure. Although she thought about engaging with the students, she decided to keep to herself and not ask the students anything about the situation. Before leaving for the day, she shared what she overheard with Isabelle, a faculty member from College Town University, who manages the volunteer schedule. Isabelle identifies as a White woman and has been a faculty member in the Department of Equine Science for three years. Isabelle has been managing the volunteers for the local equine shelter for the last two years and has recently initiated a campaign to recruit more students to volunteer.

Isabelle agreed the behavior was concerning but did not think it was her role as the volunteer coordinator to talk to the students since it did not involve the health and safety of the horses. Isabelle mentioned that this is the not the first time students have shared stories of irresponsible decisions, and she was glad as a faculty member she does not have to intervene. Brenda was a little surprised by that comment but let it go; she did not think it was her place to confront Isabelle.

The next day, Brenda mentions to her colleague Antonio what happened at the off-campus volunteer site. Antonio serves as an associate director for student conduct and his role includes following up with concerning student behavior. Antonio identifies as a Latino male. He has been working at College Town University for five years. He completed his undergraduate and graduate degrees at two smaller universities before coming to CTU.

Antonio asks if Brenda knows the names of the students and shares he wants to reach out to the students. Brenda does not know the students' names, but could find the information if she asked Isabelle. Brenda is worried that if she shares the names, she may be asked to stop volunteering because of Isabelle's views of not sharing student information and difficulty maintaining consistent volunteers. As she considers what to do, she reflects on how good the equine shelter experience has been for her mental health. Antonio is also worried about the student's comment about not being able to stay in the States and really wants the opportunity to provide support and resources to the students. Antonio reminds Brenda that as a university employee, she has an obligation to report potential student rule violations and to be careful that she is not trying to minimize this because she is embarrassed as an alumna of College Town.

What should Brenda do?

COMPLEX RELATIONSHIPS
MATTHEW BIRNBAUM

Samuel is an assistant director of Medium Size State University's (MSSU) Office of Community Standards and Compliance (OCSC). MSSU is a public, doctoral degree–granting institution located in the Southwest that enrolls fifteen thousand students. OCSC is responsible for handling all of the campus hate and bias incident reports at MSSU. OCSC was created three years ago and most staff were hired in the last eighteen months. The office was created after a campus climate assessment found many students with minoritized identities experienced hostilities that the Dean of Students Office was unable to appropriately address with its limited resources. Because OCSC is still a relatively new office and the staff have been busy addressing complaints, it has not had the time to develop policies to address some of the types of situations that might arise on campus. Samuel has been in the position for two years and has helped develop many thoughtful policies for addressing the diverse range of issues OCSC must address. Samuel has especially enjoyed helping OCSC improve its use of technology to streamline its case management.

In addition to Samuel, OCSC has three full-time community response investigators (CRI). Samuel and Linda, OCSC's director, believe in developing a highly collaborative office culture and they actively engage the CRIs in most aspects of office management, including its transition to a Restorative Justice Model for complaints that do not meet the institution's ill-defined definition of "bias." Their philosophy is that the best solutions come when those involved share information, perspectives, and then offer solutions. For example, the entire OCSC staff were involved in a series of meetings to develop new procedures for how the office would handle the increase in cases while maintaining its commitment to thorough investigations.

One way in which Samuel has streamlined case management is to automate the process of forwarding bias incident reports in the belief that too much time is spent in meetings deciding if a situation is indeed a bias incident and how to proceed. When a bias incident report is submitted through the digital portal, the system automatically forwards it to Linda and the CRIs so they can be prepared to discuss the incident and determine who is best prepared to lead the investigation.

Last year Samuel enrolled in MSSU's higher education (HE) doctoral program as a part-time student. He has completed thirty credits in the program, which enrolls numerous MSSU employees in its MA and PhD degree programs. In fact, two of the three CRIs are also enrolled in the PhD program. Samuel has taken courses with each of the HE program's three full-time tenure or tenure-track faculty members and has even co-taught a class with one.

At 4:30 pm on Thursday, Samuel, Linda, and the CRIs receive a bias incident report from Trish, a doctoral student in the HE program. The report states that Professor Swift created a hostile and harmful classroom environment by showing numerous images of recent campus-based hate crimes from across the country and then silencing her (and several other students) who raised concerns that the images were unnecessary and triggering. Trish also stated that Professor Swift had not provided enough context for each image and was therefore using the experiences and pain of marginalized students to educate majority students.

Samuel has taken classes with Dr. Swift and with Trish, and as he reads the report realizes the two other CRIs enrolled in the HE program know the student and instructor as well. Samuel thinks highly of Dr. Swift and has observed how the professor thoughtfully approaches sensitive topics and works to ensure all students feel welcome and included in the classroom. Samuel also thinks highly of Trish and has never observed any behaviors that would suggest she is not genuinely harmed by the class. Samuel recognizes that he is in a difficult position. He approaches the director with his concerns, and she indicates, "It's common to know both complainants and respondents in these situations. We're all members of the university community, and we'll often know people who come through our office. That's just the reality of our work."

What should Samuel do?

ARE CONSISTENT SANCTIONS FAIR?
MICHAEL BOTTS

David is a second-year graduate assistant in the Office of Student Conduct at Southern State University (SSU), a large public research university with twenty-three thousand students located in a conservative state in the southwestern United States. As a land grant institution, SSU is historically White, but espouses a commitment to diversity in every way. In the first year of his assistantship, David heard cases up through probation, but now that this is his second year, he is hearing more complex cases and sanctions up through recommendation for suspension.

In late October, David receives an incident report from SSU Police Officer Garvey concerning two students, Edward and Gregory. Edward is an eighteen-year-old first-year student at SSU. He is a first-generation Latino college student from a low-income family and is part of a special program at SSU, First Southerners, which provides intensive support to first-generation students who were admitted to the university with lower SAT scores, low socioeconomic status, and lower high school grade point averages. One requirement of the First Southerners program is meeting with an assigned advisor, and Edward had been attending meetings with his advisor from this program regularly during the first few weeks of the term. However, he has recently missed two of those meetings. Edward's friend, Gregory, is an eighteen-year-old first-year student as well. He and Edward met during orientation and are now close friends. Gregory is from a higher socioeconomic status than Edward and is a third-generation legacy student at SSU.

The incident report David receives documents Edward and Gregory possessing and smoking marijuana in Edward's residence hall room. The report states that in early October, SSU Police responded to a call from a resident advisor asking for assistance from the police due to the odor of marijuana coming from the fourth floor of Drummond Residence Hall, a traditional residence hall on campus that houses 560 undergraduate students; it is mostly a first-year residence hall. The report states that upon arrival, Officer Garvey could smell the odor of burning marijuana and pinpointed it as coming from Drummond 416. Officer Garvey knocked on the door of Drummond 416 and announced himself as university police. He heard scuffling in the room and then eventually Edward opened the door. Officer Garvey could see a fan blowing out an open window and a towel coming from under the door. Officer Garvey also noticed a shopping bag taped around the smoke detector in the room. Officer Garvey asked Edward if he could enter and search the room, and Edward consented. Upon searching Drummond 416, whose sole resident is Edward, Officer Garvey found ashes on the windowsill, a marijuana grinder, a roach clip, rolling papers, and two marijuana cigarettes, which were located in the corner under Edward's bed. Officer Garvey asked who the items belonged to and Edward took ownership of the marijuana cigarettes and roach clip and Gregory took ownership of the grinder and rolling papers. Edward was cited for possession of marijuana and drug paraphernalia and Gregory was cited for possession of drug paraphernalia.

After reading the incident report, David sends Gregory and Edward each an allegation letter and requests meetings with them. David alleges that both students have violated the Student Code of Conduct provisions pertaining to possession of drugs, possession of drug paraphernalia, smoking in a residence hall, and tampering with life safety equipment. Gregory responds to the email first and schedules a meeting with David to discuss the incident and options for adjudication. Gregory takes responsibility for the violations and agrees to an informal resolution. David sanctions Gregory with the standard sanctions for this type of violation: probation, a drug workshop, a community involvement activity, and a $400 fine for smoking in the residence hall and tampering with life safety equipment.

Three days later, after the appeal period for Gregory expires and Gregory has paid his $400 fine, Edward calls to schedule his meeting with David. Before the meeting, David looks at Edward's student data and finds out that Edward is receiving full financial aid including a Pell Grant. David assumes that Edward is concerned about the meeting because he receives a phone call from the director of the First Southerners program telling him that Edward is really attempting to make up his attendance from earlier in the semester, is doing fair in his classes, and is trying to improve by going to faculty office hours and attending tutoring, both of which are requirements of the First Southerners program. David asks the program director about her perceptions of Edward and she states that he is not really involved, he appears to be tired and stressed a lot, but he does not really show any other indications of troubles or concerns.

On the day of the meeting it is raining and cold outside, and Edward shows up to the meeting wearing sweatpants and a white t-shirt; he is not wearing any type of sweatshirt or jacket. Edward is obviously upset and nervous about the meeting, and David questions him about that. Edward says that he is worried about the outcome because of the sanctions that Gregory received and how much it would cost him. David asks Edward about his use history with marijuana, and Edward says that he uses marijuana about once a week to deal with stress and help him sleep. He says that he would use more often but cannot afford it. Edward says that he has used marijuana since he was fifteen. He shares that his family members sold marijuana all his life when money would get tight and that he started using because it was at home and easy to get to. When David inquires about Edward's financial worries, he tells David that he is worried that he will be kicked out of housing and will have to leave school. He also says that the $400 fine will be very hard for him to pay. Edward explains that his family cannot afford to help him with college and that he is attending college on his own. He explains that he only received enough financial aid with loans to cover the lowest meal plan, ten meals per week, does not have enough money for all hygiene essentials, and cannot afford to do laundry regularly. David assures Edward that he will not lose his housing this time and asks Edward about getting a work study job on campus. Edward explains that he has a work study job at the library, but they only employ him for twelve hours per week and that only provided around $70 per week. Edward said that he is using the money from his work study position to pay off his bill at the bookstore. David asks Edward why he never told someone about his needs or asked for help and if he knows about the basic needs assistance case manager on campus who can help with food insecurities, housing insecurities, and can help students with other basic needs as well, such as getting access to hygiene products. Edward states that he had heard something about that office but was nervous about asking for help since his family was denied public assistance due to some members of his family being undocumented. The meeting ends with Edward agreeing to an informal resolution, but David does not know what to do given the not all that unique situation that Edward is in.

David has some flexibility in sanctioning but has already sanctioned Gregory and knows that the sanctions should be consistent.

What should David do?

DISCORD WITHIN THE CONDUCT BOARD
LYDIA COULSON AND DAN HUDSON

Anthony is a first-year graduate student studying student affairs in higher education at Great Plains University, a private, mid-sized, predominately White institution located in a large midwestern city. His graduate assistant-ship is with judicial affairs, and a large part of his job responsibilities include serving as the primary advisor to the Student Conduct Board. The student conduct board is composed of all undergraduate students who adjudicate low-level conduct hearings. Each case is heard by four voting members and one chair, a more experienced board member who facilitates the hearing and only votes if there is a tie. The training for students on the board has been lackluster for the past few years. During his first week of work, Anthony's supervisor instructed him to do whatever he needed to get the conduct board running more effectively and efficiently.

At the start of the second semester, Anthony decided a more robust train-ing was a good way to help improve the Student Conduct Board. In addition to improving the beginning of semester training, Anthony wanted to provide short weekly review lessons and activities which could be facilitated in ten to fifteen minutes after the hearings were completed. When considering what topics had already been covered in training at the beginning of the semester, Anthony realized there had been no training on cultural competence, implicit bias, or identity awareness. Knowing that a strong understanding of these topics would be important to his students' work on the Student Conduct Board, he began to look for an appropriate training activity to cover this content.

Anthony settled on an activity and made copies for that evening's board. Anthony was unable to attend the hearings that night, so Shannon, a staff member from Fraternity and Sorority Life, stepped in as the advisor. Shannon is also new to Great Plains University this year, and this will be her second time advising the Student Conduct Board. In anticipation of his absence, Anthony explained the activity to Shannon and helped her prepare to facilitate it with the Student Conduct Board.

After finishing up the evening's hearing, Shannon pulled out the implicit bias activity. She pulled the copies out of the folder and explained, "I'm going to pass out the activity prompts and read them out loud. After we're finished reading, you'll get two minutes to decide on your own, and then we'll discuss as a group." She then passed the copies out to the group and began to read:

The Sinking Raft Scenario

You are sailing a small boat when you come upon a sinking life raft with six people on it. Your boat will only support the weight of two additional people. You must decide who you will save from the raft. There is not time to call for additional help or come back for others, because a large storm is about to hit and no boats will be allowed to leave harbor after you return to land. You can only select two people to save. You must decide who will be saved by choosing from the list below.

1. A fifty-five-year-old retired professional athlete who uses their notoriety to raise millions of dollars every year to support literacy programs for underprivileged children.
2. A thirty-five-year-old who runs the United States' largest legal defense fund for undocumented immigrants. He recently divorced his wife after he found out she was diagnosed with a degenerative chronic illness.
3. An ex-felon who went to prison for embezzling millions of dollars from a natural disaster relief organization who now runs an organization that helps convicts reintegrate into society. It has a proven track record of reducing recidivism.
4. A YouTuber who runs a self-help YouTube channel with more than twenty-five million subscribers and frequently helps raise money for good causes. She has been under fire for some old tweets that appear to be anti-Semitic.
5. A doctor who is known to have close ties to a White supremacist group and is on the cusp of a cure for Ebola.
6. A thirteen-year-old who is a math prodigy and just enrolled in college at one of the nation's best universities. However, in an attempt to keep up with his parents' high expectations, he had developed an Adderall addiction.

When their two minutes were finished, Shannon started the group discussion. She began by asking "What was your initial reaction to being asked to make this choice?" An especially outspoken first-year student, Mackenzie, shared that she did not think it was right to "play God like this." She then remarked that the doctor with White supremacist associations (person five) was only seen as bad because of negative media portrayal. The chair of that night's board, a senior named Yasmine, responded by sharing that as a woman of color, the doctor being a White supremacist did make her uncomfortable which is why she originally voted against him, but acknowledged that she had since changed her vote. Mackenzie replied by explaining that not all White supremacists are bad, and obviously none of them knew what the term really meant. After her last statement Mackenzie refused to continue participating in the discussion. It was clear to Shannon that all the students felt uncomfortable after Mackenzie and Yasmine's exchange. Ultimately the group, including Yasmine, decided to vote solely based on the health and contributions to society and ended up selecting individuals one and five.

As the rest of the students left, Shannon requested that Yasmine stay for a few minutes so they could talk. "How are you feeling after that?" Shannon asked. Yasmine shared that she was shocked because she had not expected their conversation to go in that direction. Shannon nodded and then asked, "Do you feel comfortable continuing to serve with Mackenzie on conduct board?" Yasmine replied, "No, absolutely not. She clearly cannot listen to others' feedback. If she's in, I'm out." Shannon sighed and shook her head.

Before heading home for the night Shannon sent an email to Anthony explaining all that had happened that evening and requested for the two of them to meet in person to further discuss the situation. Anthony opened the email at 9:00 that night, read it, and sighed. This was not the first time Mackenzie had gotten overzealous and crossed a line during board discussions. She had a history of vigorously defending her opinions and would sometimes interrupt other board members to make her point, however, this was the first time she had ever made any remarks of this nature. From their previous interactions together, Anthony knew that Mackenzie was a White student from the West Coast who was in the university honors program, and she seemed to be well off financially. He spent the rest of his night thinking about how he should handle things at work the next day.

What should Anthony do?

Appendix A

*ACPA/NASPA Professional Competency Areas
for Student Affairs Professionals*

PERSONAL AND ETHICAL FOUNDATIONS (PEF)

The Personal and Ethical Foundations competency area involves the knowledge, skills, and dispositions to develop and maintain integrity in one's life and work; this includes thoughtful development, critique, and adherence to a holistic and comprehensive standard of ethics and commitment to one's own wellness and growth. Personal and ethical foundations are aligned because integrity has an internal locus informed by a combination of external ethical guidelines, an internal voice of care, and our own lived experiences. Our personal and ethical foundations grow through a process of curiosity, reflection, and self-authorship.

Foundational Outcomes

- Articulate key elements of one's set of personal beliefs and commitments (e.g., values, morals, goals, desires, self-definitions), as well as the source of each (e.g., self, peers, family, or one or more larger communities).
- Articulate one's personal code of ethics for student affairs practice, informed by the ethical statements of professional student affairs associations and their foundational ethical principles.
- Describe the ethical statements and their foundational principles of any professional associations directly relevant to one's working context.
- Identify ethical issues in the course of one's job.

- Explain how one's behavior reflects the ethical statements of the profession and address lapses in one's own ethical behavior.
- Appropriately question institutional actions which are not consistent with ethical standards.
- Utilize institutional and professional resources to assist with ethical issues (e.g., consultation with appropriate mentors, supervisors and/or colleagues, consultation with an association's ethics committee).
- Articulate awareness and understanding of one's attitudes, values, beliefs, assumptions, biases, and identity how they affect one's integrity and work with others.
- Take responsibility to broaden perspectives by participating in activities that challenge one's beliefs.
- Identify the challenges associated with balancing personal and professional responsibilities, and recognize the intersection of one's personal and professional life.
- Identify one's primary work responsibilities and, with appropriate, ongoing feedback, craft a realistic, summative self-appraisal of one's strengths and limitations.
- Articulate an understanding that wellness is a broad concept composed of emotional, physical, social, environmental, relational, spiritual, moral, and intellectual elements.
- Recognize and articulate healthy habits for better living.
- Identify positive and negative impacts on wellness and, as appropriate, seek assistance from available resources.
- Identify and describe personal and professional responsibilities inherent to excellence in practice.
- Recognize the importance of reflection in personal, professional, and ethical development.

Intermediate Outcomes

- Identify the present and future meaningfulness of key elements in one's set of personal beliefs and commitments.
- Articulate and implement a personal protocol for ethical decision-making.
- Explain how one's professional practice aligns with both one's personal code of ethics and ethical statements of professional student affairs associations.
- Identify and manage areas of incongruence between personal, institutional, and professional ethical standards.
- Distinguish the legal and moral influences on varying codes of ethics.
- Identify and articulate the influence of culture in the interpretation of ethical standards.

- Identify and address lapses in ethical behavior among self, colleagues, and students.
- Seek environments and collaborations that provide adequate challenge such that personal development is promoted, and provide sufficient support such that development is possible.
- Identify sources of dissonance and fulfillment in one's life and take appropriate steps in response.
- Develop and implement plans to manage competing priorities between one's professional and personal lives.
- Bolster one's resiliency, including participating in stress-management activities, engaging in personal or spiritual exploration, and building healthier relationships inside and outside of the workplace.
- Explain the process for executing responsibilities dutifully and deliberatively.
- Analyze the impact one's health and wellness has on others, as well as our collective roles in creating mutual, positive relationships.
- Define excellence for one's self and evaluate how one's sense of excellence impacts self and others.
- Analyze personal experiences for potential deeper learning and growth, and engage with others in reflective discussions.

Advanced Outcomes

- Evolve personal beliefs and commitments in a way that is true to one's internal voice while recognizing the contributions of important others (e.g., self, peers, family, or one or more larger communities).
- Engage in effective consultation and provide advice regarding ethical issues with colleagues and students.
- Model for colleagues and others adherence to identified ethical guidelines and serve as mediator to resolve disparities.
- Actively engage in dialogue with others concerning the ethical statements of professional associations.
- Actively support the ethical development of other professionals by developing and supporting an ethical organizational culture within the workplace.
- Serve as a role model for integrity through sharing personal experiences and nurturing others' competency in this area.
- Attend to areas of growth relating to one's anticipated career trajectory.
- Exercise mutuality within relationships and interconnectedness in work/ life presence.
- Create and implement an individualized plan for healthy living.
- Demonstrate awareness of the wellness of others in the workplace, and seek to engage with colleagues in a way that supports such wellness.

- Serve as model and mentor for others in their search for excellence, taking measures to encourage and inspire exceptional work in self and others.
- Design naturally occurring reflection processes within one's everyday work.
- Transfer thoughtful reflection into positive future action.

NOTE

ACPA: College Student Educators International and NASPA—Student Affairs Administrators in Higher Education. 2015. *ACPA/NASPA Professional Competency Areas for Student Affairs Professionals*. Washington, DC: Authors.

Appendix B

CAS: Council for the Advancement of Standards

CAS STATEMENT OF SHARED ETHICAL PRINCIPLES

The Council for the Advancement of Standards in Higher Education (CAS) has served as a voice for quality assurance and promulgation of standards in higher education for over twenty-five years. CAS was established to promote inter-association efforts to address quality assurance, student learning, and professional integrity. It was believed that a single voice would have greater impact on the evaluation and improvement of services and programs than would many voices speaking for special interests by individual practitioners or by single-interest organizations.

CAS includes membership of over 41 active professional associations and has established standards in over 30 functional areas. It has succeeded in providing a platform through which representatives from across higher education can jointly develop and promulgate standards of good practice that are endorsed not just by those working in a particular area, but by representatives of higher education associations.

CAS often cites George Washington, who said, "Let us raise a standard to which the wise and honest can repair." CAS has raised standards; it is now time to focus on the attributes, such as wisdom and honesty, of those professionals who would use the standards. Professionals working to provide services in higher education share more than a commitment to quality assurance and standards of practice. A review of the ethical statements of member associations demonstrates clearly that there are elements of ethical principles and values that are shared across the professions in higher education.

Most of the member associations represented in CAS are guided by ethical codes of professional practice enforced through the prescribed channels of its association. CAS acknowledges and respects the individual codes and standards of ethical conduct of their organizations. From these codes, CAS has created a statement of shared ethical principles that focuses on seven basic principles that form the foundation for CAS member association codes: autonomy, non-malfeasance, beneficence, justice, fidelity, veracity, and affiliation. This statement is not intended to replace or supplant the code of ethics of any professional association; rather, it is intended to articulate those shared ethical principles. It is our hope that by articulating those shared beliefs, CAS can promulgate a better understanding of the professions of those in service to students and higher education.

Principle I – Autonomy

We take responsibility for our actions and both support and empower an individual's and group's freedom of choice.

1. We strive for quality and excellence in the work that we do
2. We respect one's freedom of choice
3. We believe that individuals, ourselves and others, are responsible for their own behavior and learning
4. We promote positive change in individuals and in society through education
5. We foster an environment where people feel empowered to make decisions
6. We hold ourselves and others accountable
7. We study, discuss, investigate, teach, conduct research, and publish freely within the academic community
8. We engage in continuing education and professional development

Principle II – Non-Malfeasance

We pledge to do no harm.

1. We collaborate with others for the good of those whom we serve
2. We interact in ways that promote positive outcomes
3. We create environments that are educational and supportive of the growth and development of the whole person
4. We exercise role responsibilities in a manner that respects the rights and property of others without exploiting or abusing power

Principle III – Beneficence

We engage in altruistic attitudes and actions that promote goodness and contribute to the health and welfare of others.

1. We treat others courteously
2. We consider the thoughts and feelings of others
3. We work toward positive and beneficial outcomes

Principle IV – Justice

We actively promote human dignity and endorse equality and fairness for everyone.

1. We treat others with respect and fairness, preserving their dignity, honoring their differences, promoting their welfare
2. We recognize diversity and embrace a cross-cultural approach in support of the worth, dignity, potential, and uniqueness of people within their social and cultural contexts
3. We eliminate barriers that impede student learning and development or discriminate against full participation by all students
4. We extend fundamental fairness to all persons
5. We operate within the framework of laws and policies
6. We respect the rights of individuals and groups to express their opinions
7. We assess students in a valid, open, and fair manner and one consistent with learning objectives
8. We examine the influence of power on the experience of diversity to reduce marginalization and foster community

Principle V – Fidelity

We are faithful to an obligation, trust, or duty.

1. We maintain confidentiality of interactions, student records, and information related to legal and private matters
2. We avoid conflicts of interest or the appearance thereof
3. We honor commitments made within the guidelines of established policies and procedures
4. We demonstrate loyalty and commitment to institutions that employ us
5. We exercise good stewardship of resources

Principle VI – Veracity

We seek and convey the truth in our words and actions.

1. We act with integrity and honesty in all endeavors and interactions
2. We relay information accurately
3. We communicate all relevant facts and information while respecting privacy and confidentiality

Principle VII – Affiliation

We actively promote connected relationships among all people and foster community.

1. We create environments that promote connectivity
2. We promote authenticity, mutual empathy, and engagement within human interactions

When professionals act in accordance with ethical principles, program quality and excellence are enhanced and ultimately students are better served. As professionals providing services in higher education, we are committed to upholding these shared ethical principles, for the benefit of our students, our professions, and higher education.

Some concepts for this code were taken from:

Kitchener, K. (1985). Ethical principles and ethical decisions in student affairs. In H. Canon & R. Brown (Eds.), *Applied ethics in student services* (New Directions in Student Services No. 30, pp. 17–30). San Francisco, CA: Jossey-Bass.

CAS Statement of Shared Ethical Principles. 2015. In Council for the Advancement of Higher Education (Ed.), *CAS Professional Standards for Higher Education* (9th Ed.). Washington, DC: Author.

NOTE

The individual items within the CAS Statement of Shared Ethical Principles (above) have been assigned numbers in order to facilitate referencing relevant aspects in other sections of this book. In the original CAS Statement, all individual items are formatted using bullets, not numbers. Our use of numbers here for referencing purposes should not be construed as assigning priority order among the individual items. This is neither our intention nor, apparently, the intention of the CAS Statement authors.

Appendix C

ACPA: College Student Educators International

STATEMENT OF ETHICAL PRINCIPLES AND STANDARDS

ACPA—College Student Educators International is an association whose members are dedicated to enhancing the worth, dignity, potential, and uniqueness of each individual within post-secondary educational institutions and, thus, to the service of society. ACPA members are committed to contributing to the comprehensive education of students, protecting human rights, advancing knowledge of student growth and development, and promoting the effectiveness of institutional programs, services, and organizational units. As a means of supporting these commitments, members of ACPA subscribe to the following principles and standards of ethical conduct. Acceptance of membership in ACPA signifies that the member understands the provisions of this statement.

This statement is designed to address issues particularly relevant to college student affairs practice. Persons charged with duties in various functional areas of higher education are also encouraged to consult ethical standards specific to their professional responsibilities.

USE OF THIS STATEMENT

The principal purpose of this statement is to assist student affairs professionals (individuals who are administrators, staff, faculty, and adjunct faculty in the field of student affairs) in regulating their own behavior by sensitizing them to potential ethical problems and by providing standards useful in daily practice. Observance of ethical behavior also benefits fellow professionals and students due to the effect of modeling. Self-regulation is the most effective and preferred means of assuring ethical behavior. If, however, a professional observes conduct by a fellow professional that seems contrary to the provisions of this document, several courses of action are available. Suggestions to assist with addressing ethical concerns are included in the Appendix at the end of this document.

ETHICAL FOUNDATIONS

No statement of ethical standards can anticipate all situations that have ethical implications. When student affairs professionals are presented with dilemmas that are not explicitly addressed herein, a number of perspectives may be used in conjunction with the four standards identified in this document to assist in making decisions and determining appropriate courses of action. These standards are: 1) Professional Responsibility and Competence; 2) Student Learning and Development; 3) Responsibility to the Institution; and 4) Responsibility to Society.

Ethical principles should guide the behaviors of professionals in everyday practice. Principles are assumed to be constant and, therefore, provide consistent guidelines for decision-making. In addition, student affairs professionals should strive to develop the virtues, or habits of behavior, that are characteristic of people in helping professions. Contextual issues must also be taken into account. Such issues include, but are not limited to, culture, temporality (issues bound by time), and phenomenology (individual perspective) and community norms. Because of the complexity of ethical conversation and dialogue, the skill of simultaneously confronting differences in perspective and respecting the rights of persons to hold different perspectives becomes essential. For an extended discussion of these aspects of ethical thinking, see Appendix B.

ETHICAL STANDARDS

Four ethical standards related to primary constituencies with whom student affairs professionals work, colleagues, students, educational institutions, and society—are specified.

1.0   *Professional Responsibility and Competence.* Student affairs professionals are responsible for promoting and facilitating student learning about students and their world, enhancing the quality and understanding of student life, advocating for student welfare and concerns, and advancing the profession and its ideals. They possess the knowledge, skills, emotional stability, and maturity to discharge responsibilities as administrators, advisors, consultants, counselors, programmers, researchers, and teachers. High levels of professional competence are expected in the performance of their duties and responsibilities. Student affairs professionals are responsible for the consequences of their actions or inaction.

As ACPA members, student affairs professionals will:

1.1 Conduct their professional activities in accordance with sound theoretical principles and adopt a personal value system congruent with the basic tenets of the profession.

1.2 Contribute to the development of the profession (e.g., recruiting students to the profession, serving professional organizations, advocating the use of ethical thinking through educational and professional development activities, improving professional practices, and conducting and reporting research).

1.3 Maintain and enhance professional effectiveness by continually improving skills and acquiring new knowledge.

1.4 Monitor their personal and professional functioning and effectiveness and seek assistance from appropriate professionals as needed.

1.5 Maintain current, accurate knowledge of all regulations related to privacy of student records and electronic transmission of records and update knowledge of privacy legislation on a regular basis.

1.6 Represent their professional credentials, competencies, and limitations accurately and correct any misrepresentations of these qualifications by others.

1.7 Establish fees for professional services after consideration of the ability of the recipient to pay. They will provide some services, including professional development activities for colleagues, for little or no remuneration.

1.8 Adhere to ethical practices in securing positions: [a] represent education and experiences accurately; [b] respond to offers promptly; [c] interview for positions only when serious about accepting an offer; [d] accept only those positions they intend to assume; [e] advise current employer and all institutions at which applications are pending immediately when they sign a contract; [f] inform their employers before leaving a position within a reasonable amount of time as outlined by the institution and/or supervisor; and [g] commit to position upon acceptance.

1.9 Provide an honest, accurate, and respectful reference. If it is not deemed possible to provide a positive reference, contact the "searching employee" to inform them of such. It is not appropriate to provide a positive reference to move an individual beyond a department or institution.

2.0   *Student Learning and Development.* Student development is an essential purpose of higher education. Support of this process is a major responsibility of the student affairs profession. Development is complex and includes cognitive, physical, moral, social, emotional, career, spiritual, personal, and intellectual dimensions. Professionals must be sensitive to and knowledgeable about the variety of backgrounds, cultures, experiences, abilities, personal characteristics and viewpoints evident in the student population and be able to incorporate appropriate theoretical perspectives to identify learning opportunities and to reduce barriers to development. Multicultural competence is a fundamental element of ethical practice.

As ACPA members, student affairs professionals will:

2.1   Treat students with respect as persons who possess dignity, worth, and the ability to be self-directed.

2.2   Avoid dual relationships with students where one individual serves in multiple roles that create conflicting responsibilities, role confusion, and unclear expectations (e.g., counselor/employer, supervisor/best friend, or faculty/sexual partner) that may involve incompatible roles and conflicting responsibilities.

2.3   Abstain from all forms of harassment, including but not limited to verbal and written communication, physical actions and electronic transmissions.

2.4   Abstain from sexual intimacy with clients or with students for whom they have supervisory, evaluative, or instructional responsibility.

2.5   Inform students of the conditions under which they may receive assistance.

2.6   Inform students of the nature and/or limits of confidentiality. They will share information about the students only in accordance with institutional policies and applicable laws, when given their permission, or when required to prevent personal harm to themselves or others.

2.7   Refer students to appropriate specialists before entering or continuing a helping relationship when the professional's expertise or level of comfort is exceeded. If the referral is declined, professional staff is not obliged to continue the relationship nor should they do so if there is not direct benefit to the student.

2.8   Inform students about the purpose of assessment and research; make explicit the planned use of results prior to assessment requesting participation in either.

2.9 Comply with the institutional guidelines on electronic transmission of information.

2.10 Provide appropriate contextual information to students prior to and following the use of any evaluation procedures to place results in proper perspective with other factors relevant to the assessment process (e.g., socioeconomic, gender, identity, ethnic, cultural, and gender related).

2.11 Discuss with students issues, attitudes, and behaviors that have ethical implications.

2.12 Develop multicultural knowledge, skills, competence, and use appropriate elements of these capacities in their work with students.

2.13 Faculty should inform prospective graduate students of program expectations, predominant theoretical orientations, and skills needed for successful program completion, as well as positions received by recent graduates.

2.14 Assure that required experiences involving self-disclosure are communicated to prospective graduate students. When the preparation program offers experiences that emphasize self-disclosure or other relatively intimate or personal involvement (e.g., group or individual counseling or growth groups), professionals must not have current or anticipated administrative, supervisory, or evaluative authority over participants.

2.15 Provide graduate students with a broad knowledge base consisting of theory, research, and practice.

2.16 Educate graduate students about ethical standards, responsibilities and codes of the profession. Uphold these standards within all preparation programs.

2.17 Assess all relevant competencies and interpersonal functioning of students throughout the preparation program, communicate these assessments to students, and take appropriate corrective actions including dismissal when warranted.

2.18 Assure that field supervisors are qualified to provide supervision to graduate students and are informed of their ethical responsibilities in this role.

2.19 Support professional preparation program efforts by providing assistantships, practical field placements, and consultation to students and faculty.

2.20 Gain approval of research plans involving human subjects from the institutional committee with oversight responsibility prior to the initiation of the study. In the absence of such a committee, they will seek to create procedures to protect the rights and ensure the safety of research participants.

2.21 Conduct and report research studies accurately. Researchers will not engage in fraudulent research nor will they distort or misrepresent their data or deliberately bias their results.

2.22 Cite previous works on a topic when writing or when speaking to professional audiences.

2.23 Comply with laws and standards common in the helping professions related to citation and attribution of information accessed electronically where public domain status may be ambiguous.

2.24 Acknowledge major contributions to research projects and professional writings through joint authorships with the principal contributor listed first. They will acknowledge minor technical or professional contributions in notes or introductory statements.

2.25 Co-authorship should reflect a joint collaboration. When involvement was ancillary it is inappropriate to pressure others for joint authorship listing on publications.

2.26 Share original research data with qualified others upon request.

2.27 Communicate the results of any research judged to be of value to other professionals and not withhold results reflecting unfavorably on specific institutions, programs, services, or prevailing opinion.

2.28 Submit manuscripts for consideration to only one journal at a time. They will not seek to publish previously published or accepted-for-publication materials in other media or publications without first informing all editors and/or publishers concerned. They will make appropriate references in the text and receive permission to use copyrights.

3.0 *Responsibility to the Institution.* Institutions of higher education provide the context for student affairs practice. Institutional mission, goals, policies, organizational structure, and culture, combined with individual judgment and professional standards, define and delimit the nature and extent of practice. Student affairs professionals share responsibility with other members of the academic community for fulfilling the institutional mission. Responsibility to promote the development of students and to support the institution's policies and interests require that professionals balance competing demands.

As ACPA members, student affairs professionals will:

3.1   Contribute to their institution by supporting its mission, goals, policies, and abiding by its procedures.

3.2   Seek resolution when they and their institution encounter substantial disagreements concerning professional or personal values. Resolution may require sustained efforts to modify institutional policies and practices or result in voluntary termination of employment.

3.3   Recognize that conflicts among students, colleagues, or the institution should be resolved without diminishing respect for or appropriate obligations to any party involved.

3.4   Assure that information provided about the institution is factual and accurate.

3.5   Inform appropriate officials of conditions that may be disruptive or damaging to their institution.

3.6   Inform supervisors of conditions or practices that may restrict institutional or professional effectiveness.

3.7   Refrain from attitudes or actions that impinge on colleagues' dignity, moral code, privacy, worth, professional functioning, and/or personal growth.

3.8   Abstain from sexual intimacies with colleagues or with staff for whom they have supervisory, evaluative, or instructional responsibility.

3.9   Assure that participation by staff in planned activities that emphasize self-disclosure or other relatively intimate or personal involvement is voluntary and that the leader(s) of such activities do not have administrative, supervisory, or evaluative authority over participants.

3.10   Evaluate job performance of subordinates regularly and recommend appropriate actions to enhance professional development and improve performance.

3.11   Define job responsibilities, decision-making procedures, mutual expectations, accountability procedures, and evaluation criteria with subordinates and supervisors.

3.12   Provide fair and honest assessments and feedback for colleagues' job performance and provide opportunities for professional growth as appropriate.

3.13   Seek evaluations of their job performance and/or services they provide.

3.14   Disseminate information that accurately describes the responsibilities of position vacancies, required qualifications, and the institution.

3.15   Adhere to ethical practices when facilitating or participating in a selection process by [a] representing the department and institution honestly and accurately; [b] periodically notify applicants of their status; [c] adhere to established guidelines, protocol, and standards for the selection process; and [d] provide accurate information about the resources available to applicants once employed.

3.16   Provide training to student affairs search and screening committee members.

3.17   Refrain from using their positions to seek unjustified personal gains, sexual favors, unfair advantages, or unearned goods and services not normally accorded in such positions.

3.18   Recognize their fiduciary responsibility to the institution. They will ensure that funds for which they have oversight are expended following established procedures and in ways that optimize value, are accounted for properly, and contribute to the accomplishment of the institution's mission. They also will assure equipment, facilities, personnel, and other resources are used to promote the welfare of the institution and students.

3.19   Restrict their private interests, obligations, and transactions in ways to minimize conflicts of interest or the appearance of conflicts of interest. They will identify their personal views and actions as private citizens from those expressed or undertaken as institutional representatives.

3.20   Evaluate programs, services, and organizational structure regularly and systematically to assure conformity to published standards and guidelines. Evaluations should be conducted using rigorous evaluation methods and principles, and the results should be made available to appropriate institutional personnel.

3.21   Acknowledge contributions by others to program development, program implementation, evaluations, and reports.

3.22   Maintain current knowledge about changes in technology and legislation that are significant for the range of institutional responsibilities in their professional domain (e.g., knowledge of privacy and security issues, use of the internet, and free speech/hate speech).

4.0 *Responsibility to Society.* Student affairs professionals, both as citizens and practitioners, have a responsibility to contribute to the improvement of the communities in which they live and work and to act as advocates for social justice for members of those communities. They respect individuality and individual differences. They recognize that our communities are enhanced by social and individual diversity manifested by characteristics such as age, culture, class, ethnicity, gender, ability, gender identity, race, religion, and sexual orientation. Student affairs professionals work to protect human rights and promote respect for human diversity in higher education.

As ACPA members, student affairs professionals will:

4.1 Assist students in becoming productive, ethical, and responsible citizens.

4.2 Demonstrate concern for the welfare of all students and work for constructive change on behalf of students.

4.3 Not discriminate on the basis of age, culture, ethnicity, gender, ability, gender identity, race, class, religion, or sexual orientation. They will actively work to change discriminatory practices.

4.4 Demonstrate regard for social codes and moral expectations of the communities in which they live and work. At the same time, they will be aware of situations in which concepts of social justice may conflict with local moral standards and norms and may choose to point out these conflicts in ways that respect the rights and values of all who are involved. They will recognize that violations of accepted moral and legal standards may involve their clients, students, or colleagues in damaging personal conflicts and may impugn the integrity of the profession, their own reputations, and that of the employing institution.

4.5 Report to the appropriate authority any condition that is likely to harm their clients and/or others.

ACPA Statement's APPENDIX A

Suggestions for Resolving Ethical Misconduct
USE OF THIS STATEMENT

• *Initiate a private conversation.* Because unethical conduct often is due to a lack of awareness or understanding of ethical standards as described in the preceding document, a private conversation between the target of inappropriate action(s) and the individual being inappropriate is an important initial line of action. This conference, if pursued in a spirit of collegiality and sincerity, often may resolve the ethical concern and promote future ethical conduct.

- *Pursue institutional resources.* If a private conference does not resolve the problem institutional resources may be pursued. It is recommended individuals work with mentors, supervisors, faculty, colleagues, or peers to research campus based resources.
- *Request consultation from ACPA Ethics Committee.* If an individual is unsure whether a particular behavior, activity, or practice falls under the provisions of this statement, the Ethics Committee may be contacted in writing. A detailed written description (omitting data identifying the person(s) involved) describing the potentially unethical behavior, activity, or practice and the circumstances surrounding the situation should be submitted to a member of the ACPA Ethics Committee. Members of the Committee will provide the individual with a summary of opinions regarding the ethical appropriateness of the conduct or practice in question, as well as some suggestions as to what action(s) could be taken. Because these opinions are based on limited information, no specific situation or action will be judged "unethical." Responses rendered by the Committee are advisory only and are not an official statement on behalf of ACPA. Please contact the ACPA Executive Director for more information.

ACPA Statement's APPENDIX B

ETHICAL FOUNDATIONS OF THIS DOCUMENT
The principles that provide the foundation for this document are:

- *Act to benefit others.* Service to humanity is the basic tenet underlying student affairs practice. Hence, the student affairs profession exists to: [a] promote cognitive, social, physical, intellectual, and spiritual development of students; [b] bring an institution-wide awareness of the interconnectedness of learning and development throughout the institution in academic, service, and management functions; [c] contribute to the effective functioning of the institution; and [d] provide programs and services consistent with this principle.
- *Promote justice.* Student affairs professionals are committed to assuring fundamental fairness for all persons within the academic community. The values of impartiality, equity, and reciprocity are basic. When there are greater needs than resources available or when the interests of constituencies conflict, justice requires honest consideration of all claims and requests and equitable (not necessarily equal) distribution of goods and services. A crucial aspect of promoting justice is demonstrating respect for human differences and opposing intolerance of these differences. Impor-

tant human differences include, but are not limited to, characteristics such as ability, age, class, culture, ethnicity, gender, gender identity, race, religion, or sexual orientation.

- *Respect autonomy.* Student affairs professionals respect and promote autonomy and privacy. This includes the rights of persons whose cultural traditions elevate the importance of the family over the importance of the individual to make choices based on the desires of their families if they wish. Students' freedom of choice and action are not restricted unless their actions significantly interfere with the welfare of others or the accomplishment of the institution's mission.
- *Be faithful.* Student affairs professionals make all efforts to be accurate in their presentation of facts, honor agreements, and trustworthy in the performance of their duties.
- *Do no harm.* Student affairs professionals do not engage in activities that cause either physical or psychological damage to others. In addition to their personal actions, student affairs professionals are especially vigilant to assure that the institutional policies do not: [a] hinder students' opportunities to benefit from the learning experiences available in the environment; [b] threaten individuals' self-worth, dignity, or safety; or [c] discriminate unjustly or illegally. Student affairs professionals are expected to understand that students from non-dominant cultures and groups that differ from the majority may feel harmed by attitudes and processes that are considered harmless by members of the dominant (i.e., majority) group.

Virtues: Habitual behavior. The virtues that student affairs educators should work to develop are based on widely accepted ideas about the characteristics of people in helping professions who are consistently ethical in their choices and behavior. Virtues differ from principles in that they are related to specific contexts and demonstrate personal characteristics that people in that context, in this case the student affairs profession, value. Virtues balance principles in that they are somewhat flexible and reflect the means by which a person acts on values. The four virtues associated with this profession are prudence, integrity, respectfulness, and benevolence.

- Self-regarding virtues. *Prudence* and *integrity* are virtues related to the behavior of a person in a particular situation. Prudence signifies thoughtfulness and unwillingness to jump to conclusions. Integrity signifies consistency and wholeness; a lack of dramatic behavioral differences from one situation to another.
- Other-regarding virtues. *Respectfulness* and *benevolence* are virtues that describe a person's treatment of others. Respectful persons are prudent—

they take time to think about appropriate responses to others in unfamiliar situations. Respectfulness is also connected to benevolence, the consistent habit of taking other people's well-being into consideration.

Context: Finding patterns of meaning and developing ethical perspectives

Because our campuses are composed of people from all over the world, have official connections with institutions in many countries, and also serve people who are Americans with significant allegiance to non-dominant cultures, it is important to take context into account when addressing ethical concerns. There are three frames of reference that should be considered: culture, temporality, and phenomenology.

- Culture. Every culture has its own ideas about values, virtues, social and family roles, and acceptable behavior. Cultures may be grounded in ethnicity, faith, gender, generation, sexual orientation, physical ability, or geographic area to name a few. Every campus also has a range of cultures based on work status or location as well as a dominant culture of its own. Ethical dilemmas often arise among or between people from different cultures. Ethical decision-making suggests that the values of relevant cultures be examined when dilemmas arise and overt conversations about conflicting values take place, if necessary.
- Temporality. This term suggests that an awareness of time-related issues be present. These include the duration of the problem, the urgency of its resolution, the time of the academic year, the duration of the relationships among the people involved, and the "spirit of the times" or *Zeitgeist*.
- Phenomenology. All persons have both cultural roots and individual attributes that shape their perspectives. Phenomenology refers to the personal and individual points of view of the persons involved in the situation. Both justice and prudence require that decision-makers do not assume anything about a person's perspective based on cultural background until that perspective is understood in both its individual and its cultural contexts.

REFERENCES FOR ADDITIONAL INFORMATION

Fried, J. (2003). Ethical standards and principles. In S. Komives, D. Woodard, & Associates (Eds.), *Student services: A handbook for the profession* (4th ed., pp. 107–127). San Francisco: Jossey-Bass.

Kitchener, K. (1985). Ethical principles and ethical decisions in student affairs. In H. Canon & R. Brown (Eds.), *Applied ethics in student services* (New Directions in Student Services No. 30, pp. 17–30). San Francisco: Jossey-Bass.

Meara, N., Schmidt, L., & Day, J. (1996). A foundation for ethical decisions, policies and character. *The Counseling Psychologist, 24*, 4–77.

Appendix D

Professional Ethics Continuum Exercise

This activity is useful in a classroom or training situation to discuss ethical issues. Below are some potentially common, or everyday, ethical situations. For each ethical situation, standards from ACPA and CAS that may be relevant to the situation are referenced as well as some general points to consider. All excerpts from the respective statements are contained in the full statements in Appendices B and C.

DIRECTIONS

All participants should stand against one wall in a room. One end of this wall will be for one extreme position; the other end of the wall is the other extreme position. Two statements representing these extreme positions will be read, and participants will need to determine where on the continuum to place themselves. Individuals may place themselves at either extreme or somewhere in the middle.

Ground Rules

- Understand that the small amount of information provided may be frustrating but may also be representative in terms of the amount of information you may receive in situations about which you will be making initial decisions.
- Be respectful and accepting of where individuals choose to put themselves on the continuum.

- Allow people to explain or share their reasoning but know that everyone is not expected to do that nor is there any need to defend your decision.
- Be prepared to share some thoughts about why you placed yourself where you did on the continuum if you are comfortable.
- Consider the potential consequences of each choice in a professional setting.
- Consider how you might engage or respond to a supervisor or peer who is on the other end of the continuum.

| 1. If marijuana is legal in the state, I would still enforce rules prohibiting its use on campus. | OR | If marijuana is legal in my state, I would not enforce rules that prohibit its use on campus. |

General points to consider: Institutional factors and values, personal values and integrity.

Refer to the statements in Appendices B and C:
    Among the relevant ACPA standards: 3.1, 3.2, 4.2
    Among the relevant CAS standards: Non-Malfeasance [3] Fidelity [4]

Other relevant guidelines, standards, principles, or considerations:

| 2. I would have a consensual sexual relationship with a student. | OR | I would not have a consensual sexual relationship with a student. |

. . . if the student is my age or older?
. . . if the student is a graduate student?
. . . if the student is in a special weekend program or attending part-time?
. . . if the student is also a fellow professional?

General points to consider—Institutional policies, professional reputation, personal values and integrity, exercises of power.

Refer to the statements in Appendices B and C:
    Among the relevant ACPA standards: 2.2, 2.4, 4.4
    Among the relevant CAS standards: Non-Malfeasance [4]

Other relevant guidelines, standards, principles, or considerations:

3. I would speak up if I   OR   I would not speak up if I
believed we were investing in   believed we were investing in
a program that has minimal   a program that has minimal
value.   value.

. . . if it was a new initiative?
. . . if it was a long-standing tradition?
. . . if I was clearly the only one with concerns?

General points to consider—Presentation of ideas/beliefs, perceptions of history and tradition, personal values/integrity.

Refer to the statements in Appendices B and C:
    Among the relevant ACPA standards: 3.1, 3.6, 3.7
    Among the relevant CAS standards: Non-Malfeasance [1], Beneficence [1,2], Justice [6]

Other relevant guidelines, standards, principles, or considerations:

4. I would contact/have a   OR   I would not contact/have a
discussion with a student's   discussion with a student's
parent if I were concerned   parent if I were concerned
about the student's well-   about the student's well-
being.   being.

. . . if the student were having physical or medical difficulties?
. . . if the student were in academic difficulty?
. . . if I had a signed release of information?
. . . if the parent emailed or left a phone message for me?

General points to consider—FERPA, confidentiality, respect for privacy or autonomy, care.

Refer to the statements in Appendices B and C:
    Among the relevant ACPA standards: 1.5, 2.1, 2.6, 4.5
    Among the relevant CAS standards: Fidelity [1]

Other relevant guidelines, standards, principles, or considerations:

5. I would accept a new job in   OR   I would not accept a new job
in the middle of the year if it   in the middle of the year if it
was the perfect job, even if it   was the perfect job, even if it
meant breaking a contract.   meant breaking a contract.

General points to consider—Obligations and responsibilities, personal values
and integrity, professional reputation.

Refer to the statements in Appendices B and C:
    Among the relevant ACPA standards: 1.8
    Among the relevant CAS standards: Fidelity [3]

Other relevant guidelines, standards, principles, or considerations:

6. I would consume alcohol   OR   I would not consume alcohol
with an of-age student   with an of-age student
enrolled at my institution.   enrolled at my institution.

    . . . if the student is my age or older?
    . . . if the student is a graduate student?
    . . . if the student is in a special weekend program or enrolled part time?
    . . . if the student is also a fellow professional?

General points to consider—Institutional/departmental expectations, professional reputation, personal values and integrity.

Refer to the statements in Appendices B and C:
    Among the relevant ACPA standards: 2.2, 3.19, 4.4
    Among the relevant CAS standards: Non-Malfeasance [2], Fidelity [2]

Other relevant guidelines, standards, principles, or considerations:

7. I would share my thoughts   OR   I would not share my thoughts
about a colleague's poor job   about a colleague's poor job
performance with another   performance with another
colleague.   colleague.

... if I noticed significant changes in his/her work?
... if I noticed significant changes in his/her personality or appearance?
... if the colleague's supervisor asked for my opinion on my colleague's performance?

General points to consider—Professional respect, collegiality, gossip, care, professional development.

Refer to the statements in Appendices B and C:
    Among the relevant ACPA standards: 3.6, 3.7, 3.12
    Among the relevant CAS standards: Autonomy [3], Beneficence [3], Justice [1]

Other relevant guidelines, standards, principles, or considerations:

8. I would agree to spend a major portion of our budget to repeat a program that had limited success and low attendance.	OR	I would not agree to spend a major portion of our budget to repeat a program that had limited success and low attendance.

... if the program targeted an underrepresented population on campus?
... if the program had yielded positive external publicity for the campus?
... if the program had been a long-standing campus tradition?

General points to consider—Fiscal responsibility, program evaluation, social justice, outreach.

Refer to the statements in Appendices B and C:
    Among the relevant ACPA standards: 3.18, 3.20, 4.3
    Among the relevant CAS standards: Fidelity [4,5]

Other relevant guidelines, standards, principles, or considerations:

9. I would share my honest opinion if I was asked by a supervisor if they should cut a full-time position that I believe had limited value.	OR	I would not share my honest opinion if I was asked by a supervisor if they should cut a full-time position that I believe had limited value.

. . . if the person currently in that position had confided that he/she is actively job searching?

. . . if some or all of those responsibilities may be added to my job?

. . . if, because of fiscal issues, a position that I value more might get cut instead?

General points to consider—Confidentiality, fiscal issues, personal values and integrity.

Refer to the statements in Appendices B and C:
    Among the relevant ACPA standards: 3.7
    Among the relevant CAS standards: Fidelity [2,4,5], Veracity [1]

Other relevant guidelines, standards, principles, or considerations:

10. I would inform my supervisor if I had recently begun counseling and taking prescription medication for a mental health–related condition.	OR	I would not inform my supervisor if I had recently begun counseling and taking prescription medication for a mental health–related condition.

General points to consider—Privacy, information disclosure.
    Refer to the statements in Appendices B and C:
    Among the relevant ACPA standards: 1.4, 3.6
    Among the relevant CAS standards: Fidelity [1], Veracity [3]

Other relevant guidelines, standards, principles, or considerations:

11. If a former supervisor agreed to be a reference for me, I would ask a friend to call him or her, posing as a potential employer.	OR	If a former supervisor agreed to be a reference for me, I would not ask a friend to call him or her, posing as a potential employer.

. . . if this person had given me both positive and negative feedback on my work?

. . . if the friend instead offered to make such a call?

... if I got a number of initially positive responses to my resume but no offers for interviews?
... if the friend called on his/her own initiative and then offered to share what was learned?

General points to consider—Honesty, confidentiality, faithfulness and respect, professional values and integrity.

Refer to the statements in Appendices B and C:
    Among the relevant ACPA standards: 1.9, 3.3, 3.7, 3.13
    Among the relevant CAS standards: Justice [1], Veracity [1,3]

Other relevant guidelines, standards, principles, or considerations:

12. If my supervisor asked me OR not to document the substandard job performance of one of my student staff members (the child of the college or university's senior vice president), I would comply.	If my supervisor asked me not to document the substandard job performance of one of my student staff members (the child of the college or university's senior vice president), I would not comply.

... if the student staff member told me he/she had accepted another job on campus?
... if my supervisor promised a raise and/or a desirable addition to my job?
... if my supervisor said this was an exceptional situation but he/she could not disclose details?
... if the substandard job performance involved alleged misuse of student funds?
... if the substandard job performance involved alleged harassment of other student staff?

General points to consider—Fair treatment, professional values and integrity.

Refer to the statements in Appendices B and C:
    Among the relevant ACPA standards: 3.1, 3.3, 3.6, 3.7, 3.10, 4.4
    Among the relevant CAS standards: Autonomy [6], Justice [4,5], Veracity [1,3]

References

ACPA-College Student Educators International. N.d. *Statement of Ethical Principles and Standards.* Washington, DC: Author.

ACPA-College Student Educators International and NASPA—Student Affairs Administrators in Higher Education. 2015. *Professional Competency Areas for Student Affairs Educators.* Washington, DC: Authors.

ACUHO-I. 2015. *ACUHO-I Standards and Ethical Principles: For College and University Housing Professionals.* Columbus: Author.

Baxter Magolda, Marcia B. 2001. *Making Their Own Way: Narratives for Transforming Higher Education to Promote Self-Development.* Sterling, VA: Stylus.

Beauchamp, Thomas L., and James F. Childress. 1979. *Principles of Biomedical Ethics.* Oxford: Oxford University Press.

CAS Statement of Shared Ethical Principles. 2015. *CAS Professional Standards for Higher Education* (9th ed.), edited by Council for the Advancement of Higher Education. Washington, DC: Author.

Chickering, Arthur W., and Linda Reisser. 1993. *Education and Identity.* San Francisco: Jossey-Bass.

Dougharty, W. Houston. 2009. "Who Is Living Here?" In *Maybe I Should . . . : Case Studies on Ethics for Student Affairs Professionals*, edited by Florence A. Hamrick and Mimi Benjamin, 87–88. Lanham, MD: University Press of America.

Eberhardt, David Michael, and Aurelio Manuel Valente. 2007. "The Moral Landscape of Student Affairs Work." *Journal of College & Character* 9, no. 2 (November): 1–6.

Gilligan, Carol. 1982. *In a Different Voice: Psychological Theory and Women's Development.* Cambridge, MA: Harvard University Press.

Hamrick, Florence A., and Mimi Benjamin, eds. 2009. *Maybe I Should . . . : Case Studies on Ethics for Student Affairs Professionals.* Lanham, MD: University Press of America.

Hirt, Joan B. 2006. *Where You Work Matters: Student Affairs Administration at Different Types of Institutions.* Lanham, MD: University Press of America.

Ignelzi, Michael G., and Melissa A. Rychener. 2018. "Why a Case Study Approach?" In *Complex Cases in Student Affairs: Preparing Early Career Professionals for Practice*, edited by Michael G. Ignelzi, Melissa A. Rychener, Molly A. Mistretta, and Stacy A. Jacob, 3–14. New York: Routledge.

Jacob, Stacy A., Stefanie M. Centola, and Kara Werkmeister. 2018. "Analyzing a Case Study." In *Complex Cases in Student Affairs: Preparing Early Career Professionals for Practice*, edited by Michael G. Ignelzi, Melissa A. Rychener, Molly A. Mistretta, and Stacy A. Jacob, 15–25. New York: Routledge.

Kitchener, Karen Strohm. 1986. "The Reflective Judgement Model: Characteristics, Evidence, and Measurement." In *Young Adult Cognitive Development: Characteristics, Environmental Influences, and Research Problems*, edited by Robert A. Mines and Karen Strohm Kitchener, 76–91. New York: Praeger.

Kitchener, Karen Strohm. 1985. "Ethical Principles and Ethical Decisions in Student Affairs." In *Applied Ethics in Student Services—New Directions for Student Services*, no. 30, edited by Harry J. Canon and Robert D. Brown, 17–29. San Francisco: Jossey-Bass.

Kohlberg, Lawrence. 1976. "Moral Stages and Moralization: The Cognitive-Developmental Approach." In *Moral Development and Behavior: Theory, Research, and Social Issues*, edited by Thomas Lickona, 31–53. New York: Holt McDougal.

Liddell, Debora L., and Diane L. Cooper. 2012. "Moral Development in Higher Education." In *Facilitating the Moral Growth of College Students—New Directions for Student Services*, no. 139, edited by Debora L. Liddell and Diane L. Cooper, 5–15. San Francisco: Jossey-Bass.

Liddell, Debora L., Diane L. Cooper, Margaret A. Healy, and Dafina Lazarus Stewart. 2010. "Ethical Elders: Campus Role Models for Moral Development." *About Campus* (March–April): 11–17.

Mathieson, Kieran. 2003. "Elements of Moral Maturity." *Journal of College and Character* 4, no. 5. https://doi.org/10.2202/1940-1639.1356.

NAFSA: Association of International Educators. (March 2019). "NAFSA's Statement of Ethical Principles." Accessed June 26, 2019. https://www.nafsa.org/About_Us/About_NAFSA/ Leadership_and_Governance/NAFSA_s_Statement_of_Ethical_Principles/.

Nash, Robert J., and Jennifer J. J. Jang. 2016. *Teaching College Students How to Solve Real-Life Moral Dilemmas: An Ethical Compass for Quarterlifers*. New York: Peter Lang.

National Immigration Law Center. 2018. *Practice Advisory: The Legal Authority for "Sanctuary" School Policies*. Accessed June 27, 2019. https://www.nilc.org/issues/immigration-enforcement/sanctuary-school-practice-advisory/.

Pope, Raechele L., Amy L. Reynolds, and John A. Mueller. 2019. *Multicultural Competence in Student Affairs: Advancing Social Justice and Inclusion* (2nd ed.). San Francisco: Jossey-Bass.

Renn, Kristen A., and Eric R. Jessup-Anger. 2008. "Preparing New Professionals: Lessons for Graduate Preparation Programs from the National Study of New Professionals in Student Affairs." *Journal of College Student Development* 49, no. 4 (July/August): 319–35. DOI: 10.1353/csd.0.0022.

Rest, James R. 1979. *Development in Judging Moral Issues*. Minneapolis: University of Minnesota Press.

Reybold, Earle L., Mark K. Halx, and Anne L. Jimenez. 2008. "Professional Integrity in Higher Education: A Study of Administrative Staff Ethics in Student Affairs." *Journal of College Student Development* 49, no. 2 (March/April): 110–24. https://doi.org/10.1353/csd.2008. 0013.

Saunders, Sue A., and Christine M. Wilson. 2017. "What Is Ethical Professional Practice?" In *Student Services: A Handbook for the Profession* (6th ed.), edited by John Schuh, Susan Jones, and Vasti Torres, 89–106. San Francisco: Jossey-Bass.

Stage, Francis K., and Steven M. Hubbard. 2012. *Linking Theory to Practice: Case Studies for Working with College Students* (3rd ed.). New York: Routledge.

Vaccaro, Annemarie, Brian McCoy, Delight Champagne, and Michael Siegel. 2013. *Decisions Matter: Using a Decision-Making Framework with Contemporary Student Affairs Case Studies*. Washington, DC: NASPA—Student Affairs Administrators in Higher Education.

Index

About the Editors

Mimi Benjamin is associate professor of student affairs in higher education at Indiana University of Pennsylvania and coeditor of the first edition of *Maybe I Should . . . : Case Studies on Ethics for Student Affairs Professionals* (2009) with Florence A. Hamrick. She served as a student affairs administrator for nineteen years in roles such as residence hall director, coordinator of residence life for academic services, associate director for faculty programs in residential communities, interim dean of students, and assistant to the vice president for student affairs. She received her PhD in educational leadership and policy studies from Iowa State University, her MA in English from Clarion University of Pennsylvania, her MEd in educational leadership from Ohio University, and her BS in secondary education/English from Clarion University of Pennsylvania. Dr. Benjamin is the coauthor of *Living-Learning Communities That Work: A Research-Based Model for Design, Delivery, and Assessment* (2018), and the editor of *Learning Communities from Start to Finish* (New Directions for Student Services, Number 149) (2015). A member of ACPA and NASPA, Dr. Benjamin has served on the editorial board for the "Research in Brief" and "On the Campus" sections of the *Journal of College Student Development* and on the ACPA Commission for Professional Preparation Directorate. In 2006 she was awarded the national Mid-Level Student Affairs Professional Award from NASPA, and in 2010 she was named an Emerging Scholar by ACPA. Dr. Benjamin served as an Elon University Center for Engaged Learning Research Seminar Co-Leader from 2017 to 2019, and her research interests include learning communities, student learning outcomes from cocurricular and on-campus employment experiences, student affairs administration, and faculty experiences.

Jody Jessup-Anger is associate professor of higher education at Marquette University. Prior to joining the faculty, she served as a student affairs administrator in roles such as residence life assignment coordinator, residence hall director, and assistant director and interim director of a women's center with an academic unit embedded in it. She received her PhD in higher, adult, and lifelong education from Michigan State University, her MS in student affairs in higher education from Colorado State University, and a BA in international studies from American University. Dr. Jessup-Anger is the coauthor of *Living-Learning Communities That Work: A Research-Based Model for Design, Delivery, and Assessment* (2018), and the coeditor of *Addressing Sexual Violence in Higher Education and Student Affairs* (New Directions for Student Services, Number 161) (2018). A member of ACPA and NASPA, Dr. Jessup-Anger has served on the editorial board for the "Research in Brief" and "On the Campus" sections of the *Journal of College Student Development* and on the editorial board for the *Journal of Student Affairs Research and Practice*. She cochaired the 2015 *ACPA Presidential Task Force on Sexual Violence Prevention in Higher Education* and served on the ACPA Commission for Professional Preparation Directorate. In 2011 she was named an Emerging Scholar by ACPA. While on sabbatical on 2017, she served as scholar-in-residence for Workshop Architects. Dr. Jessup-Anger served as an Elon University Center for Engaged Learning Research Seminar Co-Leader from 2017 to 2019. Her research interests center on how the interaction of students and the collegiate environment can support or impede student learning and development.

CPSIA information can be obtained
at www.ICGtesting.com
Printed in the USA
BVHW072323180121
598092BV00001B/51

9 781498 579025